LF

This is the only book, Russian or Western, that provides a comprehensive survey of developments in Russian prose over the last fifteen years of the Soviet regime. Deming Brown examines the work of established writers, such as Fazil Iskander and Andrei Bitov, together with many new figures who emerged during this period. Special attention is given to the evolving patterns of publication during the period: the rehabilitation of suppressed writers and the first publication of writings that had formerly belonged to the literary underground. This is an excellent introduction, of interest to scholars and students alike, to the varied writings of some eighty contemporary Russian authors, and to trends in literary criticism and publication.

THE LAST YEARS OF SOVIET
RUSSIAN LITERATURE

THE LAST YEARS OF SOVIET RUSSIAN LITERATURE

Prose Fiction 1975–1991

DEMING BROWN

Professor Emeritus of Russian Literature, University of Michigan

CAMBRIDGE
UNIVERSITY PRESS

Published by the Press Syndicate of the University of Cambridge
The Pitt Building, Trumpington Street, Cambridge CB2 IRP
40 West 20th Street, New York, NY 10011–4211, USA
10 Stamford Road, Oakleigh, Melbourne 3166, Australia

First published 1993

Printed in Great Britain at the University Press, Cambridge

A catalogue record for this book is available from the British Library

Library of Congress cataloguing in publication data
Brown, Deming, 1919–
The last years of Soviet Russian literature, 1975–1991 / Deming Brown.
p. cm.
Includes bibliographical references.
ISBN 0 521 40310 3 (hardback).
1. Russian fiction – 20th century – History and criticism.
I. Title.
PG3098.4.B76 1993
891.78′440809–dc20   92-44724   CIP

ISBN 0 521 40310 3 hardback

Contents

Preface

This book is designed as a continuation of the author's *Soviet Russian Literature since Stalin*. It aims to trace the development of Soviet Russian prose from approximately 1975 to the end of the Soviet regime in 1991.

In a work of this scope, it is necessary to confine discussion to major trends and to limit the number of authors considered. The quantity of writing published during this period is so large that a rigorous selection had to be made.

Personal interviews with twenty active Russian literary critics were helpful to me in making this selection, and I am extremely grateful to them. I am also grateful to a number of American and British colleagues whose kind advice has been invaluable. They are listed, together with those gracious Russians, in the Acknowledgments.

Acknowledgments

I am indebted to a number of institutions for help in my work on this book. The Horace H. Rackham School of Graduate Studies, the Center for Russian and East European Studies, and the Faculty Assistance Fund of the College of Literature, Science and the Arts, all of the University of Michigan, have provided generous assistance. A grant from the Kennan Institute for Advanced Russian Studies enabled me to work under its auspices as a research scholar, and a grant from the International Research and Exchanges Board supported one of my trips to Moscow.

A great many individuals have helped me at various stages. Among these, in alphabetical order, are Lev Anninskii, Aleksandr Arkhangel'skii, Galina Belaya, Marietta Chudakova, Edith Clowes, Igor' Dedkov, Ekaterina Genieva, John Givens, Helena Goscilo, Vyacheslav V. Ivanov, Natal'ya Ivanova, Konstantin Kustanovich, Alla Latynina, Lazar' Lazarev, Michael Makin, Alla Marchenko, John Mersereau, Jr., Ronald Meyer, Vladimir Novikov, Kathleen Parthé, Robert Porter, Stanislav Rassadin, Irina Rodnyanskaya, Aleksandr Rudenko-Desnyak, Benedikt Sarnov, Evgenii Shklovskii, Elizaveta Starikova, Vera Tolz, Vladimir Vigilyanskii, Josephine Woll, Margaret Ziolkowski, and Igor' Zolotusskii. I am especially grateful to Professors Parthé and Ziolkowski for their careful and constructive reading of certain individual chapters.

The person who read every word of my manuscript more than once, who gave me constant editorial help, and who steered me through my maladroit struggle with the word-processor, is my beloved wife, Glenora Washington Brown.

CHAPTER I

The literary situation: publication, genres, criticism

In an article published in 1991, the critic Sergei Chuprinin called the leadership of the Union of Soviet Writers a literary "general staff" whose function had been to "plan" and "command" the production of literature. Chuprinin was a member of the swelling chorus that demanded the extermination of the organization that had ruled over Soviet literature for nearly six decades. Through its ownership and control of publishing houses, literary journals, and newspapers, this Party-dominated monolith had served as the virtually omnipotent instrument of centralized, governmental supervision of literature. Its power was now coming to an end.

During the first dozen years with which the present book is concerned, through cronyism and patronage, reinforced by systems of censorship both formal and informal, the union's oligarchy – which writers increasingly referred to as a "mafia" – had largely succeeded in promoting the works of its adherents and stifling the publication of its enemies. Huge editions of the writings of official hacks, reinforced by commissioned, laudatory reviews, insured a wide distribution. For writers of independent temperament, accessibility to readers was difficult and often impossible.

A bold but for the moment unsuccessful challenge to this corrupt system occurred in 1979, when a group of writers, led by Vasilii Aksenov, Viktor Erofeev, Fazil Iskander, Andrei Bitov, and Evgenii Popov, assembled a large "literary almanac," *Metropol'*, containing works of twenty-three writers and poets, and demanded its uncensored publication. Refused, they sent two copies of the manuscript abroad, where it was published in

Russian and in translation. For their transgression these writers suffered exclusion from publication for varying periods, as well as other forms of persecution. Until the time when Soviet publication was restored, their writings, together with numerous other works known only through *samizdat* and *tamizdat*, became "underground" literature.

With the onset of *perestroika* and *glasnost'*, the power of this literary establishment began to erode. There were numerous and increasing challenges and uprisings within the union itself. Journals and newspapers broke away and disaffiliated from the union; new periodicals and new publishing houses mushroomed; censorship relaxed. These things did not happen all at once: the union's leadership was deeply entrenched and still had influential connections in Party and government. Moreover, it would be misleading to attribute all of the ills of the literary world to the union itself. Ultimately it was the Soviet government – the Party – that had controlled literature, and despite growing and publicly proclaimed contempt for it, the mafia was capable of a powerful rear-guard defense. For one thing, literary officials continued to arrange and promote new editions of their and their friends' work, thus retaining their perquisites, if not the readers' interest.

By the early 1990s, writers were at liberty to organize themselves, or not to organize, as they saw fit, and as a result multiple groupings had appeared. In addition to this "pluralism" and disappearance of centralized oversight, writers now experienced the liberty of the marketplace. This latter, at least in the short run, was for many writers a mixed blessing. Under strict governmental controls, they had enjoyed the security of guaranteed publication and sale of their works. Freedom from supervision also now meant freedom of the marketplace with all its perils, including the temptation – and even economic necessity – of pandering not to bureaucrats as before, but to popular taste.

No doubt the greatest achievement of the years 1985–90 was the publication of great quantities of the so-called "delayed literature" that had been previously forbidden to Soviet readers. It should be kept in mind, however, that the preceding decade, although it fell within the period of "stagnation," saw the publication of a considerable number of works of literary value. Along with Party-line "epic" novels by such establishment authors as Georgii Markov and Pyotr Proskurin that could only pretend to be serious literature, there appeared works of genuine merit by Andrei Bitov, Yurii Trifonov, Vasilii Shukshin, Viktor Astaf'ev, Vasil' Bykov, Vladimir Makanin, and others. The school of "village prose" continued to flourish during this decade. Although many of the best writers – including Vasilii Aksenov, Viktor Nekrasov, Vladimir Voinovich, and Aleksandr Solzhenitsyn – were now in exile, and although the situation was generally bleak, Soviet Russian literature had not died.

The unveiling of literary treasures began with the publication of deceased writers and poets who had previously been printed only selectively, if at all, in the Soviet Union. The list included a number of genuinely great figures, who now arose from officially imposed obscurity (the literary intelligentsia, however, had managed to know them all along) to become publicly recognized and even celebrated: Anna Akhmatova, Mikhail Bulgakov, Nikolai Gumilev, Osip Mandelshtam, Boris Pasternak, Boris Pilnyak, Andrei Platonov, and Evgenii Zamyatin. (Some of these writers had been published in part in previous years, but never fully.) Their ranks were augmented by a number of early emigre writers, most of them also deceased: Mark Aldanov, Nina Berberova, Vladislav Khodasevich, Vladimir Nabokov.

Many contemporary or recently deceased writers already known to the public had been forced by various kinds of censorship, including outright intimidation, to withhold important works from publication. A partial listing of these authors, whose suppressed works now appeared in a flood, would include Aleksandr Bek, Lydia Chukovskaya, Yulii Daniel, Yurii Dombrovskii, Vladimir Dudintsev, Venedikt Erofeev, Vasilii Grossman, Fazil Iskander, Anatolii Pristavkin, Anatolii Rybakov, Varlam Shalamov, Boris Slutskii, Vladimir Tendryakov, Yurii Trifonov, Aleksandr Tvardovskii, Boris Yampol'skii, and Anatolii Zhigulin.

Even more dramatic, indeed revolutionary, was the publication of works by recent emigres, many of whom had heretofore been branded as renegades or exiled as enemies: Vasilii Aksenov, Yuz Aleshkovskii, Joseph Brodsky, Sergei Dovlatov, Aleksandr Galich, Anatolii Gladilin, Naum Korzhavin, Eduard Limonov, Lev Loseff, Vladimir Maksimov, Yurii Miloslavskii, Viktor Nekrasov, Andrei Sinyavskii, Sasha Sokolov, Aleksandr Solzhenitsyn, Aleksei Tsvetkov, Georgii Vladimov, and Aleksandr Zinov'ev.

The list of foreign works now suddenly made available to Soviet readers is interminable, since it includes virtually everything that had previously been forbidden and was to be limited only by the capacity to print them and readers' ability to purchase them. An indication of the literary and ideological sweep of this change (which also included an opening of the gates to both the sublime – the Holy Bible, the Koran – and the ridiculous – Reader's Digest) was the printing of a translation of James Joyce's *Ulysses* and the novels of George Orwell and Arthur Koestler.

Thinkers and religious philosophers, representing the Silver Age of Russian culture that had flourished in the decades before the revolution, were now published, bringing to light ideas and names that had scarcely been known in the Soviet period – Nikolai Berdyaev, Sergei Bulgakov, Georgii Fedotov, Pavel Florinskii, Semyon Frank, Nikolai Fyodorov, Konstantin Leont'ev, Vasilii Rozanov, Vladimir Solovyov, and Peter Struve. The works of writers such as these; the opening of long-forbidden archives (those concerning Maksim Gorky, for example) whose inaccessibility had prevented a full understanding of important people, events, and trends; and the publication of newly available memoirs and works of documentary history (such as Solzhenitsyn's *The Gulag Archipelago*), all promoted a much fuller and richer understanding of Russia's twentieth-century history, thought, and culture.

The amplitude of newly permitted and rediscovered materials after 1985 stimulated an increase in public interest and demand. The circulation of thick monthly journals – the traditional media for first publication of new works – grew accordingly, sometimes doubling and tripling the size of previous printings. These journals, together with literary newspapers, also became major forums for the discussion of burning and fundamental issues, and came to be identified as much in terms of their political leanings as in terms of their strictly literary interests and values. The battle-lines were intricate and shifting, but the major periodicals could be identified with a fair degree of consistency. Liberal and more-or-less Western-oriented were *Novyi Mir* (*New World*), *Znamya* (*Banner*), *Oktyabr'* (*October*), *Druzhba Narodov* (*Friendship of Peoples*), *Yunost'* (*Youth*), and *Ogonek* (*Light*), and two newspapers, *Moskovskie Novosti* (*Moscow News*) and *Literaturnaya Gazeta* (*Literary Gazette*). On the conservative and nationalist side were the journals *Nash Sovremennik* (*Our Contemporary*), *Moskva* (*Moscow*) and *Molodaya Gvardiya* (*Young Guard*), the newspaper *Literaturnaya Rossiya* (*Literary Russia*) and often the newspaper *Pravda* (*Truth*). By 1990 some of these key periodicals had become crippled, and even threatened with extinction, by a scarcity of paper. The most distinguished journal, *Novyi Mir*, was forced to cut drastically the size of its printings, then to delay publication, and finally to omit a number of issues. The paper shortage and financial difficulties also severely damaged the main outlet for translated literature, *Inostrannaya Literatura* (*Foreign Literature*), the prominent literary and critical journal *Druzhba Narodov*, and the smaller but venerable *Voprosy Literatury* (*Questions of Literature*). Malfunctioning of the postal service brought about long delays in the deliveries of periodicals to subscribers, and even the disappearance of some issues. As of 1991 it appeared quite possible that the "thick" journals, which had been a fundamental showcase of Russian literature for 150 years, might cease to exist. It was not clear just what would come to replace these major organs of original literature, interpretation, and opinion. But smaller, non-traditional journals and newspapers had begun to spring up, together with a number of irregularly appearing "almanacs" under such titles as *Aprel'* (*April*), *Vest'* (*News*), *Zerkala* (*Mirrors*) – collections of prose, poetry, and criticism of high quality. Private or so-called "cooperative" publishing houses were proliferating. In short, the opportunities for literary publication had not been exhausted.

As economic pressure forced editors to become more cautious and market-oriented, however, these opportunities were becoming rarer. For one thing, editors became inclined to favor non-fictional works of immediate social or political import. For another, the lifting of taboos permitted the reading public to indulge its frustrated taste for less literary exotica – horoscopes, the occult, thrillers, pornography. Publishers continued, although with somewhat diminished ardor, to bring out additional works by formerly suppressed and dissident writers, and by emigres. In this transitional period, the chances for young and untried authors of serious literature to break into print were becoming more scarce.

Back in the late 1950s and 1960s, poets led the effort to restore depth and humanity to Soviet literature following the long Stalinist freeze. Love and death, and the whole spectrum of private emotions associated with the term "lyric" – subject matter that had been forcibly muffled in the Stalin era – reappeared mainly through the medium of verse. At the same time, poetry became aggressively political. Andrei Voznesenskii, Evgenii Evtushenko, and other members of a discontented and relatively daring younger generation began voicing demands for creative freedom, greater openness, and diversity of opinion. Khrushchev had partially revealed the crimes of Stalin and the evils of his regime in 1956 at the 20th Party Congress. Colorful, hortatory poetry was the most effective literary means of expressing the nation's shock over the disclosures, and of arousing national awareness of the need and potential for change.

Poetry, like every other form of political protest, became quieter during the period of "stagnation," and it remained so after 1985. Evtushenko and Voznesensky were still active, but they functioned mainly as prominent public figures campaigning in articles, speeches, and television appearances for the goals of *perestroika*, and their poetry as such lost most of its significance. In general, Soviet poetry consolidated its hard-won gains of the fifties and sixties – its right to be intimate, humane, even religious. It lost, however, its *civic* importance and entered a period which one critic characterized as "quiet lyricism."

It might have been expected that after its service as a forum and source of inspiration during the period of the Khrushchev "Thaw," poetry might once again have become a tribunal in a new time of upheaval. But, as another critic put it, prose "made the present climate." What was needed, it seemed, was not emotion, not exhortation, not flashes of poetic insight, but *analysis* of what was going on in society and in the lives and souls of its members. The public wanted information and evaluation that would help them to understand the profound changes that were taking place and that would affect their existence in fundamental ways. A precondition for such understanding was a full and truthful account of the national past, free of the heretofore dominant official formulations, distortions, omissions, and pure inventions which, they now increasingly realized, had warped their understanding of their situation. Only detailed and analytical prose, it was felt, could lead to the kind of evaluation that was urgently needed.

Russians have always enjoyed reading big novels, good or bad, and while there was little to offer the discriminating reader, there was plenty of popular material to keep the general readership occupied, such as the detective and spy novels of Julian Semyonov and the historical adventure novels of Vladimir Pikul'. Readers who expected fiction to confirm the fixed view of the world instilled by decades of official indoctrination (and there were masses of such readers) continued to subsist on the long, formulaic, primitive, and reactionary novels of such "socialist realist" hacks as Aleksandr Chakovskii, Vadim Kozhevnikov, and Georgii Markov. For more discriminating readers, however, the contemporary novel had little to offer.

Critics insisted that the *need* for good novels was greater than ever. A retrospective genre, the full-scale novel can examine, analyze, and interpret the past, give it shape and meaning, and illuminate its significance for the present. There were plenty of contemporary novels that did just this, but these novels were entirely lacking in intellectual individuality and merely illustrated prefabricated, conventional, "official" views. The people, events, attitudes, and conflicts of the Stalin era, and the Brezhnev period as well, needed to be seen through fresh and independent eyes.

The problem, critics agreed, was that the writing of a really good novel requires an original, full conception of life by an artist who is well informed and free of crippling inhibitions. The best Soviet writers, they felt, were still too bemused and aware of their own ignorance to embark on large novels with the necessary confidence. It was hoped that as fuller and more reliable information about the past, including the recent past, became available, and as the atmosphere of creative freedom improved, the "real novels" the critics longed for would begin to appear.

Meanwhile, a generous supply of serious novels, freighted with historical significance, was indeed at hand. These were the writings of authors, living and dead, which had been suppressed during the years of "stagnation," which *glasnost'* now brought to light, and which readers now eagerly consumed in large editions. These novels, by such writers as Yurii Dombrovskii, Vladimir Dudintsev, Vasilii Grossman, and Anatolii Rybakov, all focused on the iniquities of the Stalin period and featured fresh disclosures and interpretations of the events and phenomena of those years. For three or four years these novels dominated the attention of readers and critics alike. By 1990 the backlog of such fiction seemed to have been exhausted – with one exception. In that year there appeared in a rush the accumulated novels of Aleksandr Solzhenitsyn, the most articulate and arresting anti-Stalinist of them all.

During the entire period from 1975 to the present, short stories continued to be published in large numbers, by such veterans as Andrei Bitov, Yurii Nagibin, and Georgii Semenov and a number of the "village" writers. Toward the end of this period in particular the short story, as cultivated by Lyudmila Petrushevskaya, Evgenii Popov, Tatyana Tolstaya, and others, began to develop in new and extremely interesting directions. However, the most profoundly expressive prose form, at least until near the end of this period, was the short novel – the Russian term is *povest'*.

The short novel seemed to be the most appropriate response to rapidly changing times, when writers could not confidently see the world as a whole. Puzzled and disturbed by accelerating social developments and cultural instability, and lacking complete and fully rounded philosophies, writers concentrated on limited segments of human experience, emphasizing the local at the expense of the general, and dramatizing moral or ideological problems without attempting to solve them. A *povest'* is smaller, more fragmentary, less complicated than a novel, but it is no less profound. Rather, at its best, it provides a sharp focus on discrete but important issues. As employed by such writers as Vasil' Bykov, Vladimir Makanin, and Yurii Trifonov, the short novel proved to be the most eloquent Russian prose form of the time.[1]

Literary criticism, which appeared mainly in newspapers, the "thick" monthly journals, and smaller specialized journals, consisted of book reviews; topical essays; surveys of the current state of the genres; roundup assessments of a given year's literary output; articles attempting to define contemporary groupings, affinities and tendencies among writers; and retrospective analyses of literary developments. Before 1985, however, the scope of critical attention was restricted: Solzhenitsyn and Zamyatin, for example, could be mentioned only briefly and negatively. Mikhail Bulgakov and Andrei Platonov, who had been published but only in part, could be written about, but not exhaustively. Writers who had recently emigrated, such as Aksenov, had lost the right to be mentioned in criticism. The handful of most talented contemporary writers nearly all of whose works were allowed publication – Astaf'ev, Bitov, Bykov, Trifonov – were discussed extensively in criticism, as were the authors of Party-line "epic" novels such as Markov and Pyotr Proskurin.

Despite censorship and heavy editorial supervision, many critics wrote sensitive and sophisticated analyses of literature. They developed techniques of hinting and circumlocution – the so-called "Aesopian language" – that enabled them to maintain a constructive, if covert dialogue with both authors and initiated readers, and thus to encourage heretical and libertarian views. Even without resorting to Aesopian means, the best critics succeeded in maintaining and reinforcing high literary standards. Many avoided the prejudices and formulas of socialist realism, and the term itself went out of use among them. And they managed to ignore the widely promoted official hack novelists, who relied on back-scratching and sycophancy for favorable reviews and publicity.

A positive aspect of the literary scene, both before and after 1985, was the development of the semiotic and structural approach to the study of literature and culture, as developed chiefly at the University of Tartu under Yurii Lotman. This, together with the continually growing respect for the investigations and theories of the late Mikhail Bakhtin (1895–1975) concerning the influence of folk culture on literature, and on the role of the comic and the grotesque, provided a major enrichment to literary study. The particular influence of Bakhtin, with his theories of language and discourse, and his concept of the polyphonic novel and "carnival" as expressed in literature, became increasingly evident in Soviet criticism.

Further evidence that literary and cultural values had survived the Stalin years and, again, the "stagnation" of 1965–85, was the appearance, chiefly in the 1970s and 1980s, of numerous works by the scholar, critic, theoretician, and essayist Lydia Ginzburg (1902–90). Trained in the 1920s by distinguished members of the Formalist school in Leningrad, Ginzburg developed their ideas and added her own to the study of Russian and West European prose and poetry of the nineteenth and twentieth centuries. A thinker both complex and lucid, Ginzburg combined a highly disciplined and sophisticated command of literary theory and critical methodology with a keen sensitivity to cultural and social problems. Her vividly detailed and ruminative, semi-fictional book based on observations and experiences in wartime Leningrad, *Notes of a Person in the Blockade* (*Zapiski blokadnogo cheloveka*, 1984) is a profound account of the psychological and moral essence of that experience. In numerous other books and essays her commentary on the writers and intellectuals she knew and the issues she met with during her long and often difficult life forms a monument to the spiritual endurance of the Russian intelligentsia.

It became permissible, even fashionable, to cite the authority and influence of well-known but recently officially disfavored writers such as Dostoesvky, Zoshchenko, and Babel and the previously proscribed but now fully published and fully rehabilitated writers such as Platonov, Bulgakov, Grossman, and Nabokov. The freedom to refer to such writers fundamentally changed the frame of reference and *climate* of criticism, which now became intellectually richer, more variegated, and sophisticated.

In 1985 and thereafter, with new opportunities to express themselves in almost complete candor, critics began to re-examine the past of Soviet literature. They now openly deplored the corruption of the literary world, the prominence of mundane and doctrinaire "secretaries' literature" (officials of the Writers' Union held the title of "secretary"), written and published in large and lucrative editions by literary bureaucrats. The "harmony" in the writing community, many critics now proclaimed, had been merely on the surface – artificial and enforced. At the same time, some writing in the decade before 1985 had been, in the words of the critic Galina Belaya, both "deceptively simple" and "covertly polemical." In novels about World War II, "village" prose, and historical fiction, writers had carefully offered implicit reflections on a wide variety of issues. By dealing ostensibly with pan-human questions – conscience, duty, ethical choices, fate – they had deepened their readers' awareness of current moral problems.

The critics, moreover, were now able to emphasize accomplishments in past Soviet Russian literature that had not been fully recognized heretofore: the ways in which gifted poets and writers had preserved their talents and their independence by going underground, writing children's literature, and doing translations; the fact that many had kept on writing without hope of publication; the fact that despite their isolation some poets, such as Mandelshtam, Akhmatova, and Zabolotskii, had developed along modern lines comparable to Western poets. The critics were now able to declare their pride in the very staying power of a literature that had managed to overcome the restraints of a regime dedicated to the promotion of a purely utilitarian art.

Critics began to urge that the entire history of Russian literature since the Revolution be re-examined. The standard Soviet textbooks, anthologies, reading lists and syllabi for courses involving twentieth-century literature had been so badly warped by official ideological and political requirements, and by the mediocre taste of those in authority, that students, and the general public as well, had been given a seriously distorted notion of literary values and developments. It was suggested that the accepted periodization of Soviet literature (by decades or other extrinsic categories, such as "postwar literature") be reconsidered and revised in the light of aesthetic, as distinct from purely political trends. The rediscovery and restoration of such figures as Zamyatin, Platonov, Bulgakov, and the Acmeist poets, and the shrinking of such artificially inflated reputations as those of Aleksandr Fadeev, M. Bubennov, and Vadim Kozhevnikov, demanded a thorough re-evaluation and re-ranking of writers and poets. Emigre literature as well must at last be legitimized and introduced as an essential part of the total framework.

In insisting on reinterpretations and new emphases, the critics did not advocate a fixed scheme that would establish a new canon and orthodoxy. Quite the contrary: Anatolii Bocharov, for example, argued that what was required was not a new *history* of Soviet literature but new, competing *histories*, each with its idiosyncratic bias and set of concepts. There should be no single "correct" line.

An important aspect of any program of revisions, it was argued, would be a consideration of non-Marxist currents of Russian thought that had been neglected or suppressed during the Soviet period, as represented by such philosophers and religious thinkers as Berdyaev, Fedotov, and Solovyov. Expressions of interest in these and many other alternative thinkers became increasingly prominent. Scholarly reinterpretations of the history of Soviet literature in the 1920s and 1930s, tracing the ideological background, genesis, and establishment of the often pernicious mandate of literature of "social command" and the system of controls that enforced it, were written by Belaya, Marietta Chudakova, and others. And although there were a few diehards, the great majority of critics agreed that socialist realism was now moribund. Discussions now centered not on the question of whether socialist realism was relevant to the present situation, but on whether it even deserved a place in Russian aesthetic, as distinct from political, history.

The appearance of new literary histories will no doubt be delayed somewhat, because the literary world has been too preoccupied with extra-literary concerns to engage in such a massive set of revisions. Beginning with the nineteenth century, Russian literary criticism has traditionally been heavily didactic, laden with ideological, political, and moral argumentation, and it continued in this vein during the Soviet period. In 1985 criticism began to operate with a particular vehemence as an interpreter of public issues and problems, and even as a guide to behavior. Writing itself was heavily involved in civic matters, and criticism used its commentary on literature as a device for even stronger involvement.

Critics who had shown in the past that they were capable of sensitive and sophisticated discourse on the purely artistic features of a given literary text now insisted that aesthetic judgments were irrelevant for the time being. What was needed, they felt, was elucidation and evaluation of the ideas, the social, political, and ethnical implications of a novel, play, or story. But Soviet criticism sought to go even beyond the ideological explication of a literary work, by taking pains to spell out the lessons, the implications for ordinary human conduct, of a given book. This heavily didactic strain was welcomed, even demanded by readers. *Perestroika*, they felt, involved a profound transformation in everyday attitudes and behavior, a spiritual re-examination with wide, if uncertain, implications, and they looked not only to literature, but to criticism as well, for help in understanding the personal changes they were undergoing.

A major topic in criticism, addressed both directly and indirectly, was the Stalinist heritage, in its ideological aspects and in its influence on the moral and psychological climate of contemporary society. In 1990, one of the most perceptive critics, Igor´ Zolotusskii, who himself became heavily engaged in political criticism, even complained that readers were now less interested in his considered opinion of a given work than in knowing whether the work was "for or against Stalin." Now that the evils of Stalinism and their widespread consequences were increasingly a matter of public record, the theme of guilt and repentance became prominent. Literary criticism actively joined the debates over whether, and to what degree, the Stalinist nightmare should be blamed on guilty individuals and groups, or whether Soviet society at large was guilty. The question of just who should be called to account and who should repent became, in literary criticism, a major and often bitterly contested cultural issue. And even among some critics who professed to being anti-Stalinist, there were lingering attitudes and dogmatic habits of mind that, to an outside observer, seemed Stalinesque.

Ironically, at a time when critics and scholars were urging that Soviet literary *history* be rewritten with special attention to its immanent, purely aesthetic developments, many of them could not refrain from heavily political commentary on *contemporary* writing. Aesthetic criticism was not only a rarity; it often became diverted into utilitarian channels. An example is a 1990 article by Anatolii Bocharov, who had long since established his credentials as a discriminating critic. Beginning as a discussion of the use of "myth" in Soviet literature over the years, the article soon became a passionate commentary on Stalinist thought control. The "myth" that concerned this critic at this time was the system of official slogans, distortions, and lies.

At a time when both writers and readers were preoccupied with a multitude of practical, public concerns, it was natural for critics to become social and political commentators. The turn in this direction, however, was not unanimous. Some young critics objected by proclaiming their total indifference to politics. And

Igor' Dedkov, a mature critic with a long record of interest in the social implications of literature, now wrote:

I don't feel like participating in the popular competition for the loudest and strongest imprecations. Or for the most terrifying prophecy. Or for the most sensational unmasking of Lenin and Bolshevism. Or for the title of the very biggest patriot of Russia. I want something entirely different, because all these competitions have no relationship to literature.[2]

Despite feelings such as these, literary criticism became a major arena in the current ideological civil war. With the exception of periods of deepest Stalinist freeze, Soviet "thick" journals (which also frequently included non-literary material) have always exhibited varying political shadings, and after 1985 the battle-lines between what can roughly be called "liberal" and "conservative" periodicals were sharply drawn.

The conflicts between these two groups of publications, and others, were complicated by clashes, often personal and abusive, between individual critics. These quarrels were ideological in part, but they also involved innuendo, name-calling, and recriminations concerning the conduct, allegiances and associations of individuals in the pre-*glasnost'* years. Much of the denunciation and throat-cutting represented a rear-guard action by members of the threatened establishment against reformers who were trying to undermine their power and wealth. What distressed many observers, however, was the fact that conflicts were also taking place between ardent anti-Stalinists who were otherwise people of good will.

Stalin, in fact, ceased to be the issue, since the critics ostensibly agreed on the need to exorcise him. (Lingering crypto-Stalinism was another matter, about which there were numerous dark hints.) The main issue, or cluster of issues, centered on the question of the extent to which Russia, and therefore its culture, should develop along Western lines. Liberal critics, generally speaking, wrote in favor of Western democratic institutions, free enterprise, human rights, and a culture that would be open to outside influences. Their conservative opponents were national-istic, authoritarian, suspicious of the West and scornful of its culture, and imbued with a Messianic belief in Russia's superiority and special destiny. They hated not only the "mass culture" of the West but also its relative prosperity, which, if imported, might soften the Russian character. In the Soviet intelligentsia itself, and particularly among its Jewish members, they saw the pernicious influence of "cosmopolitanism" which produced a "Russophobia" that could be ruinous to the national interest. Some of the conservative critics exhibited anti-Semitism in various degrees.

A suggestion of the untidiness and complexity of the opposition between liberal-Western and conservative-nationalist critics is in the fact that when Solzhenitsyn's works reappeared in the Soviet Union in 1989 and 1990, both tendencies claimed him for their own. The liberals found in him a democrat and champion of human rights; the conservatives valued his patriotism and Russian orthodox religious beliefs. An indication of the complicated situation in the liberal camp itself was its internal disagreement about the communist heritage. All agreed about the banefulness of Stalin. Many extended their anathema to Lenin and condemned socialism outright. But there were also many who still believed in "socialism with a human face" and continued to revere Lenin. They argued, in the face of strong evidence to the contrary, that true "Leninism" had always involved the priority of "pan-human" values over class values.

By 1991, at least some of the critics had tired of using their medium as a political forum. The critic Chuprinin, who himself had been heavily involved in political commentary, now asserted that aesthetic criticism "as a form of creative activity has practically disappeared among us." Both writers and critics had become too political. Those who so desired might continue their political preoccupation, but critics who preferred to ignore politics should be encouraged to do so. Chuprinin and others noted, however, that criticism was disappearing from the pages of journals and newspapers. Its role in the contemporary literary process was diminishing, so that "the profession of criticism seems to be becoming a relic, extinct." To this Chuprinin might have added the practical consideration, noted by others, that (1) there was less new literature to write about, since little of it was being published, and (2) the journals that printed literary criticism seemed to be gradually disappearing.

Whether or not literary criticism as a political force had run its course, many argued that it was time to renew its aesthetic function. The "educative role of literature" was becoming exhausted, since readers were now tired of being taught and were no longer willing to accept sermons and ideological instruction from critics. Moreover, it was argued, Russian literature and Russian criticism had always been excessively tendentious and ideological. The world of letters now badly needed relief from this burden. What was needed, some critics now insisted, was a new aestheticism, a concentration on literature *as literature*, unfreighted with politics, philosophy, religion.

It was impossible to predict how much influence such ivory-towerism would acquire, but it was bound to stimulate debate. Thus, an article by Viktor Erofeev, entitled "A Funeral Feast for Soviet Literature," published in 1990 and clearly intended as a challenge to one and all, stated that Soviet literature had undergone "organic corruption" and was "falling apart." The cause of this was not merely the heritage of literary controls and restrictions, a crippling establishment, and the poison of an imposed ideology. True, the officially supported literary community had proved itself unable to adapt to *perestroika* and was bent on frustrating any new developments. But also liberal writers, who had grown up under the "formative influence of censorship" and through the necessity of writing between the lines had cultivated an "obtrusive allusiveness," now found it aesthetically impossible to cope with the new freedom. Moreover, Erofeev argued, the literature of liberal opposition had already accomplished its social mission. What was needed now, he concluded, was an "alternate literature" free of any social or cultural obligation.[3]

The response to Erofeev's article was voluminous and vehement. Most of the responses agreed that Soviet literature was undergoing a profound crisis and might indeed be dead. But many took exception to his more iconoclastic statements.

One wrote, for example, that Erofeev's complaint that Russian literature in general was excessively moralistic and didactic was the equivalent of criticizing Gothic architecture for being "too arched." Nevertheless, it was clear that nearly all of those who responded felt that Soviet criticism should and would develop in new directions.

It was impossible to predict with confidence how soon, and to what extent, this would happen. Many literary critics had become, and indeed may always have been, heavily oriented toward the social sciences – history, sociology, political science. Others seemed primarily interested in philosophy, ideology, or religion. Some had achieved a degree of public influence and authority; a refocusing on purely aesthetic matters would surely narrow their readership. For many it might prove impossible to cultivate new sensitivity to literature as such, or to overcome the habit of political punditry and contention. All in all, it seemed probable that utilitarian criticism and aesthetic criticism would simply co-exist, but that the latter would gain in prominence.

By the early 1990s, Russian literary criticism was still busily trying to cope with an unprecedented array of phenomena. The publication of a mass of heretofore suppressed fiction about the Soviet period, reinforced by a mass of newly available archival information, demanded a revised understanding of twentieth-century Russian history. The history of Soviet literature itself demanded a thorough reconsideration and revision. A number of rehabilitated individual writers – Akhmatova, Babel, Mandelshtam, Grossman, and many others – required new, close, and thorough study. Dozens of newly available emigre writers – including such major figures as Zamyatin, Nabokov, and Solzhenitsyn – required attention. History had conspired to confront Soviet criticism, simultaneously, with a flood of new literature from home and abroad, not only from the present but also from the past. And although established contemporary Soviet writers seemed relatively unproductive and quiescent, groups of young, experimental avant-garde writers were already on the scene.

CHAPTER 2

From "stagnation" to "openness"

It has been customary for Western commentators to discuss Soviet literature in terms of stages corresponding, roughly, to political developments within the former USSR. In accordance with this scheme, the stages represented by the present study would be (1) the so-called period of "stagnation" (*zastoi*) in the 1970s and early 1980s and (2) the period of "openness" (*glasnost'*) that began when Mikhail Gorbachev came to power. The outer boundaries of the study would be the period of the Thaw, corresponding, more or less, to the Khrushchev years and ending in the 1960s, and the collapse of the Soviet regime, in 1991.

Soviet Russian literature has indeed been sensitive to, and often governed by, political and ideological trends, and the period presently under consideration was, of course, no exception. Despite this fact, forces intrinsic to the literary process itself, and independent of extra-literary influences, were at work, as they always are to a certain degree. Although literature did undergo a time of severe doldrums under the heavy blows dealt to it by the Brezhnev regime, the strength it had acquired during the previous period largely survived the crackdown. Much of this strength remained covert until 1985, as writers either failed to publish their best and most sensitive works or published selectively and with great caution, protecting their talents and surviving by playing it safe. But even on the surface, Soviet literature, while not as lively and exciting as it had been in the late 1950s and 1960s, was vastly freer, more genuine, and original than it had been in the Stalin years.

The careers of all the writers with whom the present chapter is concerned began during the Khrushchev years and, with two exceptions, have continued to the present.[1] (Yurii Trifonov died in 1981, and Vladimir Tendryakov in 1984.) Each of them was adversely affected by the stifling atmosphere of the period of stagnation, and each, no doubt, would have fared better as a writer under freer circumstances. But in coping with a reactionary climate, each in his or her own way, they managed as a group to add new breadth to their national literature. The aesthetic discoveries they made, the standards they observed, and the modes they established represented genuine progress. Their example is a somewhat cautionary one, a testimony against the temptation to chart literary developments in terms of political landmarks.

Although the chronological span of the literary activity of the writers discussed in this chapter is roughly the same, they are a most diverse group. Three decades separate the birthdates of the oldest of them, I. Grekova, and the youngest, Andrei Bitov. Not only do they range widely in age; they represent varying degrees of talent and originality, political and social involvement, ideological tendentiousness, cultural allusiveness, aesthetic finesse. Not all of the prominent authors of the period have been included: a separate chapter is devoted to the so-called "village writers"; also, for reasons of economy I have not given space here to such writers as Ales' Adamovich, Yurii Bondarev, Vyacheslav Kondrat'ev, Viktor Konetskii, Yurii Nagibin, Anatolii Rybakov, and Vladimir Soloukhin, although several of these are treated in other chapters. Nevertheless, the eleven writers discussed here should give a profile of the period and an indication of its variety and scope.

In the 1960s and early 1970s, Yurii Trifonov (1927–81) became established as the premier purveyor of the life and mores of the Soviet urban educated classes. A master of physical and psychological detail, sensitive to the routines of city and suburban existence and the desires, anxieties, and moral problems of its participants, and with a keen eye for human weakness, Trifonov became the most prominent chronicler of the lives of what might be called the Soviet middle class.

His novellas (*povesti*) of the late sixties and early seventies displayed a sense of the historical background of the society about which he was writing, and the ways in which the times had changed. Such stories as "The Exchange" ("Obmen"), "Preliminary Conclusions" ("Predvaritel'nye itogi"), "A Long Goodbye" ("Dolgoe proshchanie"), and "Another Life" ("Drugaya zhizn'") deal frequently with family heritages and the relationships and conflicts between Soviet generations, and include references to previous periods of Soviet culture. Reading these stories one senses the totality of the Soviet experience over the decades.

Beginning with the novel *The House on the Embankment* (*Dom na naberezhnoi*, 1976), however, Trifonov became much more obvious and explicit in exploring historical dimensions. This novel, like all his subsequent works, switches back and forth in time – in this instance to include the period from the thirties to the seventies – in the attempt to encompass and interpret fundamental strains of development over the decades. *The House on the Embankment* traces the career of a literary scholar-critic who, through moral compromise and betrayal, achieves eminence in his field even though he is despised by many of his peers and contemporaries. Much is shown of the opportunistic maneuverings and intrigues in the Moscow academic world, of the corruption of everyday life and low morale of Stalinist times, and of the ways in which the young careerists of the 1930s, who came to real power in the next three decades, achieved their ends. Much of the narrative centers on the large apartment house on the Moscow River where the protagonist – and Trifonov himself – grew up, and where middle-level Soviet professionals, bureaucrats, Party officials, intellectuals, and their children resided. The house itself, which contains various essential social elements, thus becomes symbolic of an era.

The Old Man (*Starik*, 1978) is likewise preoccupied with history, although in different ways. The story alternates between the mid-1970s, depicting the vicissitudes of the elderly pensioner Letunov in the midst of his grasping, stupid, unsympathetic, and even hostile extended family, and the period 1915–20, when Letunov was involved in the Revolution and Civil War. Large parts of the narrative concern Letunov's unsuccessful attempts, through historical research and sheer memory, to reconstruct and determine the exact truth about a wartime event in which, Letunov suspects, he behaved less than honorably. A fundamentally decent man, Letunov is troubled by a vague sense of guilt not, the reader suspects, because of his own behavior but because of the misdeeds of his entire generation. Trifonov is far from clear about this, but the novel's sense of malaise suggests that the revolution itself lacked a sound moral grounding. Such a feeling is emphasized by the obvious pettiness, shallow materialism, and lack of spiritual values in the younger people – the revolution's beneficiaries – who surround Letunov.

In 1965 Trifonov published *Reflections of a Campfire* (*Otblesk kostra*), a documentary work about the revolutionary activities of his father and uncle in the early years of this century. Then, in 1973, he published a full-blown historical novel, *Impatience* (*Neterpenie*), about the revolutionary terrorist group People's Will that operated in the 1870s and 1880s. With impressive credentials as an historian, he was nevertheless clearly skeptical and even disturbed – as illustrated in *The Old Man* – over the difficulty, perhaps even the impossibility, of arriving at, and understanding, complete historical truth. His posthumously published novel, *Time and Place* (*Vremya i mesto*, 1981), illustrates this concern. Its main character is a novelist suffering the agonies of repeated rewritings of a novel – about a novelist. The work is never completed because the combined resources of imagination and memory seem insufficient to produce a satisfactory approximation of the truth.

It is not unusual, of course, for a work of literature to take the torments of creativity as its subject. In the case of Trifonov, however, the torments are obviously autobiographical. Beginning with *The House on the Embankment* his novels became not only more overtly historical in orientation, but also increasingly complex. Abrupt shifts in chronology, combined with equally sudden shifts in locale, unfilled and unexplained narrative gaps, multiple (and sometimes unidentifiable) narrators, and subtly alternating, sometimes conflicting points of view, were used more and more extensively.[2] This technique of fragmentation reached its point of greatest intensity in *Time and Place*, which consists of thirteen quite disparate and, at first glance, unrelated chapters. Clearly the writer Trifonov was struggling to find some artistic magic that could manipulate his diverse materials, taken from both past and present.

The struggle was, on the whole, successful. Despite what seems at times to be unnecessarily tortured complication, as in *Time and Place*, Trifonov's works present a gathering of vivid images of people, objects, habits, attitudes, and institutions that collectively capture the rhythms and atmosphere of an entire historic era and the periods within it. Often the smallest scenes and details are enormously evocative. In the post-humously published novel *Disappearance* (*Ischeznovenie*, 1987), for instance, we see a schoolboy in 1937 (the peak year of the Stalinist Terror and the centennial of the death of Pushkin), receiving, as first prize in a contest for memorizing lines of Pushkin, a plastic statuette of "Young Comrade Stalin Reading Pushkin."

It has been suggested that Trifonov's popularity comes from the fact that he was the first writer to make the *petty* concerns of the Soviet educated classes seem serious and significant.[3] A great deal of his narration is indeed devoted to the mental states of his urbanities – the tensions among persons who hate each other but have to live together because of the housing shortage, ugly discord between spouses, scheming to climb the social ladder. Trifonov is a subtle psychologist; his narration is seldom "objective" because it is usually done from the point of view of someone who is engaged and biased. Most of the narration in *The House on the Embankment*, for example, is done from the perspective of a moral coward who is bent on rationalizing and justifying his dishonest and predatory behavior. *Another Life*, the story of a dilettante historian who fritters away his life without completing the dissertation which has been his main goal, is told chiefly by his widow, a strong and loving woman who is unable to comprehend his character defect.

To a great extent Trifonov's later works, beginning with *The House on the Embankment*, are not only colorful portrayals of

Soviet life in historic depth, but also meditations on the heritage of the revolution and its moral consequences. The child of a veteran revolutionary who was destroyed in the purges of 1937, he included much family history, as well as directly autobiographical material, in his writings. Memory, a prominent thematic feature, is often uncertain, hesitant, and rueful, and it frequently involves episodes of personal betrayal. At the same time, these later novels feature the difficulty, even the impossibility, of finding the truth through the means of art and history. All of this would suggest that, working under conditions of political inhibition and censorship, in which he simply could not publish the full truth about the revolutionaries and their children, who were so familiar to him, Trifonov reached a painful accommodation through a kind of betrayal. He wrote abundantly and perceptively about the details of the lives of his contemporaries, their fathers, and their grandfathers, but, instead of telling everything he knew, took refuge in literary speculations about the uncertainty of memory and the impossibility of attaining the full truth.

Bulat Okudzhava (born 1924) became well known in the fifties and sixties as a poet and singer of his own songs to guitar accompaniment. At that time he also wrote several works of short fiction. In the following two decades he curtailed his activity as a poet and balladeer to concentrate on autobiographical stories and historical novels set in nineteenth-century Russia.

The stories, published in the 1980s, show the intimate and profound effects of the Stalin regime on the writer – effects that his poems and songs in the pre-*glasnost'* period had suggested only through hints and allegory. During his childhood and youth, Okudzhava's parents were imprisoned and exiled. "Girl of My Dreams" ("Devushka moei mechty," 1986) recalls the return of his mother from a ten-year camp incarceration in Karaganda to Tbilisi, where the author, a war veteran, was a university student. The mother is still handsome and affectionate as he remembers her, but she is sad, preoccupied, and non-committal about her experiences. Prison life has demoralized and fundamentally transformed her; it seems to have deprived her of most of her personality.

In "The Art of Clothes-Cutting and Life" ("Iskusstvo kroiki i zhit'ya," 1987), the author, now in 1950 a village schoolteacher in the Kaluga district, is not only haunted by his heritage as the son of political prisoners but, as a part-Georgian with a moustache, is bedeviled by the ubiquitous portraits of Stalin. In the universal atmosphere of fear and mistrust of "Western spies" he is actually arrested for a night by local police for innocuous but "suspicious" behavior.

The first of Okudzhava's historical novels, *Poor Avrosimov* (*Bednyi Avrosimov*, 1978), also known as *A Taste of Freedom* (*Glotok svobody*), centers on the trial, in 1826, of Pavel Pestel', a leader of the failed Decembrist revolution in 1825. *The Escapades of Shipov, or an Old-Time Vaudeville* (*Pokhozhdeniya Shipova, ili starinnyi vodevil'*, 1971) is a satirical account of the ridiculous activities of police spies and local gendarmes in conducting surveillance of Count Leo Tolstoy's school for peasant children in the year 1862. Tolstoy was indeed spied upon as a potential subversive by the government, but the grotesque events of the novel, culminating in a ham-handed mass search of his estate at Yasnaya Polyana for a secret printing press, are purely imaginary, and Tolstoy himself remains largely outside the narrative, serving merely as an unwitting quarry.

In both of these novels, Okudzhava concentrates on purely fictional characters, "little" people who participate in historically significant experience but do not play a leading role in them. The actual historical figures and main movers of these events remain largely in the background. The author seems more interested in evoking the atmosphere of the times, their culture, than he is in recreating essential historical personages, developments, and tendencies. He is also so preoccupied with narrative devices that the novels seem limited in historical substance and illumination. The same can be said of Okudzhava's two most recent historical novels.

The Journey of the Dilettantes (*Puteshestvie diletantov*, 1976, 1978), set in the 1840s and 1850s, features an intelligent but romantic and fractious young Prince Sergei Myatlev, a frequent irritant to the autocrat Nicholas I, who attempts to flee to Georgia with his teenaged beloved – another man's wife. The lovers are twice frustrated, and Myatlev, punished by the Emperor, ends his days in self-imposed exile on his country estate. Myatlev is a rebel against his class and its mores, but not a political revolutionary. Reared in the heady spirit of the Decembrist revolt but sobered by its catastrophic outcome, he is an interesting and complex variation on the classic nineteenth-century "superfluous man." *The Journey of the Dilettantes* is an historical novel in the sense that it is an elaboration of an actual episode of the time (Myatlev is based on the actual Prince Sergei Trubetskoi), portrays Nicholas I and his authoritarian government, and details the historical setting. It does not, however, present or analyze historical processes and focuses, rather, on such timeless topics as frustrated lovers and the opposition between authority and romantic impulses toward freedom. The novel does have a probably intentional contemporary relevance: the atmosphere of repression in mid-nineteenth-century Russia somewhat resembles that of the period of "stagnation" in the 1970s.

In *A Meeting with Bonaparte (Svidanie s Bonapartom,* 1983), Okudzhava turns back to the year 1812: Napoleon's invasion of Russia, his occupation of Moscow and its burning, and his retreat and rout amidst partisan warfare. Told in four sections containing the ruminations, memoirs, notes, and reminiscences of four widely diverse individuals who were eyewitnesses to many of the same events, it is less a panoramic history than a study of private lives and attitudes as they relate to a specific historic phenomenon. There are indeed concrete, grim, and dramatic accounts of episodes related to the struggle with the French armies, and a considerable amount of meditation and speculation, from various viewpoints, on the larger significance of what is happening. Okudzhava is deeply concerned with the spiritual, social, and historic import of the stories which his characters relate. But he seems less interested in exhaustive, objective historical verisimilitude than he is in portraying the essence of a culture in a situation of crisis. And, as in his previous works in historical settings, there is a prominent consciousness of the present-day moral relevance of past situations and events.

All four of Okudzhava's historical novels bear the marks of a conscious and experimental stylist, although each does so in different ways. In creating mood and atmosphere he sometimes uses ambiguity and the grotesque. He relies heavily on letters, diaries, notes, official reports, and other forms of documentation. He is fond of multiple narrators with contradicting biases and perspectives, and in employing them he is willing to risk excessively abrupt transitions and a sense of disjointedness. And although he seems at times to engage in undisciplined flights of fantasy, he is in fact a sophisticated writer whose apparent excesses and disharmonies are often merely a subtle form of parody.

An historical novelist of quite a different bent is Yurii Davydov (born 1924). Whereas Okudzhava's novels tend to focus on the Decembrist uprising or on the situations and attitudes that either led up to it or emerged from it, Davydov's have been largely concerned with the *Narodnichestvo* (Populism) movement of the latter third of the nineteenth century. A more fundamental difference is in the artistic use the two writers make of their materials. Although Okudzhava's concerns are genuinely historical, he freely employs fantasy to invent characters, episodes, and conflicts that are purely fictional and often quite independent of historical circumstances. On the other hand, Davydov's characters are much more often actual historical figures, and he seems to be more dedicated to the colorful portrayal of what in fact happened, or might have happened. Not only do Davydov's novels convey a sense of greater veracity; they examine persons, events, and tendencies more profoundly in terms of their moral and ideological import. Davydov is similar to Okudzhava in his obvious awareness of the relationship between Russian issues and problems of the nineteenth century and those of today, and the influence of the past on the present.

Davydov first came to prominence in 1959 with the publication of his novel *March* (*Mart*), featuring the revolutionary organization People's Will, a segment of the Populist movement distinguished by its advocacy of violent, conspiratorial, terrorist means. His works have continued to focus on questions of revolutionary ends and means. *The Slack Period of Autumn* (*Glukhaya pora listopada*, 1970) extends his depiction of People's Will and introduces the character of German Aleksandrovich Lopatin, a complex and enterprising revolutionary who continues as a prominent figure in later novels of Davydov. Lopatin, a friend of Marx and Engels and the first translator of *Das Kapital* into Russian, embodies for Davydov the best qualities of Russian revolutionaries – social idealism, humanity, a democratic spirit, courage, and absolute integrity. He serves as a touchstone by which other prominent revolutionary figures of various stripes are tested, and usually found wanting.

In *The Fate of Usol'tsev* (*Sud'ba Usol'tseva*, 1972) Davydov introduced a purely fictional character, Nikolai Nikolaevich Usol'tsev, whom we are also to see in a later work. Usol'tsev becomes associated in the late 1880s with an unsuccessful expedition of a small group of Russian peasants and intellectuals to Ethiopia for the purpose of founding a socialist colony. The enterprise, organized and led by a scheming and ruthless authoritarian demagogue, collapses in an atmosphere of thought control and spy-mania. The story is narrated through the journals of Usol'tsev himself, a callow but honest and well-meaning young Populist, and is ingeniously documented and authenticated by frequent authorial footnotes, which provide archival background material and commentary lending the narrative an historical perspective which Usol'tsev himself could not have possessed at the time. The novel thus combines the freshness of the personal, eyewitness report of a participant and the sophistication of the author's historical knowledge and hindsight.

In *Two Sheaves of Letters* (*Dve svyazki pisem*, 1982) Davydov again returns to German Lopatin and People's Will. The novel portrays revolutionary activities ranging from St. Petersburg to the provinces, to emigre colonies in Western Europe, and to Siberia (where, for example, is shown the unsuccessful attempt to free Nikolai Chernyshevskii from exile). Both idealists and cynics, upright fighters and predatory intriguers are displayed. As usual with Davydov, the major theme of the novel is that of revolutionary morality. A prominent character is the manipulative and murderous terrorist Sergei Nechaev, who stands as the moral antagonist of Lopatin. Davydov takes pains to show how the revolutionary movement could indeed breed and encompass such polar opposites – could promote democracy on the one hand and dictatorship on the other. In this as in his other novels, Davydov invites the reader to share his own investigative mental processes as he discovers and interprets archival documents and evaluates behavior. The reader becomes closely involved in, and convinced by, the author's moral judgments, and his comprehension of historical processes and their consequences.

Davydov's most recent novel, *Evenings at Kolmovo* (*Vechera v Kolmove*, 1988), returns to the notebooks of Nikolai Usol'tsev. By now, his African experience long behind him, Usol'tsev is a doctor in a rural mental hospital organized on permissive, democratic principles, and is a disciple of the Populist writer Gleb Uspenskii, who is also his part-time patient. The narrative burden is shared by Usol'tsev through his journals, and the author himself, who contributes numerous chapters in his own person. Although both the "Usol'tsev" and the "Davydov" chapters contain numerous brief portraits of such historical figures as the revolutionary Vera Figner and the writers Nekrasov and Saltykov-Shchedrin, as well as a spectrum of purely fictional characters from various sectors of the Populist movement, the center of attention is Uspenskii – his strong though somewhat disturbed personality and his generous and intelligent humanity. Loosely organized as a series of scenes and portraits rather than a plotted narrative, *Evenings at Kolmovo* is a panorama of Russian intellectual life, in its liberal and radical shadings, in the latter decades of the nineteenth century.

It is instructive to compare the novels of Davydov about People's Will with Yurii Trifonov's *Impatience* (*Neterpenie*, 1973). Trifonov's novel is structurally complex with a multitude of characters, and is stylistically more intricate. Although

Trifonov, like Davydov, is concerned with the problems of political morality which terrorism involves, his approach is much more heavily psychological. Trifonov seems preoccupied with what terrorists feel, how they (largely in the person of his central hero) develop within themselves the moral justification for the acts of political murder in which they engage, while Davydov is preoccupied with the moral import and historical consequences of their bloody frame of mind and their acts.

Although he is known as a short-story writer, critic, and essayist, and as editor of the leading journal *Novyi mir* during the years of its distinguished revival under *glasnost'*, the reputation of Sergei Zalygin (born 1913) as an author is based largely on his novels. The range of his topics is wide – including his psychological novel *The South American Variant* (*Yuzhnoamerikanskii variant*, 1973), about the problems and adjustments of a professional woman in her middle years – but he is best known for his historical novels about the social and ideological conflicts and developments in the 1920s. His interest in the decade following the October revolution involves later versions of the fundamental problems treated by Okudzhava, Davydov, and Trifonov, and in this sense his historical novels are thematic successors to theirs. Zalygin, however, favors agrarian settings and the ideological and moral issues relating to them. Born and educated in Siberia, and originally a practicing agronomist and hydrologist, he has affinities with the school of "village prose" and writes primarily about the effects of the revolution on the countryside.

In his novel *On the Irtysh* (*Na Irtyshe*, 1964), Zalygin had examined the forced collectivization of agriculture in 1931, emphasizing the sacrifices and injustices to which Siberian peasants were subjected. *Salt Valley* (*Solyonnaya pad'*, 1968), set in the period of the Civil War, had explored the issue of revolutionary means mainly through the character of a punitive, dogmatic, and dictatorial commissar. The novel *The Commission* (*Komissiya*, 1975), a sequel to *Salt Valley*, continues Zalygin's critique of harsh Bolshevik tactics, which are particularly incompatible with the folk culture against which they are directed. In his detailed depiction of peasant society at a time of revolutionary upheaval, in which a budding, locally generated utopia is crushed by the growing Soviet power, the author uses numerous individual members of a village community as representatives of various attitudes toward life in general and revolution in particular. At stake are a way of life and a set of community attitudes that are in harmony with and respectful of the natural environment as they face revolutionary change that threatens to destroy them.

After the Storm (Posle buri, 1980, 1985) is a return to the period following the Civil War. Embracing the whole time of the New Economic Policy, from 1921 to 1928, it is Zalygin's most comprehensive and panoramic novel. Through a spectrum of characters many of whom are former White Guard officers now in the service of the Soviet government, it lays out the various attitudes toward the future which the Soviet regime should take, and the sets of moral and political values behind these attitudes. Much of the novel depicts the ways in which the new Soviet regime made use of "former" persons – the defeated Whites – and the practical and ideological adjustments which these educated individuals had to make in order to adapt. At the heart of many of these changes in values are questions of "proletarian morality" versus pan-human ethics. There is also a strong critique of the Marxist–Leninist belief that progress must involve man's "mastery" of nature.

The novel is a strong endorsement of Lenin's New Economic Policy and an implicit argument that a similar partial restoration of private enterprise is the proper prescription for the 1980s. Zalygin was clearly a liberal in the contemporary Soviet context, and in writing his historical novel he no doubt had the present in mind. In fact, he appended to the end of the novel a long letter to the author by a "reader" who, it turns out, is really the novel's main character, now in deep old age. The letter expresses Zalygin's own view of the political and international situation of the 1980s.

Zalygin is not as gifted a historical novelist as Okudzhava, Davydov, or Trifonov: the characters in *After the Storm* (and, to a lesser extent, in *The Commission*) are somewhat schematic spokespersons for representative points of view, and they spend an inordinate amount of time arguing and debating their positions. But, although intellectually contrived, they do seem historically authentic, as does the Siberia in which their fates develop, and as do the problems in the morality of power which they discuss.

Both *The Commission*, with its microcosmic Siberian village, and *After the Storm*, with its greater temporal and geographic sweep, display a rich variety of well-individualized characters (with their regional speech peculiarities) and an impressive knowledge of the land – its history, traditions, and myths – and are full of narrative interest and color. As historical novels, however, their main contribution is in their presentation of an extensive and detailed ideological landscape of their time.

In the late 1950s and early 1960s Vladimir Tendryakov (1923–84) established a reputation as a probing examiner of values and behavior. His prose used both rural and urban settings and characters with various occupations and stations in life. Although topical and politically liberal, his stories and short novels surpassed mere social criticism. What distinguished them most of all was their pervasive concern with such matters as duty and personal responsibility, unexplained evil, and the ultimate sources of human conduct. Tendryakov's works were sometimes lacking in economy and delicacy, but their moral earnestness and keen sense of the tragic often made them interesting and powerful.

During his lifetime, Tendryakov had seemed to be a writer who, although firmly anti-Stalinist and somewhat critical of Soviet conditions, remained within the bounds of acceptable dissent. He had begun to display an open interest in matters of spiritual motivation and religious belief, but this, too, was not a rarity in a Russian literary community that had now been allowed to embrace such a work as Bulgakov's *The Master and Margarita*. A number of Tendryakov's posthumously published works, however, show him to have been a more original thinker, a more caustic social critic, and a more vivid and arresting portrayer of the evil of his times than he had seemed to be. This is true, as we shall see, of many writers, such as Vasilii Grossman and Yurii Dombrovskii, whose most powerful works were forced to remain "in the drawer" for long periods. But Tendryakov, who had ostensibly remained a fairly tractable literary figure during the period of "stagnation," dramatically illustrates the difference between appearance and reality in a writer of talent under Soviet conditions.

The publication in 1987 of his novel *Attack on Mirages* (*Pokushenie na mirazhi*, dated 1977–80) disclosed a Tendryakov who was profoundly skeptical of Marxist–Leninist utopianism and the teleological cast of mind that underlay the conventional Soviet historical optimism. The novel's narrator is a distinguished physicist, Grebin, who is distressed by the fact that his own son, presumably the product of a progressive society based on technological advancement, has turned out to be a materialistic lout. Grebin's distress leads him to seek the causes of historical development in an attempt to find the laws of social existence. Is human behavior governed purely by the social and economic environment, or does the inherent human moral sense play a decisive role in shaping the course of history? Are "great men," including moral leaders, really important?

To study these problems Grebin, together with his laboratory assistants and with the aid of computer programs, attempts to reconstruct certain fragmentary historical events as they would have developed in the absence of Jesus Christ and His teachings. These fantasies, of course, fail to produce conclusive answers. It does not become clear just how influential are will and choice in the affairs of mankind, or the degree to which man's moral consciousness is influenced by technological and social change. Morality is indeed important, but its ultimate source remains a mystery. But these experiments in fantasy seem to suggest that great personalities (and implicitly such figures as Lenin and Stalin) are of little significance in history, and this is probably the reason why Tendryakov failed to publish the novel during his lifetime.

Tendryakov also turns out to have been a more profound and

cutting satirist than he had seemed to be. In works published during his lifetime there had been some elements of sarcastic social commentary, but nothing that would indicate more than a mild satirical streak. However, in the story "The Clear Waters of Kitezh" ("Chistye vody Kitezha," dated 1977–80, published in 1986), he produced a work of sharp and full-scale social satire. The setting is a sleepy provincial town that subsists on, and is dominated by, a huge factory complex that has been increasingly polluting the local river which is the town's water supply. The docile populace has fatalistically accepted the situation. One fine day, however, there appears in the local newspaper a fiery article, written by a local poet but inspired and planted by some unspecified higher authority, that expresses alarm over environmental damage in general and the pollution of the town's river in particular. The townspeople awaken and begin to organize initiatives to combat the industrial monster. But just as the movement gathers steam and shakes up the civic lethargy, the newspaper editor takes fright and writes, under a pseudonym, a threatening "letter to the editor" suggesting that the central authorities are greatly displeased by the town's revolutionary effort. The populace, which immediately assumes that the ominous letter has in fact been generated from on high, quickly sinks back into its usual passivity. The story is indeed a sad one, but the petty calculations and self-serving maneuverings of local functionaries in their attempts to evade responsibility, and the reactions of the populace to this temporary stirring-up of its energies, are given a distinctly comic cast.

In the latest stages of his career Tendryakov began writing stories based on his two-year experience as a field-telephone specialist in several battles of World War II. "A Day that Ousted a Life" ("Den', vytesnivshii zhizn'," 1985) is the competent, carefully detailed but otherwise unremarkable account of a rookie's crowded first day of military action and the psychological transformation it brings about. A more profound and memorable story is "Donna Anna" ("Donna Anna," dated 1969–71, published 1988), which combines the same detailed depiction of battlefield atmosphere with a portrayal of the disastrous effects of a Stalinist mentality on military behavior.

"Donna Anna" is actually one of a series of eyewitness stories, autobiographical in nature, all published posthumously, that convey Tendryakov's most vivid, bitter and eloquent social criticism and include much of his best writing. The first three of these, all published in 1988 but written much earlier, are set in rural Russia. "The Pair of Bays" ("Para gnedykh") takes place in 1929 and tells, in fascinatingly colorful concreteness, of the reactions of a community of peasants to the incipient collectivization of their farms and property, and of the conflicted attitudes of the young man (the narrator's father) who serves as the local Party enforcer. The second story, and the most grim, "Bread for a Dog" ("Khleb dlya sobaki") portrays the ghastly suffering and death of "kulaks" in 1933 from officially decreed starvation, as seen through the eyes of the now ten-year-old son of that same enforcer. "Paranya" ("Paranya"), set in 1937 at the peak of the Stalin Terror, depicts a village madwoman who confuses Stalin with God and Christ, but whom everyone, in fear of political retribution, refuses to challenge until she is publicly murdered, causing general relief. The fourth of this series of stories, now depicting Stalinism in wartime, is "Donna Anna."

With the work "The Hunt" ("Okhota," dated 1971, published 1988), Tendryakov moves to the year 1948, when, as a student at the Gorky Literary Institute in Moscow, he passively witnessed the anti-Semitic, anti-"cosmopolitan" campaign of denunciation, secret and open, that poisoned the lives, ruined the careers, and sometimes killed Soviet intellectuals, in this case the literati. Not a work of fiction, but rather an indignant (and sometimes self-accusatory) memoir of a period of social insanity, "The Hunt" recounts the torments and also the perfidy of a number of actual persons. The most prominent of these was the novelist Aleksandr Fadeev, an official of the Writers' Union who, against his better instincts, carried out the purge of "cosmopolitans" and died, in 1956, a remorseful suicide.

In 1961 Tendryakov wrote "On the Blessed Island of

Communism" ("Na blazhennom ostrove kommunizma," published 1988), the acid description of a lavish picnic-reception thrown the year before by Khrushchev for the literary intelligentsia. Numerous sycophantic literary bureaucrats are portrayed, and Khrushchev himself is shown as a drunken bully and a fool. The essential argument is that when such things still go on and such people still thrive, Stalinism cannot be dead. In "People or Non-People" (*Lyudi ili nelyudi*, dated 1975–6, published in 1989), which consists of sketches and memoirs, the author continues his candidly negative appraisal of the corrupt literary world, among other things, and, in a spirit of confession, tells of his own cautious behavior and circumspect writing. And indeed, only after he was dead did the full animus of his attitude toward the system in which he lived become evident.

Among the handful of most prominent Soviet authors in the three decades before the nineties, Daniil Granin (born 1918) may also have been the most visible. Not only an extremely prolific writer, he was also for many years an official in the Leningrad section of the Writers' Union, a People's Deputy during the Gorbachev regime, and in general an ubiquitous public figure generally identified with the literary establishment. Both his fiction and his non-fiction have managed to be timely, topical, and searching without being markedly daring.

In the 1960s and early 1970s he had already become well known as a writer of novels and short stories, articles about the social aspects of science and technology, travel essays (he has been an assiduous globe-trotter), and commentary on environmental issues. His fiction was known for its exploration of moral problems involved in scientific and industrial activity, as well as his examination of the individual conscience in conflicts involving complex ethical choices. During the middle and late 1970s and all of the 1980s Granin continued to maintain all of these interests and, in addition, published documentary biographical narratives about outstanding scientists and scholars; stories with a speculative, philosophical bent; fiction about World War II; and, together with Ales' Adamovich *A Book of the Blockade* (*Blokadnaya kniga*, 1979, 1981), a collection of reminiscences and diaries of persons who had gone through the 900-day siege of Leningrad.

Granin's best-known novel is *The Picture* (*Kartina,* 1979). Its central figure is Losev, the mayor of a provincial city in northwest Russia. An energetic official who gets things done and strongly believes in industrial progress, Losev has a rather sudden revelation in which he comes to fear the cultural costs of such progress. Specifically, he sees that the planned expansion of a local factory will involve the demolition of a large and beautiful pre-revolutionary house and the destruction of the picturesque creek on whose banks it is situated. The major conflicts in the novel spring from Losev's dilemma over whether he should sacrifice the economic welfare of his city (which badly needs the expanded enterprise) for the sake of preserving a valuable cultural monument and its setting for the benefit of future generations. A complicating factor is that if he tries to build the new factory in a different place (a feasible alternative) he will risk defying the central authorities by disrupting their plans, and thus jeopardize his own career.

Losev does not face his problems alone. Pulling him in the direction of preservation is, among others, the rueful old former commissar Polivanov who, in the 1930s, had led the burning of religious books and icons in the city square and who now wants to restore his reputation for posterity by leading the conversion of the house into a provincial historical museum. The tug in the opposite direction comes from Uvarov, a driving and powerful industrial official with a reputation as a "robot," who is devoted exclusively to building up society's material base, who admires Losev's administrative abilities, and who can greatly enhance Losev's career. The moral and ideological conflict of the novel develops along the lines represented by these characters, with several additional variations. After extensive exploration of the values represented in this conflict and the depiction of a great amount of local politics and bureaucratic infighting, the novel ends with only a partial resolution. The house is preserved as a museum and the town is to be developed as a tourist site, but Losev, who has been burdened with problems of self-esteem, simply leaves town and fades away.

Open-endedness, however, is not a major flaw in this novel. Its deficiencies are in its schematically dialectical structure and sometimes wooden characters, and in its frequent verbosity.

One of Granin's most accomplished works of the 1980s was the short novel *The Track is Still Noticeable* (*Eshche zameten sled*, 1984), in which a middle-aged Leningrader – the war veteran Dudarev – and a Georgian woman – Zhanna – recreate the image of a lieutenant Volkov, whom they had known decades before, in World War II. Although Zhanna had never met Volkov in person, she had conducted an extensive wartime correspondence with him; Dudarev had known Volkov at the front and had disliked him. By reading a thick packet of Volkov's letters to Zhanna, Dudarev comes to realize that Volkov had been in fact a highly intelligent, impressively cultured, courageous, and honorable man, badly misunderstood by both his comrades and his superiors. Granin's adroit use of a combination of reminiscences and old letters to reveal, gradually, the true character of an abused and underestimated man, creates a suspenseful, psychologically interesting, colorful, and moving story.

The book of Granin that caused the greatest stir in the 1980s was *The Bison* (*Zubr*, 1987), published during the general wave of revelations about the iniquity of the Stalin period. Labeled as a *povest'* but based closely on actual characters and events, it combines a profile of the distinguished but eccentric geneticist Nikolai Timofeev-Resovskii with an account of the twentieth-century Russian scientific intelligentsia. What is most striking about his hero's career was his decision to work in Germany from 1925 to 1945, remaining there during the entire Nazi period in preference to returning to work under oppressive Soviet conditions. *The Bison* portrays vividly Stalin's terrorization of the scientific community through his favorite, the charlatan Trofim Lysenko. However, in its strained attempts to emphasize the hero's colorful traits and to make him a legendary figure, the work seems at times both artificial and attenuated.

I. Grekova is the pen name of Elena Ventsel' (born 1907), a

distinguished mathematician and specialist in probability theory who has maintained both her scientific and her literary careers for many decades. She became well known as a writer in the 1960s, and her production of stories and short novels has continued into advanced age. A political liberal with a sharp sense of fairness and justice, she has a keen eye for human weaknesses and strengths; a fine, ironical sense of humor; and a vast understanding of and compassion for frustration and suffering. Although she is a frankly female writer (her narrator is usually a middle-aged woman), Grekova seems equally strong in creating both male and female characters, of all ages. One of her prominent strengths is her treatment of the relationships between generations. As a rule, she favors urban settings, and her stories often center on a scientific institution or workplace. She is obviously attracted to small, complicated collectives, which she portrays as turbulent organisms full of conflicts, infighting, and intrigue. Her authorial stance is usually that of an objective observer, but her narrators often display various shades of amusement, exasperation, or indignation, as well as an ingratiating quality of self-irony.

One of Grekova's most popular novels is *The Faculty* (*Kafedra*, 1978). It can be seen as a collection of vignettes, life-stories, and episodes, loosely unified by the academic department (cybernetics) of the institute in which all of the novel's characters are researchers, teachers, and students. The novel combines a treatment of serious academic issues – such as administration, standards of research and teaching, grading, advancement and promotion, plagiarism – with a wide variety of more personal, "human" issues in the private lives of individuals of all ages – a variety that gives the narrative a panoramic quality. A major character is the recently deceased head of the department, a scientist of great accomplishment and benevolent, grandfatherly figure whom we come to know through generous excerpts from his diary. In contrast is his successor as head, who fails and is removed because of his rigid inability to work with people. The central and focusing character in the novel, whose point of view dominates the narrative, is Nina Astashova, a highly intelligent faculty member who combines honesty, enterprise, and aggressiveness with an element of uncertainty and defenselessness, and whose private life is complicated by her three children and a talented but drunken and womanizing lover. In *The Faculty* we see many of Grekova's greatest strengths, including the ability to create fascinating characters and to show how people's private lives affect their working, professional lives.

The narrator of *Ship of Widows* (*Vdovii parokhod*, 1981), which is set in the immediate postwar years, is Ol'ga Flerova, who has lost her husband at the front and the rest of her family in a German bomb attack, and who has lost her profession as a pianist because her fingers became paralyzed in that same bombing. Ol'ga lives with four other widows and the spoiled son of one of them in a tumble-down communal flat, because none of them has anywhere else to live. As individuals they are very dissimilar, and as a group they are incompatible: their joint existence is poisoned by squabbling, jealousy, duels of wills, spite, and paranoia. But – and Ol'ga is able to see this generously and compassionately – they are all simply human. Despite their frequent nervous estrangement from one another, they do help each other in times of trouble. These women are not abnormal – merely poor, unlucky and, above all, deprived of privacy. Little kindnesses provide some relief, and the spoiled and obnoxious boy grows up to take extraordinarily devoted care of his dying mother. *Ship of Widows*, however, is Grekova's starkest work, even though it is a compassionate work of great social and psychological profundity.

Thresholds (*Porogi*, 1984) takes place in a cybernetics institute in Leningrad. The main part of the novel tells of the spiritual rehabilitation of an engineer who had undergone a nervous breakdown after a piece of apparatus in his previous place of work had exploded and killed some of his colleagues. For this accident he had been punished but later cleared; his troubles, however, had been compounded by his wife's love affair with his best friend, and he had become a misanthropic loner. Other threads in the novel are an anonymous campaign of denunciatory letters accusing the management of bungling and corruption (the culprit is exposed and resigns) and an account of the career of the institute's head, a model leader. To a great extent the hero of the novel is the institute itself – its social climate, the personalities of its individual members, their interreaction, tensions, affinities, and dislikes, and their relationship to the bureaucracy and the engineering group as a whole. Although a variety of devices – first-person and third-person narration, documents, transcripts of meetings, decrees (in officialese), extensive dialogue, and interior monologue – add plausibility and interest, the novel seems of lesser weight than *Ship of Widows* or *The Faculty*.

A departure from Grekova's usual pattern of group-oriented stories with a female point of view is "The Pheasant" ("Fazan," 1985), which is an account of the life of a dying man, as told through his subjective reminiscences. An intelligent, aesthetically gifted person, he has never lived up to his promise because he is lazy, irresponsible, pettily dishonest, and a user of people. The main focus of his deathbed thoughts are the women in his life – his mother, sister, wives, and numerous other women he has conquered and exploited. He thinks of his sunny childhood and of his first love – the only woman who thoroughly understood him and might have saved him. As his recollections wander randomly over time, he bitterly evaluates his life (he has also been a heavy drinker) and considers it a "waste." Grekova, somewhat mechanically and without apparent justification, also reconstructs through her hero's reminiscences the various periods of twentieth-century Russian history, an excursion that seems to have little relevance to what is essentially a moral and psychological portrait.

The onset of *glasnost'* seems to have had little effect on the tenor of Grekova's writing. Although she had been forced to withhold some of her works from publication prior to 1985, she seems never to have compromised her skeptical, and sometimes sharply critical, interpretation of Soviet life. When the story "Without Smiles" ("Bez ulybok") appeared in 1986, therefore, it was only slightly more caustic than her previously published works. It differed, however, in other respects. Her wryly humorous, self-critical narrator – the victim of a temporary shunning (for an unspecified ideological deviation) at the scientific institute where she works – identifies other persons not by name but by nicknames she gives them, based on what she subjectively perceives to be their most important personal attributes (e.g. Streamlined, Thin, Puffed-Up). The story is populated not by Grekova's usual characters but by personified abstractions, or caricatures. Nevertheless, her satirical account of the process of bureaucratic harassment, which includes lengthy public hearings against her heroine, back-stabbing, various kinds of petty abuse, and being treated by many as a pariah, gives the impression of full social and psychological verisimilitude. Her spunky heroine has found herself in a grotesque situation and, most appropriately, she portrays it grotesquely.

Grekova is clearly a highly intelligent, perceptive, candid, and courageous writer. An indication of what she *might* have said in earlier years, had she been permitted to, is the story "Masters of Life" ("Khozyaeva zhizni"), dated 1960 but published only in 1988. On a train the narrator, obviously Grekova herself, meets a man who tells her his pathetic life-story – how the Stalin regime hounded and imprisoned him, and destroyed everyone dear to him and everything meaningful in his existence, including his identity. In her usual manner, Grekova manages to make this poor man a very interesting and individualized character, and not just the faceless victim of a common tragedy.

For thirty years the stories of Georgii Semyonov (1931–92) have served as illustrations of the fact that literature in the Soviet Union was not obligated to have political, social, or ideological significance, much less to display a partisan bias. Although Semyonov's works bear a discernibly Soviet cultural imprint and are recognizable in their Russian time and place, they seem to have no extra-literary agenda. Semyonov has been interested simply in how human beings think and feel, in how they react to each other, and how they behave in the natural and social environment.

An example is the story "The Smell of Burnt Powder" ("Zapakh sgorevshego porokha," 1984). In 1947 in a postwar

Moscow still suffering from a severe food shortage a boy, almost sixteen, buys a shotgun with money he has saved by scrimping on meals. His motive is twofold: he has long had the single-minded goal of owning a shotgun, and he has long dreamed of bringing meat to the table of his mother (a war widow) and younger brothers. A friend takes him to the city zoo, where the friend has made a deal with the keepers to kill ravens and jackdaws which are stealing the meat set out for bears and tigers. In making his kill of two fat ravens, the boy wanders near a busy boulevard, where his hunting exploits, in the midst of the city, are witnessed by an astonished crowd. He is arrested and taken to a police station, where the officer in charge, himself a hunter, sympathetically releases the weeping boy with some fatherly advice. The ravens, roasted, delight the boy's family.

These are the bare bones of Semyonov's story. What makes it a moving one is its structure and close attention to physical and psychological detail. By the time the boy gets a chance to use his new weapon, we know a lot about him, like him, and are at one with him in his obsession to own and use the gun and help his family; we share his emotions during the hunt and, crushed, at the police station. Rich in urban social atmosphere, "The Smell of Burnt Powder," through a series of carefully developed and unified episodes of increasing tension, dramatizes an important stage in the development of a most sympathetic and convincing boy. The author does not dwell on the self-evident irony of the fact that the boy, to prove himself to himself, has joined a chain of predators, both animal and human, and that the city in which he lives is, in some respects, a jungle.

As a rule, Semyonov portrays ordinary people in everyday situations in which very little happens. At the same time, the events that do take place and the people who participate in them often have an enigmatic quality. The author seems reticent about providing full motivation or displaying characters in their entirety. In "A Play of Fancy" ("Igra voobrazheniya," 1979), the narrator, at a national conference, meets a charming, very talkative young woman who tells him at length about her three little daughters and especially her husband, a struggling artist some of whose paintings have been inspired by extremely strange, even supernatural, experiences he claims to have had. The woman says she believes her husband completely and stands in awe of him, but is frankly puzzled by him. The narrator is captivated by the woman and about to fall in love with her, when, before the end of the conference, she suddenly flies home. So many questions about this woman and her husband remain unanswered, despite her ebullience, that the bemused reader can only guess and ponder.

Not only does Semyonov present characters who cannot understand one another and often remain a mystery to the reader, the author himself can seem frankly bewildered. In "The Cuckoo Called" ("Kukovala kukushka") a man who has gone to the countryside to fish and rest from the hectic bustle of the city where he lives suddenly finds himself uneasy and confused about just why he has done this. He feels vaguely that there must be some more complicated but undefined reason for his presence in the village, and leaves in psychological chaos; the author, too, seems unwilling to provide enlightenment. In "A Pleasant Habit" ("Priyatnaya privychka," 1985) the author is even franker about his inability: he interrupts his narrative with an extended digression in which he confesses that he cannot explain one prominent but somewhat mysterious character. On the other hand, in this same story he presents, with clarity and in depth, the image of a posing, self-dramatizing woman who plays with life but is afraid to live it honestly.

More often than not, Semyonov's stories are melancholy, dominated by a sense of human inadequacy and feelings of loss. At times there is a feeling of horror. "The Collection" ("Kollektsiya," 1985) tells of a middle-aged bookkeeper, divorced, living alone, and friendless. He has intellectual pretensions and goes on talking jags in which he decorates his cheap, stupid philosophizing with pseudo-literary verbiage. Only at the end of the story do we discover that his apartment is crammed with birds, in action poses, which he has killed and stuffed. This is a man not merely unable to appreciate beauty in its live, natural state; he is, in fact, a moral cripple.

Semyonov's style is graceful and polished. His stories have abundant sensory detail, and his portrayal of nature is sensitive and animated. Both his knowledge of human psychology and his moral sense are impressive. It is irritating, however, when he breaks into a narrative, as he does in "A Pleasant Habit," to expatiate on matters of literary theory in a manner that might be suitable in a novel but is not appropriate to a short story.

Andrei Bitov established himself in the 1960s as a writer to whom conventional labels did not seem to apply. Born in 1937, he was only slightly younger than such militant iconoclasts and satirists as Vasilii Aksenov, Anatolii Gladilin, and Vladimir Voinovich, but he avoided their style of sharp social protest. Although he is a near contemporary of Valentin Rasputin, Vladimir Makanin, and Anatolii Kim, his work bears no resemblance to theirs. He himself has said that he does not belong to any literary "generation," and his writing continues to remain outside any formal grouping.

Before he had reached the age of thirty, Bitov had become known as a prose stylist, a delicate psychologist, and a subtle and complicated thinker about aesthetic, moral, and philosophical concerns. In more recent years he has become a versatile, authoritative man of letters – short-story writer, novelist, literary scholar, critic, poet, and essayist on ethnography, geography, history, and ecology, and other cultural matters. From 1975 to 1985, because of his participation in the *Metropol'* project, he was virtually blacklisted by Soviet publishers, but with the coming of *glasnost'* his works have appeared prominently and frequently. His novel *Pushkin House* (*Pushkinskii dom*), which had been published abroad in 1978, finally appeared in Russia in 1987.

Much of Bitov's writing is so cerebral and intricate that he has been accused of being excessively intellectual in his approach to his art. He indeed seems to be more self-consciously "literary" than most of his contemporaries. *Pushkin House*, for example, is so heavily laden with literary allusions and cross-references that a reader who is not equipped with a knowledge of Russian writing, particularly that of the nineteenth century, may find himself seriously handicapped. Even works that are not so specifically literary in orientation, such as the recent story "The Man in the Landscape" ("Chelovek v peizazhe," 1987), are often compounded of speculations, direct and indirect, on such a multiplicity of interconnected themes, that they sometimes seem abstruse and deliberately mystifying. However, Bitov makes no apology to his readers. In an interview in 1988, he admitted that his works are not for the "mass reader," but coolly explained, "I am busy with my own business."

This business, it must be added, is not as exclusive and esoteric as the above remarks might indicate. Although Bitov is clearly an intellectual and an aesthete profoundly interested not only in the philosophy and fine points of his craft but also in its relationship to the other arts and to culture in general, he is also deeply concerned with the human condition in both its contemporary and its historic manifestations.

Bitov's stories frequently focus on the mental and emotional processes of an intelligent, educated, young, or early middle-aged man. As a rule they involve, in varying degrees, this man's relationships with women, his attitude toward his work and creativity (he is often a writer), his speculations on aging and death, his feeling toward his parents, his wife, and his own fatherhood, and, in general, his spiritual evolution. The external characteristics of this hero – his name, age, occupation, place of residence, marital status – sometimes vary, but despite his different guises he is essentially the same person. Keenly observant of the outside world, he is also self-centered, endowed (or possibly cursed) with a powerful talent for introspection and self-analysis. Bitov shows in detail his reactions to usually undramatic, ordinary life experiences that result in self-revelation and mark stages in his psychic and moral development.

The development is not easy: the hero is a vacillator, given to self-doubt and, despite a degree of fallibility that is no greater than ordinary, to periods of self-loathing. On the surface a normally functioning, creative, responsible individual, Bitov's hero is often lonely and tormented, puzzled over his own behavior and its ethical implications. Although at times his analysis of himself can lead to periods of consoling revelation, at others, as in the story "The Taste" ("Vkus," 1987), it can lead to a rage of guilt and despair.

There is, however, nothing pathological about the hero. It is simply that he feels with a particular intensity the doubts, confusion, and feelings of inadequacy that bedevil many sensitive individuals. Bitov makes no secret of the fact that his hero, although not strictly autobiographical, is a man who internally resembles the author himself. And while Bitov is quite capable of creating interesting characters who are totally unlike the author, he seems incapable of going very deeply into their psyches. At least until recently, he has preferred to concentrate on a figure whose mental landscape is close to his own. This figure seems frequently to be asking himself "Why am I like this?" and sometimes to go on to the question "Why do I ask myself why I am like this?" This is not idle narcissistic curiosity: the hero's preoccupation with his own motivation springs from an active conscience and ethical sense, a feeling of the need to relate decently and respectfully to other human beings and living creatures, and a sense that he is doing this inadequately. He is in fact not sure of the dividing line between real and unreal, or between good and evil, and it is this unease that leads him to examine so closely his own mental processes.

Critics who demand that writing be socially oriented have often accused Bitov of being excessively subjective. It is true that although the hero of many of his stories (frequently his name is Monakhov – derived from the Russian word for "monk," suggesting his isolation) is a separate entity, his voice is often tantalizingly close to that of the author. One reason for this closeness is that the hero's view of things is often in fact that of the author. Another is that Bitov is especially fond of detailing, examining, and evaluating thought processes, and the intimacy with which he does this can give the impression that writer and hero are identical.

In general the writer's presence is often very prominent in Bitov, and frankly so. He is fond of little authorial asides and of longer digressions in which he complains of his trouble with his plot and characters, poses alternative strategies, and ponders about matters that are only loosely related to, and sometimes remote from, his main narrative. It is in these deviations that we see the author as a restless, far-ranging intellectual, an assiduous aesthete whose sense of artistic discipline, paradoxically, is flexible to excess.

Bitov's interests, which extend from art to Zoology and which include a profound concern for ecology and the place and destiny of the human race, are so interconnected that any attempt to single out separate topics is bound to seem somewhat artificial. It should be noted, nevertheless, that a strong sense of history, and particularly of cultural history, governs much of his work. Writing about the present, he deftly inserts references that provide a historic dimension to his characters and situations. In the story "The Doctor" ("Doktor," 1978), for example, his admiring portrait of an elderly Jewish woman physician carefully points out that much of her devoted service to humanity took place in the Stalin period – information that subtly increases her stature. Just as subtly, he indicates that his troubled hero Monakhov suffers from anxieties that, in part, come from the malaise of the Soviet intelligentsia in the Brezhnev period of "stagnation." Bitov's consciousness of Russian cultural history is most evident in the novel *Pushkin House*, which is based largely on a contrapuntal usage of materials from the nineteenth and twentieth centuries.

A sense of history, in combination with a respectful fascination with the cultural traits of the former Soviet Union's ethnic minorities, permeates Bitov's numerous travel writings, and especially *Lessons of Armenia* (*Uroki Armenii*, 1968). Here the writer emphasizes not so much the exotic aspects of these non-Russian peoples as he does the ways in which a knowledge of their cultural history can help him understand his own nationality. In these travel notes the questionings, attitudes, and changing impressions expressed by Bitov the narrator create a chronicle of spiritual development that is similar in kind to that of his fictional heroes. His travelogues are, in large measure, intellectual and spiritual autobiographies.

The very process of writing – its psychology, its means of groping for truth, its potential for overcoming time and space, the search for suitable forms and structures – is one of the major themes of Bitov's work. He seems to be constantly striving to find new dimensions, new angles of vision, some way of overcoming the intrinsic limitations of the written word, and he seems eager to share with the reader the delights and agony of his struggle. An impressive stylist, he writes prose that is graceful and rich in sensory imagery. He is particularly effective in creating physical atmosphere, and in showing how the weather, the landscape, and man-made objects – houses, furniture, even pots and pans – affect the human psyche. Bitov can be a show-off: occasionally his turns of phrase seem more elegant than necessary, and his psychological analysis overly elaborate. He can also be a tease: his sense of fun sometimes leads him to startle the reader by breaking the rhythm and sequence of narration, or by confiding that he simply cannot resolve some writing problem.

A problem that Bitov indeed seems frequently unable to solve is the naming of his characters and stories, and the grouping and dating of the latter. An examination of numerous editions of his works suggests that he is an inveterate shuffler, re-arranger and re-namer who is often unwilling to leave well-enough alone. While Bitov seems fond of picking at and partially re-writing his published stories, there are other reasons for his apparent confusion. Some of his works, and notably large parts of the novel *Pushkin House*, could not have passed censorship at the time they were completed. Others were finished at a time when publishers were boycotting him because of the *Metropol'* affair. As a result, some of these works had to be published much later than the author intended, and out of the intended sequence. It is true that, as published, his individual stories have an impressive integrity and completeness of their own. But Bitov seems naggingly uncertain about how they all fit together.

To date, Bitov's most ambitious attempt to put together a multiplicity of characters, ideas, moods, and strains is *Pushkin House*. This is a work of great historical and cultural depth, arresting social relevance, and considerable, although not consistent, aesthetic interest. Its main event is the partial trashing of Russia's most famous literary museum, on the eve of the annual celebration of the October revolution, by a young scholar who has been assigned to watch after the museum over the holiday. The young scholar, Lyova Odoevtsev, is then killed in the museum in a drunken duel by the young man who has been his nemesis since childhood. Or, if we are to choose an alternate version of the affair which Bitov provides in an epilogue, Lyova is merely stunned, revives, and manages to repair the damage from the trashing before anyone notices.

Whatever the outcome, the scandalous episode is farcical. The weapons in the clumsy, inebriated duel are antique museum pistols similar to the one by which Pushkin himself died, and the duel itself is a wild parody of Pushkin's own. In fact, the whole novel makes extensive parodic use of such nineteenth-century Russian classics as Turgenev's *Fathers and Children*, Lermontov's *A Hero of Our time*, and Pushkin's *The Bronze Horseman*. It also refers, in parodical fashion, to dozens of other writers and works of that century. The purpose, however, is not to ridicule this literature, but to employ it as an ironic framework in which to examine the situation of a twentieth-century Soviet Russian intellectual, his family, and his acquaintances.

Lyova Odoevtsev, age thirty, is a philologist and a hereditary member of the Russian intellectual aristocracy. His father is a prominent and well-established literary scholar, and his grandfather, who has recently returned from many years in the Gulag, was an even more distinguished scholar before his imprisonment. Blue-blooded and protected from many of the harsh realities of life, Lyova is making a career as a scholar and critic, working in the hallowed archival museum known as Pushkin House. But Lyova has a complicated private life. He is fitfully, jealously and hopelessly in love with the sexy Faina, who perfidiously toys with his affections. He is unable to respond adequately to the worthy and intelligent Albina, who has been selflessly devoted to him for many years. And he is alternately cajoled and bullied by the crafty and vulgar Mitishat'ev, whom he has known since their schoolboy days, and who is to be his duelling opponent.

Lyova is not a bad fellow, but he is not particularly admirable. He is honest, highly cultured, and intelligent enough to appreciate his valuable heritage, but he is indecisive and rather feckless. (One reason for his disorientation may be his faint but disturbing realization that his heritage is tainted: his father, to save his own skin, turned on his grandfather at the time of the latter's political incarceration.) He seems to lack a really fundamental set of beliefs and sense of purpose – as a schoolboy, he was even apathetic over the death of Stalin. His hothouse childhood has made him naive; he is completely unable, for example, to understand his grandfather, an eccentric transformed by years of prison life that Lyova cannot conceive of. Despite his years of acquaintance with Mitishat'ev, he seems incapable of fathoming the sheer malice which Mitishat'ev represents. In sum, Lyova is a mixture of the classic nineteenth-century "superfluous man" and a Russian intellectual of the second half of the twentieth century who seems unable to save himself from drowning in the surrounding vulgarity.

Although there are subplots, numerous supporting episodes, and a few interesting additional characters, these are the essentials of Bitov's story. The rest of the 400-page novel is devoted to literary play, some of it witty and light-hearted, some of it fairly ponderous, but all of it devoted to a kind of literary exercise. The work is packed with overt and covert allusions to Russian literature (Dostoevsky, Tolstoy, Blok, Nabokov, etc.) and to a lesser extent to foreign literatures (Proust, Joyce, Hemingway, etc.). There are chatty little essays on cultural and moral topics, and on writing and writers in general. Bitov toys with his plot, offering hints and foreshadowings, repeating whole passages, commenting on his authorial difficulties, discussing alternative versions of episodes and developments, and inviting the reader to choose between them. The sum total of all this is a kind of literary compendium focusing on St. Petersburg and designed to make a statement, in historical perspective, about the condition of Russian culture in the 1960s.

There is abundant evidence that Bitov is still a dynamically developing writer. His abiding interest in Pushkin, whom he obviously considers to be the pinnacle of Russian culture, is shown in his constant references to the author, essays about him, and, most recently, the fantastic story "Pushkin's Photograph

(1799–2099)" ("Fotografiya Pushkina (1799–2099)," 1987).
At the end of the twenty-first century, on Pushkin's three
hundredth birthday, young Igor Odoevtsev, a descendant of
Lyova and Faina (he *did* marry her, after all!), and therefore a
"hereditary Pushkinist," is dispatched by a space-time machine
to the early nineteenth century for the purpose of obtaining a
live photograph and voice recording of the great poet. After a
number of bewildering, and often comic, adventures in which
he leaps about in Pushkin's times and locales in search of his
quarry, manages several brief and inconsequential encounters
with Pushkin, and actually resides in the old Russia for an
extended period, Oleg finally returns to his own time – with
blurred and fragmentary photographs and unintelligible tape
recordings. His attempt to meddle in history (among other
things, he has tried to prevent Pushkin's fatal duel) has been a
complete flop. As it often is with Bitov, this story is a vehicle for
the examination of Russian cultural history and the author's
meditations on its implications for the present, as well as a
medium for further subjective authorial musings on the process
of literary creation – its moral values, psychology, and means of
cognition.

There have often been opaque patches in Bitov's writing,
passages inviting a variety of interpretations, and sometimes
simply unintelligible. The confusion, I suspect, largely results
from the author's multiple allusiveness, his effort to combine
widely diverse thematic material in an optimally compact
package. The confusion is compounded by the author's constant
search for new ways of seeing things and saying things. A case in
point is his story "The Man in the Landscape," which begins
with the authorial narrator's encounter and long conversation
with a voluble and eccentric painter, a meeting that degenerates
into a drunken evening of nightmarish proportions. The author
and his chance acquaintance discuss, often in an alcoholic haze,
a large number of fundamental questions. Among them are God
and the Devil and man's relationship to them; the nature of
creativity and numerous allied questions of aesthetics; reality
versus beauty and illusion; man versus nature; Russia's past in
opposition to her present; the erosion of culture; and, of course,

the short-term and long-term effects of alcohol on human cognition. Both the intellectual dimensions and the unwieldiness of the complex thematics of this thirty-six-page story are suggested in a question which, fairly early on and before they get drunk, the painter poses to the author: "Where is man? who is man? and why is man?"[4]

The most prominent representative of ethnic minorities among Soviet writers in the 1970s and 1980s was Chingiz Aitmatov. A Kirghiz born in 1928, Aitmatov first wrote in his native language and then gradually switched to Russian. By 1975, he was a fully established and highly popular Russian-language writer, known primarily for his short stories and novellas, the most distinguished of which was *The White Ship* (*Belyi parokhod*, 1970). Aitmatov had also established a career as an influential public figure and member of the official literary establishment, a career which he continued to pursue into the 1990s. Among other things, he became an adviser to Gorbachev and served as the Soviet ambassador to Luxemburg. Although he steadily remained within the bounds of Soviet orthodoxy (for example, dutifully signing public letters condemning Andrei Sakharov and Aleksandr Solzhenitsyn), his public position and his fiction have often come close to overstepping the bounds.

Aitmatov often writes of the pain of personal and social injustice and the oppression and suffering of innocents. He relates human tragedies with unblinking candor, and his stories have often had such a pessimistic cast that it is difficult to find any gleam of affirmation in them. The element that preserves them from the blackest gloom is the author's obvious love and respect for simple, good people and their aspirations. It should also be added that, at least in his earlier works, Aitmatov was careful to bow in the direction of socialist-realist orthodoxy by inserting rays of hope: in the end an idealistic but still powerless young communist would take note of an injustice or an evil situation for possible future remedial action.

The greatest strength of Aitmatov comes from his observant affection for the landscape of Central Asia and its folk tradition. His dynamic descriptions of the steppes and mountains of

Kirghizia and Kazakhstan, the workings of the weather and seasons, the behavior of animals and birds, are poetically powerful. The stories themselves are often inspired by, or at least closely integrated with, folk legends of ancient vintage, which not only lend the narrative an aura of ethnic authenticity but also serve as a parabolic commentary on a story's events and conflicts.

Aitmatov's talent for close observation of nature and of people who are intimate with it is not confined solely to the settings of his native Central Asia. One of his finest stories, "A Spotted Dog, Running by the Seashore" ("Pegii pes, begush-chii kraem morya," 1977), is located in the Far East, on the Sea of Okhotsk. A boy, his father, his uncle, and an old man, in a four-oared boat on the boy's first seal-hunting expedition, become lost for days in a great fog. To preserve the meager supply of fresh water for the boy, the men abstain from drinking it and each of the men, in turn, disappears overboard. Rich in physical and psychological detail, it is a story of men against nature, of noble love and self-sacrifice. Typically, the story makes extensive use of local customs, myth, and legend. As is frequently the case with Aitmatov, the story's remote setting emphasizes the intensity and timelessness of its spiritual drama.

The Day lasts More than a Hundred Years (*I dol'she veka dlitsya den'*, 1980) is the first, and more successful, of Aitmatov's two novels. Set in the early 1950s at a remote siding in Kazakhstan consisting of a handful of railroad buildings and workers' houses, it combines four time levels. The first is patriarchal antiquity, from which comes the legend of the *mankurts* – victims of a ghastly form of torture that leaves them as virtual robots devoid of both memory and will. This legend and other equally ancient ones underline both the current and the timeless thematics of the novel. In the second time level – the early years after World War II – a number of tragic events caused by Stalinism take place. The chief of these is the destruction of a good man, and the orphaning of his family, in a frameup by the KGB on a charge of disloyalty. The third time level is the narrative present, during which the novel's main character, a steadfast, ordinary workman, endeavors to find burial for the body of his best friend in an ancient, legendary Kazakh cemetery, only to discover that the cemetery is sealed off and about to be leveled as part of a government military-scientific reservation. In the fourth time level we have the near future in a science-fiction framework. A Soviet–American team of cosmonauts inadvertently discovers a benevolent civilization in another galaxy, which wants to make contact with Earth. The prospect of such an unknown so frightens the two terrestrial governments that they terminate contact with their cosmonauts and create a defensive ring of satellites around the earth.

The novel works. Its various elements, which in outline may seem impossibly disparate are in fact integrated by their common concern over the history and destiny of humans and all living things. Not all of the human characters are adequately developed – for example, the two cosmonauts. There is some authorial preaching; the political values are so impeccably anti-Stalinist that they seem somewhat dutiful. (The victim of the frameup is posthumously rehabilitated.) But the vigor and vividness of the narration are so great (the hero's magnificent camel goes on a heroic rampage in rutting season), the treatment of human suffering and tragedy so compelling, and the ethnic aura so charmingly pervasive and cohesive, that the inadequacies are easily ignored. Central Asia, its traditions, and its creatures – both human and wildlife – and their linkage to all creation, are displayed most vividly and memorably.

The greatest strength of the novel *The Execution Block* (*Plakha*, 1986, published in English in 1989 as *The Place of the Skull*), which takes place in both Kirghizia and Kazakhstan, is its portrayal of a pair of wolves and their natural environment. Its greatest weakness is diffuseness: in addition to the wolves, who are victimized by human greed, we have gangs of rapacious hoodlums – drug-runners gathering Central Asian hemp for the Russian market and officially sponsored meat hunters, who slaughter herds of antelope with machine guns from helicopters; an erstwhile, heretic theological student and Christ-like figure, who disastrously tries to persuade these predators to mend their ways; and an exemplary, independent, and enterprising shepherd whose life is ruined by a drunken lout who is jealous of his success and family happiness, and by a mean-spirited Party secretary who resents what he considers the shepherd's defiance of the collective.

This novel became one of the most widely discussed and controversial works of Soviet literature of the 1980s. A main reason was its topicality. It was, for example, the first work of Soviet literature to deal with the drug trade and drug abuse. It raised alarms about man's senseless exploitation of the environment and interference with ecology, his blind worship of technology and industrialization. Such currently fashionable targets as tight control over the press and rigid, dogmatic, centralized management of the rural economy were prominent in the novel. Of more profound topical interest was Aitmatov's portrayal of Soviet society as morally empty, dominated by an official ideology that was inadequate to contemporary needs. In featuring a proselytizing Christian (albeit a naive and not-too-bright one) as his major character, the author was accused of pernicious "God-seeking."

Equally controversial were the novel's aesthetic characteristics. Although its two main sections (the account of the ex-seminarian and his losing fight against iniquity, and the tragic tale of the shepherd's destruction) are thematically connected, if loosely, they are really separate stories. The presence of the two wolves in both stories, which is intended to provide cohesion, is inadequate. The writing is often wooden and clumsy: particularly awkward and jarring is the insertion of a dream featuring a dialogue between Christ and Pontius Pilate – a lame borrowing from Bulgakov's *The Master and Margarita*.

Although they do not save the novel, there are strong points. The pair of wolves, if somewhat implausibly humanized, are nevertheless noble and touching as representatives of the natural world and victims of human thoughtlessness and cruelty. Once again, Aitmatov's use of myth and legend, and his loving description of the Central Asia terrain, are poetically moving. Also, his moral alarm and forebodings are convincing, but they have the flavor of journalism more than art.

In a seemingly leisurely fashion over the course of nearly three decades, Fazil Iskander (born 1929) has written what, for want of a better term, can be called an epic novel, *Sandro of Chegem* (*Sandro iz Chegema*, 1983). The work is a loose accumulation of novellas set in the author's native Caucasian region of Abkhazia and centering (although not consistently) on Sandro, a roguish local character who embodies many of the most colorful traits of his small, exotic, Muslim ethnic group. Iskander's Abkhazia is a mythical construct that is nevertheless, like William Faulkner's Yoknapatawpha County, authentically rooted in a regional culture. The stories Iskander tells about it extend over nearly the entire twentieth century, although they concentrate on the past fifty years. They are lively, often improbable, full of adventure, arresting characters, and local color, and packed with robust humor. Until 1988, when the Sandro epos was finally published in full, it had been printed in the Soviet Union only in fragments; many of its stories, especially those featuring wickedly sly satires on Stalinism, had been rejected by the censors.

The episodes in this huge and growing work (Iskander keeps on adding to it) are arranged in no particular sequence. They leap back and forth in time and place (the mountainous interior of Abkhazia and its more urbanized valleys and seashore), characters appear and disappear at random, digressions are the rule rather than the exception. Iskander himself has written that the work began as "a gentle parody of the picaresque novel," but that "the concept gradually became more complicated, overgrown with details." Iskander's most perceptive Western critic, Laura Beraha, has called the work a "compilation" based on the principle of "stacking" or "piling up."[5] Such is Iskander's magic that this seeming welter does not, in the end, give the impression of disorder. Cumulatively, through multiple associations and judicious repetition, they create a rich and complex portrait of an entire society and culture in historic depth.

Although a comic, ironic tone predominates as Iskander pokes fun at nearly everything involving human nature and its vivid Abkhazian manifestations, a tragic sense underlies the whole. The violence of social disorder and blood vengeance; the deleterious effects of the Soviet regime, collectivization, and the Stalinist Terror on the native way of life; and the common human misfortunes of poverty, illness, and death frequently come to the surface. Sandro, the hero, an unreliable neer-do-well, petty operator, and trickster who supplements occasional small, part-time employment with jobs as a professional *tamada* (toastmaster) and dancer, is a charming, vital embodiment of human frailty. His vast array of relatives (including his father, who is a much better man than Sandro), and the family customs, folkways, and national traditions they embody, provide much of the thematic cement that holds the novel together. Likewise, the prominent element of satire, directed not only at Soviet ideology and the cliches that accompany it but also at universal human foibles, helps to unify the novel.

Perhaps the most engaging feature of *Sandro of Chegem* is the personality of the author himself. Despite its precise, detailed, and authentic ethnic and geographical background, Chegem is clearly a mythical world, the product of one writer's fertile, lively, and unfettered imagination. The very whimsicality of Iskander, his tall tales, his wry (although sometimes garrulous) flights of philosophizing, his fondness for parodying Soviet officialese, his love for creating oddball characters, and his pervasive humanity, all are compellingly endearing.

While he was accumulating the stories that make up *Sandro of Chegem*, Iskander was also writing a cycle of semi-autobiographical stories about childhood. Most of them focus on the experiences of Chik, a bright, lively, and perceptive schoolboy who grows up in the Black Sea city of Sukhumi. Chik is no paragon. He has a normal capacity for mischief, saying the wrong thing, credulity, and disobedience. But he is also curious, gregarious, and an independent thinker. For him the world is fundamentally a sunny and fascinating place, but its adult sector, as seen from Chik's point of view, is puzzling and often fails to make sense. Chik *wants* to believe that the world of adults is rational and just; the evidence tells him it is not.

The stories about Chik are free of didacticism, but they show the boy to be very much the child of his tragic times. Like his

classmates in the 1930s, Chik wants to believe that what his
teachers, textbooks, and other sources of public information tell
him is true. He believes, therefore, that the Soviet Union is
constantly menaced by foreign spies and "wreckers," since "he
had heard much about secret saboteurs' signs cunningly
insinuated on cigarette boxes, medical posters, books about the
revolution, and even children's blocks." When a classmate
suggests to him that the cover of an exercise book, illustrating a
poem of Pushkin, actually contains the cabalistic message
"Down With Stalin," Chik eagerly, but unsuccessfully, tries to
decipher it. When a group of children on the street surround
and taunt an unknown man as a "saboteur" simply because he
has an unpleasant face, Chik too is swept up in the excitement.

Chik lives in an Abkhazia of the 1930s and 1940s that is in
many respects warm and "normal," providing the boy with
delights, and inculcating in him beliefs and loyalties. He is
romantically inspired by what he has been told about the
revolution and its mythical heroes. At the same time, he learns
gradually that the adult life about him is tainted with anxieties
and sorrows, occasioned by an atmosphere of suspiciousness,
mysterious disappearances, and sudden exiles. We are thus
shown a world, as seen from a child's perspective, that is both
benevolent and ominous.

Iskander's stories abound in animals and birds. One of the
best tales in *Sandro of Chegem* is the monologue of a mule. The
author's long "philosophical tale," *Rabbits and Boa Constrictors*
(*Kroliki i udavy*, 1982), is a clever, often hilarious allegory of the
revolution, the developing Soviet power, and their moral
consequences. It portrays a community of rabbits, ruled by a
corrupt King and his unsavory court, and a contiguous
community of boas, ruled by the Great Python, which feeds
upon the submissive rabbits. The intrigue begins when, one fine
day, a swallowed rabbit refuses to be digested, stands up inside
his embarrassed boa, kicks, and makes loud, impertinent
remarks about the Great Python, who proclaims (in a parody of
Soviet jargon) that "a boa out of which a rabbit speaks is not a
boa we need." From then on, the story becomes an elaborately
figurative commentary on Soviet society and its institutions,

ideology, and psychology, enlivened by a multitude of reptilian, avian, and animal characters speaking salty, colloquial Russian. *Rabbits and Boa Constrictors* was published in the United States in 1982 but in the Soviet Union, not surprisingly, only in 1987.

Iskander was probably the most effective humorist and satirist in the Soviet Union during its last three decades. Beneath the genial exterior of his stories, and despite their relaxed manner, he has been a bitter opponent of injustice, privilege, official deception, and the bullying of a police state. It would be a mistake, however, to think of him mainly as a political writer, for his works convey an understanding of the human condition that far transcends their time.

The eleven writers in this chapter have been observed as individuals, representing a wide variety of topics, temperaments, styles, and interests. Several of them seem fairly traditional and conventional in the context of Soviet literature; Granin, Zalygin, and Aitmatov, in their narrative manner, appear to have emerged from socialist realism and can be considered as revisionist offshoots of that tendency and mode. The same could be said of Davydov and Trifonov, although they seem farther removed from socialist realism. In this respect, such writers as Bitov, Okuzdhava, and Iskander seem to represent an extreme reaction against literary practices inherited from the Stalin period; the only trace of socialist realism in their works is clearly parodic. In terms of literary history, the most important feature of these eleven authors are their roots, not in socialist realism, but in the Russian classical writers – Pushkin, Gogol, Dostoevsky, Tolstoy, and Chekhov – and in such twentieth-century exemplars as Bely and Zoshchenko. In this sense these eleven, each in his or her own way, represent the continuation of the best strains in the Russian literary heritage.

As a group, these writers represent a consolidation of the gains which Russian literature had accomplished in the 1950s and 1960s, but only a modest advance beyond these gains. Some of them did engage in a degree of further experimentation in literary form and style. This was most notable in Trifonov, Bitov, Iskander, and Okudzhava, and in the largely unsuccessful structural experimentation of Aitmatov's *The Execution Block*. And although all of these writers cultivated some new subject matter and often took bolder stances toward social, ideological, and moral problems than they had in the past, much of their increasingly sharp criticism was simply not published until the era of *glasnost'*. Thus, although these writers continued to develop, they often could not show it.

The satirical element seems notably lacking among these writers in general, and in this respect they are representative of this period as a whole. With the exception of Iskander and Bitov and small portions of Grekova and Tendryakov, their works are not satirical. Even the satire of these four writers represents delayed publication of works written in earlier days and only recently come into print. In the period of "stagnation," many of the best satirists – Voinovich, Aksenov, Aleshkovskii – had gone abroad, voluntarily or involuntarily, because of a climate hostile to satire. Later, in the period of *glasnost'*, social conditions were so ominous and outright grim that there was little incentive to make fun.

The works of Trifonov, Okudzhava, Davydov, Zalygin, Tendryakov, and Bitov are testimony of the increased interest in Russian history of the nineteenth and twentieth centuries, specifically as it relates to the October revolution, the forces that made it, and its consequences. It is probable that writers of fiction actually surpassed the professional historians in their degree of candor and the extent to which they contributed to a revised view of these epic and tragic national developments. It is notable that in their treatment of relatively recent history – such as that of the 1930s – such authors as Tendryakov, Trifonov, Okudzhava, and Iskander often wrote autobiographically, interpreting historical developments through the personal experiences of themselves and their families. There is a profound sense of tragedy, usually with an unmistakably anti-Bolshevist bias, in their stories.

CHAPTER 3

Retrospective writing about the Stalin period

Soviet commentators often and fondly quoted Woland's statement in Bulgakov's *The Master and Margarita* that "manuscripts
don't burn." Many of the works mentioned in the present
chapter were originally "repressed" manuscripts that had been
accumulating in archives and desk drawers for decades. In the
mid-1980s, such works flooded publishing houses and were
consumed eagerly by rapidly increasing numbers of Soviet
readers.

The newly discovered works included many that had long
been known in the West. Examples are Evgenii Zamyatin's
dystopian novel *We*, Boris Pasternak's *Doctor Zhivago*, and Anna
Akhmatova's *Requiem*, a cycle of poems about the suffering of
Russian women under Stalin's terror. These works, and many
other newly revealed treasures from twentieth-century Russian
writing, had been known in varying degrees by the Soviet
literati, who for years had been reading them in circulated
manuscript form or in foreign editions smuggled into the USSR.
For the broad reading public, however, such works were a
revelation.

Until the Gorbachev era, these works were all politically and
ideologically taboo. So were a great many writings by more
contemporary authors, living or recently deceased, whose
criticisms of the Stalin era in particular were thought to be too
vivid, frank, and powerful to bear the light of day. Under the
new circumstances, this literature represented a massive re-
examination of the national experience. Soviet *historians*, by
their own admission, had until very recently been so heavily
indoctrinated with official dogma, and so intimidated by

ideological and political restrictions, that they had often been much less reliable in their testimony than writers of imaginative literature. It was natural, therefore, for literature to assume, at least in part, the burden of chronicling the events and developments that had led up to the turbulence of the 1980s.

The publication of "repressed" literature was a response to pent-up curiosity about a grim and mysterious past which had shaped the lives of everyone. It was also a response to the need for a purging of the national conscience and a prerequisite for the healing of national psychic wounds. For writers, this literature, often autobiographical or partly so, described their most painful, dramatic, and formative life experiences, about which they had heretofore been forced to be silent.

In this climate, aesthetic refinement was less highly prized than information and analysis. What interested both readers and writers was the search for truth, and works were received enthusiastically because of their revelations, even though their artistic quality might be inferior. A key word in critical parlance was *dokumental'nost'* (documentariness) – which meant the writer's reliance on the display of facts rather than the workings of his imagination. The critics were inclined to brush aside the question of whether a piece of journalism can be a work of art, or whether the presentation of information is less worthy, aesthetically, than a writer's invention. It was not that literary standards had fallen, or that writers and critics had somehow become coarse, negligent, or obtuse about literary matters. Many simply felt that the times so urgently demanded a literature of factual disclosure that, for the moment, verifiable truth was more important than finesse and fantasy.

Personal memoirs were an important aspect of documentary literature. These, published by the hundreds, included works that had long been known in the West, such as those of Nadezhda Mandel'shtam, the widow of the great poet; Evgeniya Ginzburg, who survived many years in the Gulag; and Nina Berberova, an emigre in the West who recalled the people and culture of Russia's Silver Age and the intelligentsia in exile. Newer discoveries included the memoirs of the widow of Nikolai Bukharin, one of the major political opponents whom

Stalin executed; Konstantin Simonov, a novelist, dramatist, poet, editor, and war correspondent with high political connections in the Stalin period; Natal'ya Rappaport, the daughter of a great pathologist who was imprisoned in 1953 as a member of the trumped-up "doctors' plot" and released only after Stalin's death; and Lidiya Chukovskaya, an intimate of Anna Akhmatova and distinguished literary figure in her own right.

War literature is a prominent, traditional Russian genre, but the continuation of writing about World War II, nearly half a century after the event, was remarkable. There seem to be a number of reasons for this phenomenon. First, the war was an enormous blow to the nation, a shock whose pain continued to reverberate to the present. Moreover, it was the only event in seventy years of Soviet history when the entire people were united by a common ideal and purpose. During the war, governmental controls and restrictions over the citizenry were somewhat relaxed, so that a whole generation felt freer than either before or after. The war continued to be examined, despite its horrors, as both a liberating and a uniting experience that brought out many of the best qualities of the Soviet people. The coming of *glasnost'* provided a new impetus for writing about the war. Heretofore, despite temporary bursts of candor, many tragic aspects of the conflict had been shrouded in official obfuscation, secrecy, and lies. During and immediately following the war, some literature about it had been relatively candid and free of ideological dogma – one thinks of Simonov's *Days and Nights (Dni i nochi)*, Vasilii Grossman's *The People are Immortal (Narod bessmerten)*, Vera Panova's *The Train* (the English title which was given to her novel *Sputniki*), and Viktor Nekrasov's *Front-Line Stalingrad* (the English title of his *V okopakh Stalingrada*). Soon, however, Stalin's postwar crackdown on all intellectual endeavor turned war literature into a distorting tool of official policy. Then, in the Thaw of the late 1950s and early 1960s under Khrushchev, many good and honest works about the war came out, by writers who had fought in the front lines, such as Georgii Baklanov, Yurii Bondarev, Vasil' Bykov, Ales' Adamovich, and Bulat Okudzhava. Under Brezhnev, war literature was once again muzzled, and the mediocre and self-serving memoirs of Brezhnev himself became touted as the greatest achievement in Soviet literature about the war. The major result of the Brezhnevian controls, however, was not a cessation of good writing about the war but rather the postponement of its publication until more liberal times.

The backlog of literature whose publication was delayed under Brezhnev was large and extremely informative. It included many valuable works of a documentary nature, such as *A Book of the Blockade* (*Blokadnaya kniga*, 1984), by Daniil Granin and Ales' Adamovich – an account of life and death in besieged Leningrad, based on various factual materials, letters, and memoirs of those who experienced the blockade. Another such work is *War's Unwomanly Face* (*U voiny ne zhenskoe litso*, 1983) by Svetlana Aleksievich, a collection of interview accounts of the war by female participants – most of them nurses and medics but many of them combatants. Starkly realistic, convincing in its emotional authenticity, it provides a compassionate, admiring, and powerful cumulative portrait of Byelolrussian womanhood in wartime. Works such as these, through a kind of montage, create collective images of the populace as they fought and endured the war. They also augment and correct the record by providing largely eyewitness accounts of the facts about military events and wartime conditions. In 1990, Aleksievich wrote a similar work about participants in the war in Afghanistan, and their families – *Boys in Zinc* (*Tsinkovye mal'chiki*).

A work that combines the documentary method with personal memoir is Elena Rzhevskaya's *Berlin, May 1945* (*Berlin, Mai 1945*, 1988). A translator with the Soviet army as it took Warsaw and advanced to Berlin, Rzhevskaya was present when Hitler's charred body was found outside his bunker (and was entrusted with the Führer's teeth, which she carried in a box for two days during the search for dentists who could identify them). Her eyewitness account of the taking of Berlin, reinforced by her extensive archival work done decades later, is vivid and detailed. In a companion piece, the author tells of an admiring interview with General Georgii Zhukov in retirement, in which the General, who commanded the entire Berlin campaign, reveals that Stalin, for unknown reasons, kept his commander completely in the dark about the finding of Hitler's remains.

As I have indicated, the period of Thaw under Khrushchev produced a body of superior fiction about front-line warfare, told intimately from the points of view of direct participants. The school of "trench truth" (*okopnaya pravda*) was indeed a kind of memoir literature in fictional guise, since its authors had been soldiers and junior officers who themselves had been combatants. Although this literature was frequently criticized by reactionaries for "deheroization" of the war and "Re-marquism," and although its authors were outnumbered by more orthodox writers who continued to produce large novels in the tradition of socialist realism, this school, which was sometimes called "lieutenants' literature," had succeeded in becoming well established.

The trend of "trench truth" seemed either to have been officially discouraged or largely to have exhausted itself in the Brezhnev years. Exceptions were the writings of Vasil' Bykov and the short novel of Vyacheslav Kondrat'ev *Sashka* (*Sashka*, 1979), whose central figure is a rank-and-file infantryman engaged in the fierce action around Rzhev. What is unique about Kondrat'ev's hero is his modest dignity, selflessness, steadfastness, active kindness, and feeling of his own worth – qualities developed during his harsh life of deprivation and heavy labor as a peasant in the 1930s, and keenly tested by the shortages of food and military equipment he must endure at the front and as he makes his way on foot to hospitals in the rear.

A story that shows the effects of Stalinism in the war effort is Vladimir Tendryakov's "Donna Anna." In its central episode a young officer with a rigidly ideological cast of mind kills his superior, who has been defying – with good reason – an order to advance. The young officer then takes command and leads the troops out of the trenches into a suicidal, futile attack. It matters little that he is subsequently executed for insubordination and murder: the damage his Stalinist personality has done is irreparable.

In *A Cloud Spent the Night* (*Nochevala tuchka zolotaya*), completed in 1981 but published in 1987, Anatolii Pristavkin wrote what is perhaps the most pathetic and disturbing of the war novels. It is the story of very bright twin boys – homeless and apparently orphaned – who are swept up in the mass evacuation of children from European Russia to the Caucasus. Despite individual instances of kindness and solicitude for these innocents, the atmosphere of official administrative neglect and callousness is appalling. So, too, is the reaction of the Soviet populace, who simply fear to notice, much less protest against, this manifest evil. The cruelest and most dramatic episodes in the novel, and its most daring political revelations, center on the fate of the native peoples of the Caucasus, notably the Chechens, whom Stalin, doubting their loyalty, deported wholesale to Siberia during the war, but some of whom remained on their land as pockets of resistance against a genocidal central government.

Vasil' Bykov, one of the most accomplished of the writers who have depicted front-line military action, has also specialized in fiction about guerilla warfare and life in occupied territories. Three novels he published in the 1980s display his remarkable talent for combining fierce anti-Stalinism with an appreciation of the suffering and courage of ordinary Soviet people in wartime. His *Sign of Misfortune* (*Znak bedy*, 1983) related the grim experience of a middle-aged peasant couple, tormented and finally destroyed by the German occupiers and especially by the sadistic local punks who have become Polizei (police in the service of the Germans). What gives the story its particular depth and meaning, however, is the picture of the couple's life in earlier years. Here it becomes evident that the war and Nazi occupation are in fact the culmination of a series of misfortunes that have formed the characters and marred the lives of these peasants. The decade of the thirties, with its unfair expropriation of peasants' property, forced collectivization, purges, and terror, has plagued their existence. The story can easily be interpreted as arguing that the authoritarian process of change in the decade before the war was a cruel, unjust, stupid failure, and that the war itself was just a sharper, more violent version of what had already been done to the people for many years.

Bykov's *The Quarry* (*Kar'er*, 1986) studies the remorse of an officer who, wounded in action, is hidden and protected by Byelorussian villagers and then, in his efforts to return to the Soviet forces, exploits one of his protectors and probably causes her death. Long after the war, he realizes that he has sacrificed a principle to become a more effective fighting man. In 1941, moral scruples had become devalued and inhibitions weakened. It was a time of shocked confusion after Hitler's attack on a woefully unprepared nation and of general suspiciousness among the Soviet people, resulting from the social nightmare of the 1930s. The novel is rich in revealing glimpses of wartime Byelorussia and its social fabric, which includes the widow of a priest who had suffered a lifetime of persecution under the Soviets, and who herself is a fearless, active supporter of the partisans. The hero's initial suspicion of this representative of the "class enemy" is symptomatic of the times.

In the Mist (*V tumane*, 1987) features three Byelorussian villagers, two of them partisans who have been assigned to execute the third – a neighbor who is mistakenly thought to have informed on the guerillas. The two, however, die in action; the third, knowing he cannot prove his innocence, kills himself. The bleak novel, however, is more than a study in hopelessness. Its three characters are clearly products of Soviet culture. One of the would-be executioners is initially willing to kill his neighbor, whom he has known and admired all his life. Only after great moral anguish does he abandon his habit of unquestioning obedience and decide to try to spare his man. The second executioner is sneaky and suspicious, eager to believe the worst about people. He rationalizes his rapacious and cowardly behavior with formulas from the social paranoia of the twenties and thirties, and thinks in Stalinist patterns and cliches. Even their intended victim, a man of dignity, devotion, and courage, has been scarred by the fatalism of the down-trodden. His suicidal resignation to his lot shows him to be as much a victim of social conditioning as of fate.

The most highly acclaimed Soviet novel about World War II is Vasilii Grossman's *Life and Fate* (*Zhizn' i sud'ba*), which was completed in 1960, published abroad in 1985, and finally in the USSR in 1988. A vast, panoramic work centering on the Battle of Stalingrad in 1943, *Life and Fate* is much more than a military novel. Although its battlefield accounts are detailed, vivid, and authentic, based on Grossman's own eyewitness experience, what distinguished it from hundreds of other Soviet war novels is its huge sweep, its social and moral depth. It devotes much more space to life behind the Russian and German lines than to actual combat. The main focus is on the Soviet population (especially the scientific intelligentsia, although all classes are included), but there are numerous portrayals of Germans, including Hitler. There are scenes of the Nazi gas chambers, and poignant characterizations of their victims among Soviet Jews, as well as extensive depictions of the Soviet Gulag system as it operates in wartime. The parallels between Nazism and Stalinism in the novel are numerous.

Life and Fate contests the myth of wartime unity and harmony among the Soviet people. Anti-Semitism is shown to operate at all levels behind the Russian lines. Although the novel includes abundant accounts of Soviet steadfastness and heroism, it also shows brutality, venality, opportunism, and political intrigue among both the military and the civilian populace. Grossman is not an impressive psychologist, but his portrayal of the numerous moral tensions, choices, and compromises which Soviet citizens are forced to make is powerful. With its large and varied cast of characters and depiction of Soviet wartime society as a historically conditioned, complex organism, it is a work of great depth. The novel has the additional distinction of having been "arrested" by the KGB in manuscript form shortly after its completion, and of having been denounced by the high Party official Mikhail Suslov, who assured the author that it would not be published before two or three centuries had elapsed.

It would be incorrect to represent the war writing published in the 1980s as solely a literature of debunking and disparagement. Writers continued, as in previous decades, to display respect and admiration for Soviet soldiers and ordinary civilians. However, the new freedom from the shadow of official formulas enabled them to show both soldiers and civilians as psychologically complex and often morally confused individuals, whose morale was compounded not only of hatred for the Germans and love for the motherland but also of trauma from life under Stalin's dictatorship.

It is interesting that at least one writer has extended a literary olive branch to the former German enemy. Anatolii Genatulin's novel *Tunnel* (*Tunnel'*, 1987) traces the painful evolution of the attitudes of a Russian whose sweetheart had been raped and murdered by Hitler's troops. Obsessed by his loss and a violent hatred of Germans that has made him generally unruly and anti-social, he finds himself employed, in 1949, at a dam construction site where a number of German prisoners of war are also working. Their faultless behavior, which culminates in saving the hero from a drunken suicide attempt, finally causes him to regard them as decent human beings.

Even in the periods of tightest state control, literature about the countryside, the so-called "village prose," had been somewhat more candid than that which was devoted to other aspects of the Soviet scene. Still, readers had been kept in the dark about many features of rural life. The most carefully hidden area of secrecy was the collectivization of agriculture that took place in the early 1930s. Now the new freedom to publish permitted writers, for the first time, to pursue the full truth about this era.

It is clear that a number of village writers, despairing of publishing completely frank works about the period of collectivization, simply stored them in hopes that they might eventually come out. Works of Vasilii Belov, Boris Mozhaev, and Fyodor Abramov that come within this category and were finally published after 1985 are discussed in Chapter 4. Also, the first three in a posthumously published cycle of seven semi-autobiographical stories by Vladimir Tendryakov are about the period of collectivization, in which the author's own father was a rural Party enforcer. As seen through the eyes of the young son, the process of "dekulakization" is grotesque, insane, and often ghastly. The most powerful of these stories, "Bread for a Dog" shows dispossessed peasants dying of starvation on the streets of a rural center, ignored by a callous populace who "no longer consider them people" because they are the "class enemy."

An uncomprehending, pathetic victim of the times is the central figure in Vasil' Bykov's *The Cordon (Oblava*, 1990). A simple peasant buys a threshing machine which he rents for small sums, and often simply lends, to his neighbors. One of them jealously denounces him to the authorities as a kulak; his machine, and then his farm, are confiscated through unbearably heavy taxes, and he is driven from his village. A few years later he attempts to return from his exile. The villagers, now members of a shabby kolkhoz, join the police in hunting him down, and he drowns himself in a swamp.

No less secret than the details about the agrarian tragedy of the early thirties were those about the system of prisons and concentration camps known as the Gulag. This theme had been briefly opened to literature in 1962 with the publication of Aleksandr Solzhenitsyn's *One Day in the Life of Ivan Denisovich (Odin Den' Ivana Denisovicha)* and then quickly suppressed. In the decades before the arrival of *glasnost'* in the USSR, Western readers had become well informed about the Gulag system through the works of Western researchers, the memoirs of expatriates, and such works as Evgeniya Ginzburg's *Journey into the Whirlwind (Krutoi marshrut)*, Anatolii Marchenko's *My Testimony (Moi pokazaniya)*, Georgii Vladimov's novel *Faithful Ruslan (Vernyi Ruslan)*, and, above all, Solzhenitsyn's *The Gulag Archipelago (Arkhipelag Gulag)* – none of which had been allowed Soviet publication. Now these works, and many others on the subject, began to appear.

Solzhenitsyn's *The Gulag Archipelago* had the greatest impact. A mammoth work of research and compilation, prepared with the assistance of a network of collaborators who had extensive and often first-hand knowledge of the Gulag system, and written in moral indignation but also with a passionate concern for historical truth, this work achieved instant popularity and authority. Equally factual and vivid, but much more compact and dispassionate in manner, are the Kolyma stories of Varlam Shalamov. These stories, which often emphasize the total hopelessness of camp existence, present portraits of a wide

variety of the Gulag's victims. A similar variety is included in
the memoirs, in the form of a series of stories and sketches, of Lev
Razgon – like Shalamov a long-term veteran of the camps –
entitled *Not Invented* (*Nepridumannoe*, 1988–89).

Some writers who had direct knowledge of the Gulag, or of its
concomitant – exile in remote regions – chose the medium of
fiction, usually with a prominent factual, autobiographical
ingredient. Such is Anatolii Zhigulin's *Black Stones* (*Chernye
kamni*, 1988), told from the point of view of a student in his late
teens, falsely convicted of anti-Soviet conspiracy and sent to the
Siberian camps. Semi-fictional also is the section of Anatolii
Rybakov's *Children of the Arbat* (*Deti Arbata*, 1987) that tells of its
young hero's experiences in Siberian exile. Yuri Nagibin's short
novel *Arise and Go* (*Vstan' i idi*, 1987), which, the author has
testified, is 90 percent autobiographical, includes several
poignant scenes in which a son goes to visit his father, first in a
camp and later in exile. A less direct but even more striking
evocation of the Gulag is Bulat Okudzhava's story "Girl of My
Dreams", an account of the behavioral change and apparently
profound psychological transformation – both touching and
shocking – which his own mother underwent during her ten
years as a *zek*. As the above-mentioned works and numerous
others indicate, the inhumanity of the Stalinist system of prison
and exile had now become a standard topic of literature.

Similarly, the Great Terror of 1937 and its aftershocks, which
poisoned the social atmosphere until well after the death of
Stalin, became a prominent element in retrospective fiction.
Even works that did not directly focus on this theme often
referred to it indirectly or in background narration.

Nearly all of the works dealing directly with the terror had
been written long before they were finally published. Thus,
Yurii Trifonov's incomplete novel *Disappearance* (*Ischeznovenie*)
was not printed until 1987, several years after the author's
death. A major part of the novel details specifically the events of
1937 – the sudden and secret night arrests of innocent people as
"spies for Germany and Japan," "enemies of the people,"
"Trotskyists," "saboteurs," and "provocateurs," with ac-
companying searches and denunciations. The victims are

chiefly professionals, bureaucrats, and intellectuals, and the novel shows how even well-meaning individuals, under the growing pressure of terror, gradually lose their generosity, human responsiveness, honesty, and sense of justice.

The absurdity of the atmosphere of terror is treated with mordant humor in a number of the stories of Fazil Iskander. In *The Old House Under the Cypress* (*Staryi dom pod kiparisom*, 1987), for example, he shows schoolchildren daily deleting from their textbooks the names of persons who have disappeared as "proven" enemies of the state. In a more somber vein Nagibin's *Arise and Go* emphasizes the absurd fact that all who are engaged in operating the police and prison system of terror *know* that the arrested are innocent, but maintain the pretense that they are guilty.

Sections of Andrei Bitov's *Pushkin House* depict the fate of a professor who was seized in 1937 and languished for three decades in the camps. The terror and its aftermath have transformed him into a bitter, repulsive isolate whose only close associate, in freedom, is his former camp guard. The most interesting psychological portrayal of the Terror, however, is Boris Yampol'skii's *Moscow Street* (*Moskovskaya ulitsa*, 1988). Written in the 1960s and set in 1958, it features an innocent man who is stalked by plainclothes police agents – both real and imaginary – who are furtively pursuing him for an unspecified crime. The setting combines the nasty, hostile, suspicious crowdedness of a Moscow communal apartment with the ominous emptiness of the streets about which the terrified and increasingly paranoid hero wanders at night – an emptiness that is clearly intended to suggest the spiritual desolation of Soviet society of the time.

In many of the aforementioned works, the machinery of the police state is shown in operation. Secret-police surveillance is at the heart of Yampol'skii's novel, and NKVD arrests and interrogations are prominent in Rybakov's *Children of the Arbat*. Zhigulin's *Black Stones* not only depicts the interrogation (including torture) of its young hero but also emphasizes the wild absurdity of his arrest, of the charges brought against him, and of the sentences given to him as well as many others. The most exhaustive and morally penetrating fictional portrayal of the NKVD, however, is in Yuri Dombrovskii's *The Department of Unnecessary Things* (*Fakul'tet nenuzhnykh veshchei*, published in Paris 1978, Moscow 1988). (This novel is a sequel to Dombrovskii's *The Keeper of Antiquities* (*Khranitel'drevnostei*, 1964).[1]) Large sections of the novel concentrate on police interrogations, including beatings, special punishment cells, trickery, and deprivation of sleep in the effort to induce confessions to false charges. Particularly strong are the depictions of individual prisoners, their interrogators, and the relationships between them. The police establishment, and the system that administers it, are shown to be totally cynical and absolutely devoid of moral values. Law and ethical norms, as one interrogator announces, are simply "unnecessary things."

Throughout much of this retrospective literature there are portraits of Joseph Stalin himself, in varying degrees of depth, detail, and persuasiveness.[2] In Dombrovskii's novel, the young hero frequently ponders on Stalin and his significance, and even holds imaginary conversations with the Leader, as with a kind of devil. There are only glimpses of Stalin in Grossman's *Life and Fate*, but his unseen presence permeates the novel. Stalin is a background figure in Vladimir Dudintsev's novel *White Robes* (*Belye odezhdy*, 1987), but a baneful one: the charlatan who is the villain has maintained his spurious plant-breeding empire on the strength of frequent tea-drinkings with the dictator. Stalin's intrusions into the realm of the arts are described in the posthumous memoirs of Konstantin Simonov, *Through the Eyes of My Generation* (*Glazami cheloveka moego pokoleniya*, 1988), in which we see him prescribing and then closely supervising the content of one of Simonov's plays.

In Aleksandr Bek's novel *A New Assignment* (*Novoe naznachenie*, 1986, first published in Frankfurt, 1971) Stalin appears frequently in person, but as an essentially wooden figure. The Leader's impact on the novel, however, is enormous, because his image looms large as the model on which the main character has tried, self-destructively, to base his career. To date the three most prominent fictional treatments of Stalin, all successful in different ways, are those of Solzhenitsyn, Iskander, and Rybakov. In Solzhenitsyn's *The First Circle* (*V kruge pervom*, Soviet publication 1990), Stalin appears as a menacing, fascinating but fundamentally grotesque character – a portrait somewhat lacking in psychological subtlety and profundity. In contrast to Solzhenitsyn, Iskander, in the episode "Belshazzar's Feast" from *Sandro of Chegem*, does not attempt to enter Stalin's mind extensively, but his external portrait is vivid and sharp in its emphasis on the dictator's sadistic treatment of his inner circle. A convincing Stalin is that of Rybakov's *Children of the Arbat*, which combines interior monologue – relating Stalin's musings, paranoid suspicions, and manipulative calculations – with accounts of his conversation and demeanor. The most detailed and intimate, although somewhat clumsy, fictional portrait of Stalin to date is in Ales' Adamovich's "Understudy: Dreams with Open Eyes" ("Dublyor: sny s otkrytymi glazami," 1988). Adamovich, too, uses interior monologue and, occasionally, stream-of-consciousness to recount the daydreams and imaginary conversations of Stalin with various individuals, including family members, who were important in his life from time to time. In many respects this is the starkest picture of Stalin to date, with its emphasis on his megalomania, obsessive fears, and total contempt for the people under his rule.

The moral devastation of society at large during the Stalin period is emphasized in many works. In Nagibin's *Arise and Go*, the grimy provincial town of his father's exile has a predatory, suspicious, jealous populace that is eager to destroy any individual who finds an opportunity to liberate himself from it. Yampol'skii's Muscovites are a grotesque wolf-pack, brutalized, scheming, and full of mutual hatred. Aleksandr Bek's *A New Assignment* features a high-level *apparatchik*, a fundamentally honest man who is so slavishly devoted to the service of Stalin that he becomes morally obtuse, unable to notice or consider the cost – in terms of terror and the destruction of human life – of the industrial and military might he is helping to create.

Rybakov's *Children of the Arbat* provides an example of ingrained immorality in the rise of a jealous, resentful, cunning young man who finds a career in the NKVD. A more thoroughgoing exposure of pervasive moral corruption, centering in this instance on the year 1949, is Dudintsev's *White Robes*, which concerns a scientific-academic empire similar to that of the notorious plant-breeder Trofim Lysenko, built on falsification of evidence, spying, misinformation, denunciation, and suasion and reinforced by chauvinistic, anti-Western, anti-Semitic dogma.

The depredations by the Stalin regime against the Soviet creative intelligentsia remain, even today, a major topic of discussion among intellectuals. This havoc is a major topic of the retrospective literature published in the Gorbachev era. Vladimir Tendrytakov's novella "The Hunt" is an auto-biographical account of the persecution of fancied "enemies of the people" and the anti-Semitic baiting of "cosmopolitans" in 1948, which devastated a cowed and corrupted Moscow literary community. Dombrovskii's *The Department of Unnecessary Things* features an insane attack by the NKVD on an innocent archaeological enterprise in Central Asia, through the arrest of a young philologist-historian and the unsuccessful attempt to destroy him by means of an elaborate frameup and show-trial. Throughout the novel, freedom of intellectual endeavor, and the forces that frustrate it, are matters of deep concern.

The ordeal of science under Stalin is depicted in detail in *White Robes*. Not only does the novel portray the repressive measures – including the destruction of careers and, literally, book-burning – employed to maintain a fradulent scientific empire; it also shows how honest scientists went underground and camouflaged their work in an effort to preserve it. Daniil Granin's *Bison* is the sympathetic documentary profile of a famous Russian scientist who went abroad in the 1920s and chose to remain in Hitler's Germany, knowing that Stalinist policies and controls, and the cancer of Lysenkoism, would have brought about his professional demise. In Grossman's *Life and Fate*, a prominent physicist who is the victim of an anti-Semitic intrigue is saved from extinction, ironically, because Stalin decides that he needs him for research that has potential military significance.

The confusion and psychological strain of life under Stalin are major topics of retrospective literature. Particularly prominent is the theme of divided allegiance, which often leads to betrayal and subsequent remorse. Four stories already mentioned will illustrate. In Tendryakov's "Bread for a Dog" we are given the wrenching picture of a boy who adores his father – a hero of the revolution and commissar who now serves as an enforcer of Stalin's cruel collectivization. Torn between love of his father and pity for his father's victims, the boy guiltily sneaks food to starving "kulaks" in the streets, and, when the effort fails, attempts to salve his conscience by feeding a stray dog. In Bykov's *Cordon*, the manhunt that pursues the victim into a swamp is commanded by his own son, who had repudiated his "kulak" father and changed his name in his rise to local power. A profoundly remorseful son appears in Abramov's "Journey into the Past," in which a boy, induced by elders to renounce his father as a traitor and class enemy, learns as a man that his father had actually been a hero in defying repressive authorities. He becomes an alcoholic and finally, in a drunken gesture of repentance, freezes to death on his father's grave.

Nagibin's *Arise and Go* is the moving and psychologically penetrating account, largely autobiographical, of a son and father during the Stalin years, from the point of view of the son. The father, a good and courageous man, was exiled in the early 1930s, and then imprisoned in the Gulag in 1937, because in the previous decade he had been employed in private business (the commodities exchange). He was forced to spend the rest of his life in restricted areas away from cities. To protect themselves, the son and other members of the family hid their relationship to the "criminal" father and saw him only on rare occasions, under circumstances of elaborate and humiliating secrecy. The story focuses primarily, however, on the increasingly remorseful attitude of the son toward his father. He gradually learns how cruelly and unjustly his father has been treated, and comes to understand not only the moral suffering which prison, exile, and estrangement from his family have brought to his father, but also his quiet fortitude in enduring this suffering. The son becomes overwhelmed by feelings of guilt over having misunderstood and neglected and, in effect, betrayed his own parent.

It is important to note that retrospective literature about the Stalin period does not create an unrelieved atmosphere of demoralization. The memoirs of Natalya Rappaport, for example, show great resilience in the human spirit under terrible pressure. Dudintsev's honest scientists have just been mentioned. The boy in Tendryakov's "Bread for a Dog" is so sickened by the suffering and death about him that he becomes hysterical, but he remains sensitive and does not succumb to callousness. In Nagibin's autobiographical story, his father, and the father's fellow-veterans of the Gulag, retain their dignity and do not complain about their torment. The twins in Pristavkin's *A Cloud Spent the Night* are lively, bright, and attractive in the face of extreme adversity.

In Zhigulin's *Black Stones*, the student group of naive idealists to which the narrator belongs, and which, absurdly, is an NKVD target, is touching and inspiring in its moral purity. The narrator himself is endowed with the courage, sense of humor, balance, and intelligence of a survivor. The most interesting and inspiring of them all, however, is Dombrovskii's young archaeologist. Incarcerated on a ridiculous charge, he resists his interrogators (and torturers) with a dignified sense of his own worth (he wins a hunger strike), ironic humor, a bold willingness to speak his mind under extremely dangerous circumstances, and a morally acute belief in his own values.

It would be an exaggeration to say that the positive human qualities depicted in this literature were responsible for the decline of Stalinism. But they surely helped.

CHAPTER 4

Village prose: its peak and decline

In the fifties, sixties and seventies, the authors of "village prose" – literature about the Russian and Siberian countryside – created a rich body of writing about the age-old, but now threatened, peasant way of life.[1] Often this was a literature of protest over the harsh and unfair lot of the farmer, herded into collective and state farms, deprived of volition, frustrated by the ignorant and impractical demands of central planners, and neglected and exploited by arrogant urban authorities. As a censored literature, it seldom was able to tell the whole truth about the cruelty and malfunctioning of the agricultural system dictated from above, but it did achieve more candor than did writing about any other sector of Soviet society.

At the same time, this literature re-examined in great detail the way of life of rural Russians – their traditions, customs, values, psychology, and aspirations. Most of the village writers were themselves of peasant origin, proud of their roots and eager to celebrate the best of their heritage, but also unafraid of exploring its dark sides. On the whole, village prose displays an intricate mixture of filial affection and solicitude for the countryside and its inhabitants on the one hand, and sadness, revulsion, and anxiety about their future on the other.

Many Soviet critics have argued against the use of the term "village prose," and many writers who have been said to belong to this school have either expressed their discomfort or disavowed membership altogether. The reason is that the term has become a large umbrella, covering a great variety of writing and diverse ideological tendencies. It can justifiably be argued, in fact, that literature should not be categorized in terms of the locale in which it is set. Also, numerous writers are concerned only *partly* with village themes and often write about totally different matters. Nevertheless, with due allowance for abundant exceptions, one can find a fairly common core in much of this writing.

As a rule, village literature is oriented on peasant *families* – their antecedents and traditions, their formation and ferment, and often their alienation and breakup. Village writers like to dwell on memories of a rural childhood and youth – sometimes idylically happy, sometimes confused, deprived, and impoverished. The contrast, and frequently the conflict, of generations is emphasized. Particular prominence is given to elderly persons, especially women, who are shown to embody the best elements of peasant culture and serve as the last repositories of ancient Russian spiritual values. It is they, for example, who know the songs, tales, superstitions, and legends of old, and who demonstrate a sensitivity, respect for custom, wisdom, and fortitude far superior to those of their children and grandchildren. And it is they who are most closely attached to the land and its farmsteads, are most alert to the rhythm of the seasons and attentive to the surrounding natural beauty, and who lament most profoundly the passing of the village way of life.

Most often, these old people convey the author's own alarm over a perceived cultural loss, or the threat of it. The village writers lovingly describe their own birthplaces and the fields, forests, meadows, rivers, lakes, and living creatures around them. Their characters speak in local dialects; the characters' folk beliefs and their arts and crafts display regional peculiarities. In paying such close attention to ethnic detail, writers are not only attempting to preserve a cultural heritage but also pleading against the obliteration of the culture itself. They are also asserting, in varying degrees of insistence, the special claim of the Russian peasant for attention, his unique worthiness as a human being. Although village writers do not, as a rule, argue that the Russian peasant is intrinsically superior to other human beings, their works have frequently been used by nationalistic literary critics and chauvinistic commentators as evidence illustrating this superiority.

Nostalgia for the rural Russia of yesterday and anxiety over its cultural transformation are found in connection with other strains of village writing: environmental and ecological concerns and anti-urbanism. The poisoning of the atmosphere, and the land itself, with industrial effusions; the diversion of rivers and drying-up of lakes; and the flooding of farmland and settlements to build hydroelectric projects all appear in this writing as evils that are extremely ominous. The nuclear disaster at Chernobyl in 1986 has recently become a favorite point of reference. As peasants leave the land and flock to the cities, moreover, the moral costs are thought to be high. Millions of people lose their rural identity and integrity and find nothing substantial to replace them in the cities. In the writing of extreme anti-urbanists the cities themselves are a major source of moral depletion and mass degradation.

The phenomenon of village prose had virtually run its course by the early 1980s. Its most prominent living members continued to write, but they had either turned to other topics or, like a great deal of current Soviet literature in general, had become more publicistic than aesthetic. In the atmosphere of *glasnost'*, some writers now published revelations about the countryside, and particularly about the early years of collectivization at the beginning of the 1930s, which they had long been forced to withhold. A number of works of this kind were brought to light posthumously. There was, however, one particularly disturbing development. Some of the very best village writers began to display strains of narrow nationalism, anti-Westernism, and anti-Semitism, which made them congenial to militantly chauvinistic and proto-fascist elements in Soviet society. For some writers, the appeal may have been inadvertent, but others became openly associated with these ugly and dangerous tendencies.

Valentin Rasputin (born 1937) was the best of the village writers. He stood out in his ability to combine local, specifically Soviet Russian topics with timeless, universal concerns. The sensitivity and breadth of Rasputin's humanity, in fact, is one of his major strengths. Another strength is the discipline and

compactness of his writing. Although his works are rich in detail
that gives the flavor of village life, they are also tightly knit and
thematically unified.

Rasputin established his reputation with four medium-length
novels (*povesti*) and several short stories, all set in his native
Siberia. The first novel, *Money for Maria* (*Den'gi dlya Marii*,
1967), is an examination of a peasant community's response to
the emergency of one of its families, an emergency that can be
met only through comradeship, generosity, and self-sacrifice.
Maria, an honest and simple woman, has been persuaded by
her neighbors to take the job of village storekeeper even though
she totally lacks the necessary experience and is fearfully
reluctant. An inventory discloses a shortage, and although
everyone knows she is not guilty of embezzlement, she faces a
prison term if she cannot cover the shortage. The heart of the
story is the attempt of her husband Kuz'ma to save her (and
therefore their family) by borrowing 1,000 rubles from their
friends and neighbors, and ultimately, with little reason to
hope, from his brother in the city. Kuz'ma is only partially
successful, and the story ends with his and Maria's problem
unresolved. Within the framework of this test of communality,
the story offers a fascinating and sharply individualized gallery
of characters as they react in various noble and ignoble ways to
Kuz'ma's timid appeals for help. The story is written with
unassuming compassion, leavened with humor and irony, and
gives an impression of great social and cultural authenticity.

The Final Term (*Poslednii srok*, 1971, also translated as *Borrowed
Time*) recounts the last days in the life of Anna, an old Siberian
villager. Four of her five living children (she has borne thirteen)
come to her deathbed. A temporary improvement in her
condition enables three of her children to persuade themselves
that Anna is not yet dying, and they leave abruptly. They have
come not to comfort their mother but to bury her, and are
frustrated, disappointed, and even angry at her stubborn refusal
to die. That night Anna does die.

We are shown a family that has become fragmented and has
lost its soul in the process. Anna's children have not merely been
geographically dispersed and out of touch; they are spiritually

remote from one another and are clearly unworthy of their mother. One wonders, in fact, how such an exemplary peasant woman could have produced such an ugly and shallow brood. At the same time, they are a fascinating group, acutely individualized and vividly memorable. Each of them represents a different form of alienation from the maternal village. Although all of them are callous and lacking in spiritual depth, the most repulsive is the quarrelsome daughter Lyusya, a hardened, self-righteous city-dweller who views everything in the village with an attitude of critical superiority.

The eighty-year-old Anna, who with her old friend Mironikha represents a disappearing generation and its values, is a profoundly conceived character, particularly in the portrayal of her steadfast approach to death. In her last hours, nature remains the strong source of wonder and consolation it has been all her life, and death itself for her is not only elemental but also something mysteriously welcome.

Rasputin's talent for the dramatic is best shown in his skilful construction of a tragedy in *Live and Remember* (*Zhivi i pomni*, 1974), the story of a front-line deserter, Andrei Gus′kov, who hides out near his native village with the aid of his wife Nastyona. A loving, loyal woman whose purity of heart blinds her to her own welfare, Nastyona sacrifices herself by becoming an accessory to her unworthy husband's crime. As an outlaw, Gus′kov becomes vicious; his humanity disintegrates. Increasingly tormented by guilt, fear of apprehension, and mental torture sadistically inflicted on her by Gus′kov, Nastyona kills herself and their unborn child by drowning in the river Angara. The movement of the story is masterful in its relentless accumulation of harrowing circumstances that lead to Nastyona's suicide.

In all three of the aforementioned novels, Rasputin shows a remarkable sense of the social organism – the rhythms and unwritten laws of its existence, its cohesive and divisive forces. His works gain authenticity from the ingredient of village culture that is embodied in them. Folk beliefs and standards of conduct, traditional ways of doing and seeing things, in large measure motivate the behavior of his characters, particularly the older ones. What lends his works a special authority in this respect is his ingenious use of the local language, in the speech of his narrator as well as that of his characters, to suggest, intimately, his villagers' points of view. Particularly noteworthy is his sensitive use of the natural environment – vegetation, the river Angara, the seasons and the weather, birds – together with domestic animals and crops. The critic Starikova has pointed to the striking quality of *animation* in his portrayal of nature, which lends a dynamic, poetic aura to his depiction of the environment and man's relationship to it.[2] The acuteness of Rasputin's eye for detail in both the natural and man-made worlds, and his subtle emphasis on the close relationship between these two worlds, endow his writing with an extraordinary sense of life.

All of these qualities are especially prominent in the novel *Farewell to Matyora* (*Proshchanie s Materoi*, 1976). A new hydroelectric dam is about to flood an island in the Angara river which has been farmed for centuries by the same families. The peasants are about to be resettled in a "modern" but faceless *sovkhoz*, miles from the river. The novel recounts the island's last days – the final harvest (some peasants weep as they mow), the preparation of the village for burning and the conflagration itself, the destruction of the ancient cemetery – and features the sad and bitter reaction of the oldest inhabitants.

The work is a loving tribute to a disappearing way of life and set of values and a poetic lament over their passing. The author uses landscapes of varying dimensions, to create atmosphere, to establish mood, and as indirect moral commentary. An example is the mysterious nocturnal prowl through the ill-fated village by the goblin "Master" (*Khozyain*) – an account which captures the subtle sounds, smells, sights, and the very feel of the place as it breathes in its sleep. The charming descriptions of Matyora make its impending passing all the more deplorable.

The main protagonist is Darya, a deeply spiritual old woman whose Christianity includes pagan folk elements and who bemoans contemporary mankind's arrogant violation of nature for the sake of material progress. Ideologically opposed to her is her grandson Andrei, who unquestioningly accepts material values and seems indifferent to his grandmother's anxiety over the countryside and its threatened culture. Between the two is Darya's son Pavel, a responsible man who enjoys the advantages of urban living but has lingering misgivings about its lack of spiritual substance. The sentiments that dominate this elegiac novel, however, are those of Darya, who ritually whitewashes and scrubs her house just before it is put to the torch.

Farewell to Matyora is primarily a work of social protest, directed against those who are altering the environment and disrupting a time-honored mode of existence in the name of material progress. The undertone of moral indignation over the drowning of this beautiful, fertile island and the centuries of peasant civilization it has nourished, of hatred for the planners who are forcing this ugly transformation, is unmistakable. In this respect, the novel is closer in spirit to much of the rest of village prose than any other work of fiction by Rasputin. At the same time, *Farewell to Matyora* is now generally agreed to have marked the highest point in the development of village prose in general.

In 1985 Rasputin published *The Fire (Pozhar)*, a short novel of vehement social criticism that is artistically his weakest work. The locus is a workers' settlement along the Angara, near a drowned island village similar to Matyora. The inhabitants do not farm (even kitchen gardens are rare) but work as loggers, together with bands of itinerants on the criminal fringe, tearing down pine forests. In the central episode, the settlement's warehouses, containing all its supply of consumer goods, burn to the ground because of the community's lack of preparedness and inability to organize a fire-fighting effort. Some supplies are saved, but there is drunken looting, and one of the oldest settlers is murdered. The fire and the people's behavior in its presence are symbolic: the community, removed from the land and its beneficial discipline, has lost its soul and has become a mob, and the fire itself is a retribution.

The conflagration and the human circumstances surrounding it are shown vividly and dramatically. For the significance of the situation and events, however, we are asked to rely on the lengthy broodings of Ivan Petrovich, one of the community's few upstanding citizens, on the spiritual decline of his country-men. As a character, Ivan Petrovich is merely an awkward and tedious device for conveying Rasputin's own preachments about the moral state of his nation. Whether or not the author's indictment is accurate and valid, his means of presenting it represents a serious aesthetic flaw.

One of the first works to employ the new candor permitted by *glasnost'*, *The Fire* signaled sweeping changes in Rasputin's career. In recent years he turned from a writer of fiction into a publicist and prominent political figure in Gorbachev's Russia. Although his fiction itself has been free of strident nationalism, xenophobia, and anti-Semitism, his journalism, public utter-ances, and association with reactionary ideologists indicate that these elements are prominent in his recent attitudes.

The best-known work of Viktor Astaf'ev (born 1924) is *Tsar-Fish* (*Tsar'-ryba*, 1972–75), a collection of stories, essays, and personal memoirs that received a State Prize in 1978. Set along the Yenisei river and its tributaries, it depicts the harsh, often desperate and sometimes degenerate lives of Siberians in a land that is rich in natural resources and often scarred by extreme poverty and suffering. The title story, "Tsar-Fish," is the vivid and detailed account of a lone fisherman's long battle with a huge sturgeon, which nearly drowns the man before escaping. Several other stories involve the men who fish for a living, often illegally, in these teeming waters, and their struggle against the wardens whose job it is to catch poachers.

The most prominent character in several of the stories is Akim, a courageous young man who has endured a childhood of extreme deprivation and who stubbornly scratches out an existence variously as a laborer, fisherman, river-boat crewman, and trapper. Both the high and low points in his life of constant, bitter hardship come when he chances upon a dying young woman in a remote trapper's shack, nurses her, falls in love with her, brings her back to civilization through the frozen taiga (and incurs a horribly disfiguring frostbite), and loses her when she gratefully leaves for home in Moscow.

Running through *Tsar-Fish* is a tragic paradox: the natural abundance of fish, game, nuts, and berries in this land of taiga and tundra, and the frustration of the human potential. Astaf'ev is sensitive to the might and beauty of Siberia – its terrain and vegetation, the extremes of its seasons – which he describes with great delicacy. He is equally eloquent in portraying the cruel shabbiness of human conditions – a fish depot in the far north, where the children are devastated by malnutrition and scurvy, a dingy airport in a squalid town whose populace is crude, hopeless, and brutal, poisoned by the all-pervasive Siberian alcoholism. Astaf'ev is alarmed, moreover, by mankind's threat to the environment; he is clearly an enemy of urban "progress" and the physical and spiritual despoliation he thinks it entails.

A wounded veteran of World War II, Astaf'ev has written several works with military settings. The best-known of these is the short novel *Shepherd and Shepherdess* (*Pastukh i pastushka*, 1974). Subtitled "a modern pastoral," it is the story of a brief, radiant love affair between a young lieutenant and a girl he meets in a Ukrainian peasant hut in a lull between fierce battles. The author's best works, however, are set in Siberia, and often have elements of autobiography. Such is his large collection of stories about childhood and later years, based largely on his recollections of relatives and other Siberian villagers, *The Final Bow* (*Poslednii poklon*), initially published in 1968 but periodically augmented until 1989. Such also is the story "To Live One's Life" ("Zhizn' prozhit'," 1985), whose hero, a simple man orphaned as a child and reared by foster parents in harsh circumstances, goes to war and is severely wounded, returns to a variety of modest jobs (finally as a buoy tender on the Yenisei), marries, is widowed, and dies. In the hands of Astaf'ev, this ostensibly colorless, obscure life is the subject of a vigorous, interesting, although unsparingly cruel narrative. The hero is dogged by obstacles, frustrations, and disappointments. He is surrounded by inhumanity and crime, and endures only through enormous, active moral strength. The story gives a tangible sense of the texture of Siberian life, and although it displays extensively the negative and ugly aspects of human behavior, it is ultimately a humane tale of great spiritual depth.

Early in his career Astaf'ev established himself not only as a concerned environmentalist but also as a moralist. In recent years, however, he has gained a reputation as an outright scold with more than a shade of bigotry. This reputation is based mainly on *A Sad Detective Story* (*Pechal'nyi detektiv*, 1986), a "novel" which is actually an extended diatribe against the moral flaws of his countrymen. Set in a provincial Russian city and its environs, the work ostensibly tells of the experiences and observations of a retired policeman who has become a writer; in fact it is a crude vehicle for the direct expression of the author's own indignation as he parades and comments upon a succession of local drunks, pseudo-intellectuals, thieves, rapists, and cutthroats who are intended to represent the shortcomings of society at large. In this and other recent effusions Astaf'ev has come out as an open anti-Semite and has thus displayed his own moral and intellectual limitations.

There is powerful evidence, however, that Astaf'ev has not lost his talent as a writer of fiction. He remains despondent about the present moral state of his country, but he has recently embodied his gloom in a genuine work of art that may well be aesthetically the finest thing he has ever written. This is the story "Lyudochka" ("Lyudochka," 1989), the grim, bitter, and extremely disturbing account of the rape of a girl by a gang of hoodlums, and of her subsequent suicide. The provincial town in which the girl is destroyed is run-down and filthy, its police are indifferent and corrupt, and the punks who terrorize its central park are horrifying. The victim is a warm-hearted waif whose weak constitution comes from an alcoholic father. Out of these circumstances Astaf'ev has woven a story that is devoid of special pleading and therefore all the more shocking and heartbreaking.

Recent developments in the career of Vasilii Belov (born 1933) illustrate the fragmentation of village prose in the 1980s. He is the author of distinguished works of fiction about his native Vologda region in northern Russia, and of ethnographic portraits of the same area. In 1966 Belov became well known with the novel *That's How It Is* (*Privychnoe delo*), the intimate, deeply moving, and tragic account of an industrious but hopelessly impoverished peasant, his large brood, and his steadfast wife who dies young from overwork. Belov further enhanced his reputation in 1968 with the publication of *A Carpenter's Stories* (*Plotnitskie rasskazy*), which center on the lives of two elderly peasants, representing positive and negative sides of the rural Russian character, as seen by a visitor from the city who had grown up in their village. Both of those works were notable for their careful attention to the conditions and routines of folk culture, and both the good and the evil to be found in the countryside.

Belov had always shown a keen interest in the ways of the Russian north, and in 1982 he published *Harmony* (*Lad*), a volume of ethnographic sketches based on memories of his own childhood, the reminiscences of his mother, and the accounts of elderly people in the area. It is an exploration of the world of these peasants – their arts and crafts, their rituals and customs, their sense of time and the ways it is marked. Various occupations and skills are described: carpenters, well-diggers, potters, shoemakers, horse-doctors, traders. Belov tells about the food they eat, the ways in which they play, the processing of their crops, the seasonal rhythm of their work, their holidays and celebrations, their rich folk tales and their techniques of telling them. A tribute to the spiritual power and beauty of his people, *Harmony* intentionally fails to mention the dark aspects of their life.

For more than fifteen years Belov worked on a large historical novel, *Eves* (*Kanuny*), which he began publishing in 1972 and whose third part appeared in 1987. The time is the late 1920s, when Lenin's New Economic Policy had brought relative stability to the farmers of the Vologda region, but when Stalin's devastating campaign to collectivize agriculture was on the horizon. Belov's usual ethnographic material, such as weddings and holiday celebrations, is lovingly presented, and the cast of characters is large and colorful. The narrative concentrates on the majority class of independent and cooperative farmers – the so-called "middle peasants," who are neither rich nor poor, and who constitute the backbone of the rural economy. It is this majority that is to be the chief victim of the coming upheaval –

denounced as "kulaks," stripped of their land and possessions, banished, imprisoned, starved, and slaughtered. The novel itself depicts little of this activity, which came later: rather, it concentrates on the atmosphere of conflict and foreboding that preceded the wrecking of the village community.

A more arresting work is Belov's continuation of *Eves* in the story "A Year of Great Change: A Chronicle of Nine Months" ("God velikogo pereloma: khronika devyati mesyatsev," 1989), a grim picture of the collectivization itself, showing not only the harsh and inhuman measures taken against the entire peasant class of the Vologda region but also the murderous deportation of Ukrainian peasants to this frozen northern area. In *Eves*, depicting the centrally directed Party and government agents of the coming collectivization, Belov had singled out urban Jews as being particularly active and malicious. This story also includes passages displaying Belov's notorious anti-Semitism.

Belov's novel *Everything Lies Ahead* (*Vse vperedi*, 1986) is a major departure from his previous work. Its *dramatis personae* are the Moscow intelligentsia, addicts of mass culture imported from the decadent West, given to sexual excesses and aberrations, marital infidelities, rock music, abortions, and White Horse Scotch. Moscow itself is an asphalt and concrete nightmare, frenetic, polluted with gasolene fumes and tobacco smoke and poisoned by soulless cosmopolitanism. The title is ironical: everything does *not* lie ahead. Russians should not live by the illusory promise of the future, but in the present, respectfully conscious of the values that have been inherited from the simpler and purer Russian past. The world Belov presents to us is populated by "natural people" – those who repudiate the physically and morally unhealthy city – and "devils," who embrace its pernicious charms and try to seduce others into sharing them. The chief villain of the novel is a Jewish scientist-turned-bureaucrat, who steals a Russian's wife and children and aspires to emigrate to America.

As a work of art, *Everything Lies Ahead* is vastly inferior to Belov's previous work. It is really a polemical tract, with schematic characters who are often merely caricatures, and a great amount of undisguised authorial rhetoric. Like Rasputin in *The Fire* and Astaf'ev in *A Sad Detective Story*, Belov in this work was clearly willing to sacrifice aesthetic values in the effort to sermonize.

It is significant that these three writers, all highly accomplished veterans of the school of village prose, should recently have abandoned the village *as such* for their settings, and at the same time should have turned to angry, didactic, argumentive fiction with a prominent admixture of publicism. This development illustrates the fact that village prose had indeed run its course, but it also suggests that conditions in Soviet society had become so disturbing that good writers were willing to turn themselves into bad writers in an effort to sound the alarm.

Belov was not the only village writer to undertake a work of historical fiction about the early years of collectivization. This was done also by Boris Mozhaev (born 1923) in his two-volume novel *Peasant Men and Women* (*Muzhiki i baby*, 1976–87). Mozhaev had established his credentials as a village writer with a militant, semi-journalistic talent in the fifties and sixties, notably with the publication in 1966 of his story "From the Life of Fyodor Kuz'kin" ("Iz zhizni Fedora Kuz'kina").[3] Also known as "Alive" ("Zhivoi," Mozhaev's original title for the story), it tells of the battles of one stubbornly courageous and resourceful peasant against stupid and often vicious political authorities in the mid-1950s.

Peasant Men and Women, which Mozhaev calls a "chronicle," is set in the author's native region of Ryazan' in 1929–30. Book I, which ends before the onset of collectivization, presents a generally positive picture of peasant life and the social order in the late 1920s, while Book II features the conflicts and horrors of collectivization. With a large cast of characters representing a variety of occupations and stations in rural life, Mozaev details and affirms the Russian cultural heritage with a genuinely nationalistic ardor. He portrays the collectivization drive not only as an onslaught against that heritage but also as a grave political error on the part of the Party and its leadership. Not only is the authorities' classification of peasants into purely political-economic categories shown to be schematic and doctrinaire: as events unfold, it is also demonstrated to be brutally unjust and impractical.

Angry and full of pain, with a narrator who often directly addresses the reader in his indignation, *Peasant Men and Women* portrays collectivization as a rape and pillage of the countryside by drunken Party activists and corrupt bureaucrats. Families are destroyed wholesale, children suffer, and the dispirited peasants are gripped in bitter hopelessness. Although it is a work of fiction, the novel uses the documentary devices that were to become popular in the literature of *glasnost'*, quoting excerpts from speeches, proclamations, pamphlets, and the like. It combines history and political analysis and frankly condemns the policy of collectivization as ill-conceived, a violation of the nation. It is not surprising that Mozhaev had great difficulty in publishing Book II, which he completed in 1980 but which was allowed to see the light of day only in 1987. This novel, together with that of Belov and the recently published stories of Tendryakov, Nagibin, Bykov, and others, serves as an antidote to the myths about collectivization fostered by such writers as Mikhail Sholokhov, Fyodor Panferov and their legions of socialist-realist colleagues.

One of the most prolific and authoritative village writers was Fyodor Abramov (1920–83), a literary scholar and critic who turned mainly to fiction during the last twenty-five years of his life. Among the earliest to insist on writing the unvarnished truth about the countryside, Abramov was the author of numerous stories and sketches, and of the tetralogy of novels *The Pryaslins* (*Pryasliny*, 1958–78), an epic treatment of life in his native remote northern region of Arkhangelsk. Abramov left behind an archive of unpublished fiction, diaries, and miscellaneous commentary that has gradually come to light, showing this writer, who was often somber in tone, to have been even more troubled and bleaker in outlook than his previously published works had indicated.

Abramov's short stories are often little more than portraits of interesting and memorable people and places. In describing them, he relies heavily on the local point of view and the local language. Characters, objects, and scenes are shown and judged by the peasants who know them best, and the author does not visibly interfere. The writing is factual and tangible, avoiding intellectual abstractions about such things as the village spirit and character. Still, these qualities become clear through material evidence and through the depiction of acts and deeds. Thus, we see the heroine of "Pelageya" ("Pelageya," 1967–69), who labors in a village bakery for twenty years to support an ailing husband and ungrateful daughter. However, Abramov's narrator does not always remain aloof. In "Wooden Horses" ("Derevyannye koni," 1969) we are shown a resilient, lovingly generous, selfless, and dignified old woman who has endured a life of hardship, an arranged, loveless forced marriage, the loss of some of her children in the war, and neglect and disappointment from her other children. We also discover a narrator who is so moved by her that he resolves to try to emulate her ancient peasant virtues.

For an epic, *The Pryaslins* is remarkably confined in space. The village of Pekashino, along the Pinega river, is the unchanging center of the novels' activity. In time the novels span three decades, from 1942 to the early 1970s, in the lives of several local families and especially the Pryaslins. The first novel, *Brothers and Sisters* (*Brat'ya i sestry*, 1958), shows the women, old folks, and children of Pekashino, with all their menfolk away at the front, struggling to provide food and wood for the war effort, avoid starvation, and survive as families and as a community. *Two Winters and Three Summers* (*Dve zimy i tri leta*, 1968), the second and artistically the most successful novel in the tetralogy, depicts the immediate postwar years. In this novel Mikhail Pryaslin, a stripling but still the eldest son, emerges as the extremely hard-working, devoted, and self-sacrificing anchor of this now fatherless family. Faced with impossible demands from corrupt regional authorities for the rebuilding of the village economy, the community struggles on. *At the Crossroads* (*Puti-pereput'ya*, 1973), set in the fall of 1951, shows village conditions scarcely less harsh than they had been before, with repressive, meddlesome, and blatantly unjust government and police measures hampering the development of the collective farm and the community it purports to serve.

The final novel, *The House* (*Dom*, 1978), shows the community of Pekashino after a lapse of two decades. By now the story has picked up dozens of characters and parted with many of them. The collective farm has been engulfed by a state farm, and many families, including the Pryaslins, have at least partially dispersed. Mikhail is still the head of the family, but the family is now demoralized and fragmented. Although still firm and honorable in his role as authority, Mikhail is disappointed, bitter, and cantankerous. He has even turned his back on his loving sister Liza, the innocent victim of marriage to a conniving lout who has periodically caused great damage to the Pekashino community. Mikhail's other siblings, one of whom is an outright criminal, have become alienated in varying degrees, but as the novel ends there are indications of a possible general reconciliation.

Throughout the four novels Pekashino, which has undergone the ravages of wartime, governmental abuse, and time itself, has become a microcosm of all of Russia. Abramov has paid close attention not only to the natural setting, the interaction and evolution of families, and the change in the organization and methods of work as agriculture becomes more industrialized, but also to the very spirit of the community as an organism influenced by outside historical developments. The title of the novel, *The House*, refers not only to the Pryaslins' ancestral home – partially destroyed but now being restored – but to Russia itself. Despite the melancholy tone of this final novel, Abramov is suggesting that in the hands of the gloomy but sturdy Mikhail, with his unsophisticated, earthy practicality, this remote bit of Russia, and symbolically Russia itself, will find salvation.

As a rule, Abramov's narrative manner is undramatic and objective. He obviously identifies with and respects the peasant milieu out of which he himself came, but he does not idealize it. His writing seems free of the nostalgia and ideological bias which underlies that of Belov or Rasputin, and he seems content simply to describe the lives of his peasants, their traditions, their work, and the objects that surround them. However, the articles he wrote in his last years, and the posthumously published diaries, indicate he felt that in his fiction he had been too generous with his peasants, too tolerant of their shortcomings, that in truth they were more inert, lazy, and indifferent to their best interests than he had shown them to be. It also turned out that, as with other village writers, political circumstances had simply prevented him from disclosing the whole truth about the countryside. In 1974 he completed and tried to publish the painful, gloomy story "A Trip to the Past" ("Poezdka v proshloe"), which appeared only in 1989. The story depicts the cultural and moral devastation that accompanied collectivization – the senseless razing of churches, the murder of children.

A departure from the conventionally realistic village prose is a novel of the fantastic, *Living Water* (*Zhivaya voda*, 1980), by Vladimir Krupin (born 1941). It tells of the discovery, in a remote forest settlement where trains never stop, of a miraculous spring whose waters rejuvenate the populace, making everyone uniformly handsome and decent, and, above all, eliminate the craving for alcohol. Only one man – the sixty-year-old watchman and stable-tender Kirpikov – remains unaffected by and uninterested in the magic elixir. When an earthquake destroys the spring, the inhabitants revert to their normally flawed, fallible, and drunken visages and way of life. Only Kirpikov, who has found a new serenity on his own, has been permanently changed.

These are only the barest outlines of *Living Water*, which is in fact a remarkable blending of realistic detail, folklore motifs ("living water" is traditional in Russian legend), sophisticated social satire, moral and philosophical exploration, comedy, and phantasmagoria. The plot centers on Kirpikov, who for years has earned himself a steady supply of home-brew by plowing, with his ancient gelding, his neighbors' kitchen gardens, and whose drunkenness, like that of his neighbors, has driven his wife to despair. Suddenly the sobering realization that he is mortal and in his sixties impels Kirpikov to seek a meaning in his life, a justification. He stops drinking, tries unsuccessfully and with comic ineptitude to persuade his neighbors to follow suit, and retreats underground to his root-cellar to read books on history and biology and to engage in "archaeological" digging, all in an effort to understand why he has lived. The rudimentary self-knowledge he gains is sufficient to enable him to see that "living water," however seductive its promise may be, is a fraud, and that purity and beauty can come only from the careful nurturing of one's own soul.

One of the great virtues of *Living Water* is that its characters think and talk like those we have known in standard village prose but also show the influence of social change in their use of official stock phraseology and newspaper cliches coming from the city. The moral confusion of their little settlement (which can be taken, allegorically, for Russia itself) enhances its willingness to embrace the irrational phenomenon of "living water" as a universal panacea to replace the ubiquitous alcohol. The story is grim, but it is also lively, funny, and, in the character of the stumbling but earnestly seeking Kirpikov, heartwarming.

In the past decade Krupin has become a well-known writer of fiction and essays on a wide variety of topics. He shows conservative inclinations and a deep devotion to the Russian Orthodox church. In terms of the history of village prose, however, it is instructive to consider two works published in 1981: the story "The Handbell" ("Kolokol'chik") and the "novel in letters" *The Fortieth Day* (*Sorokovoi den'*). Both are in the first person and appear to be autobiographical. In "The Handbell" the narrator, with a group of fellow-writers from the capital, pays a ceremonial visit to Vyatka (the Krupins' family seat) to celebrate the town's 600th anniversary. The story's main burden is the author's growing shame as he hears two of his own works, previously tape-recorded, played over the local public address system. Not only do the stories seem false and superficial to him; he is embarrased by his and his colleagues' condescending role as urbanites "going to the people." *The Fortieth Day* consists of the narrator's letters to his wife during a visit to his ill and aged parents in the countryside, and includes ruminations on a wide variety of journalistic and literary topics, together with accounts of his experiences during his extended visit. There are frequent notes of frustration and remorse over his failure to tell in print what he thinks is the truth about the countryside, and over his inability to add anything important to what the major village writers have already said. These feelings are another reflection of the fact that by the early 1980s village prose was already in its twilight period.

All of the writers mentioned in this chapter developed ideological biases and established distinct points of view on issues related to the countryside. Although not all of them were explicitly tendentious, their interpretations of village life and its changes made them the spokesmen for trends in contemporary thought about Russia's past, present, and future. There is one writer, however, who seems to be exceptionally free of such bias and to be content with presenting discrete, clear, and trenchant glimpses of village existence. This is Boris Ekimov (born 1938), who specializes in short stories.

Ekimov's writing is laconic and economical, but his love for the countryside is evident in his accounts of its natural beauty, its tranquil sights and sounds, and the unhurried pace of village existence. He deeply respects the things that peasants have built, such as a cowshed in the story "Solonich" ("Solonich," 1986) whose floor is made of oaken blocks more closely fitted than parquet. Such objects, however, and the way of life they represent, are threatened: the man who built and owns this magnificent cowshed must sell out the family holdings and move to a larger settlement. The population of his native village has shrunk so badly that it can no longer support proper schools, and this peasant has been forced to make the heart-rending choice of uprooting for the sake of his children.

Ekimov is no less attentive than other writers to the passing of a way of life. In "The Boy on the Bicycle" ("Mal'chik na velosipede," 1984) we see an engineer who has come to his village to visit his mother and who becomes engrossed in bittersweet nostalgic reminiscences. Many of Ekimov's characters are oldsters whose families have left the village, such as the lonely widow in "House for Sale" ("Prodaetsya dom," 1986), who stipulates such impossible conditions for the sale of her house that it will most likely remain unsold until she dies. The author's approach to such characters, however, is unsentimental. He respects their emotions and conveys them deftly, but he is more interested in understanding their psychology than in pleading that they be pitied.

As a rule, Ekimov's stories focus on social and moral problems, illuminating them without attempting to solve them, and simply inviting the reader to ponder them. In "The Meeting is Postponed" ("Vstrecha otmenyaetsya," 1986), a schoolteacher has arranged to have her mother, who is a locally renowned and richly rewarded champion milkmaid, visit her class as an example of high accomplishment. She discovers that her mother is to be tried for stealing milk and fodder from the collective farm where she works; the mother freely admits her guilt – "everybody does it." The situation remains unresolved, but the meeting is postponed. In "What's All the Crying About?" ("O chem slezy?," 1989) a widow who lives with her ancient mother-in-law makes vodka, which is a prominent local currency, to pay for such things as a winter's supply of straw and a carpenter's services. The militia confiscates the still and exacts a heavy fine, and the story ends with the two women tearfully bewailing their fate. It is typical of Ekimov that in neither of these stories is there any kind of lyrical coloration or authorial intrusion.

Although Ekimov seems to have no ideological axe to grind, he has a fine sense of the community, its moral makeup, and its psychology. In "The Chelyadins' Son-in-Law" (*Chelyadinskii zyat'*, 1986) a released convict appears in a village to settle in with a local woman who has known him only through correspondence. He shirks his job tending the collective farm cattle, but his intimidation and threats force the community to accept him. The peaceful peasants simply cannot cope with him; he is a wolf among sheep. The story ends on an ominous note of menace and alarm. Although social commentary can be derived from the tale, it is essentially a study of the timeless power of evil.

In outlining recent developments in village prose and its

declining prominence, I have not mentioned several writers who are commonly associated with this school, notably Aleksei Leonov, Vladimir Lichutin, Viktor Likhonosov, Evgenii Nosov, Aleksandr Prokhanov, Vladimir Soloukhin, and Sergei Zalygin. The themes, arguments, and aesthetic traits of these writers, however, are such that a discussion of them would not alter the general picture this chapter has presented.

Although village literature was clearly waning in the eighties, it was by no means extinct, as the writings of Boris Ekimov, for one, attest. As long as Russians live together in small agricultural communities, some writers, at least, will find them interesting. The tradition of philanthropic writing, of finding significance in the lives, customs, and aspirations of simple people in modest circumstances is a deep one in Russian letters, and it will surely continue.

As it developed in the seventies and eighties, village literature accumulated political and ideological baggage peculiar to the times: belated revelations about and protest against collectivization and the social injustice and terror that marked its establishment in the early 1930s; a nationalistic affirmation of grass-roots culture that developed, in some cases, into outright chauvinism; a sense of alarm about the environment that became transformed into anti-industrialism. These manifestations, however, were essentially secondary. Although such writers as Rasputin and Astaf'ev turned their attention from the village to the grim, semi-urban non-agricultural settlement, and although Belov began writing about the hated city, these changes did not vitiate their major accomplishment, which was to portray, with devoted care and in colorful detail, the culture of the peasant community. This accomplishment, which they share with Mozhaev, Abramov, Krupin, and Ekimov, is their essential contribution to Russian literature.

CHAPTER 5

The "forty-year-olds"

Like most twentieth-century commentators on literature throughout the world, Soviet critics have been fond of classifying contemporary writers into groupings, tendencies, and schools. Some kinds of writing lend themselves readily to such classification – examples are the schools of "village prose" and "military prose," although even in these categories some works do not fit neatly. In the late 1970s critics began referring to a loose grouping of writers whom they called, variously, the "forty-year-olds," the "Moscow school," and the "urban school" (*gorodskaya shkola*). The critics themselves were manifestly dissatisfied with such groupings and readily admitted to their lack of real, much less permanent, cohesion. Such categories, however, provided a convenient and not ineffective means of identifying current literary tendencies, ephemeral as they might prove to be.

This chapter will discuss seven writers who have generally been associated with at least two, and usually all three, of the categories mentioned above. (The approximate nature of such categories is indicated by the fact that although their dates of birth range from 1935 to 1944, they were all identified as "forty-year-olds" in the late 1970s.) Their interests, ideological configurations, and manners of writing vary greatly, but they do have several things in common. All of them are too young to have immediate memories of World War II, although some refer to its indirect effects on their childhood. On the other hand, all of them are old enough to have participated in, or at least to remember, the exciting and hopeful years of Khrushchevian reform in the late 1950s and early 1960s, and to have retained the democratic aspirations of that period while experiencing the disillusionment and frustration of the Brezhnev years.

All of them have lived in Moscow (or, in one case, Leningrad) for long periods and frequently use the large city as background and social-psychological motivation, and sometimes as a character in itself. Although they write about people of all ages and stations in life, they tend to feature heroes who themselves are in their forties and whose thoughts and motivations are characteristic of that pivotal stage in life. About all of these writers there is an absence of dogmatism, an ideological tentativeness, and lack of doctrinal certainty. They do not fear ambiguity and ambivalence, and in some cases they in fact cultivate such attitudes. To a great extent they seem to feel that as artists their task is investigative and cognitive, not didactic. As interpreters, for the most part, of a period (the 1970s and early 1980s) in which social stagnation had deprived their countrymen of belief in the future and had fostered attitudes of futility and cynicism, they wrote largely about individuals who had learned to adapt to a way of life they could not hope to change, and of the means by which such individuals made the necessary accommodations. Such pragmatic adjustments often involved a degree of moral compromise or even outright corruption. As a rule, the writers in this group avoided directly passing judgment on such behavior and maintained, rather, an ironic attitude toward it.

It should be emphasized that the overlapping categories of "Moscow," "urban," and "forty-year-old" prose are unstable and, no doubt, will ultimately disappear from histories of this period. Some writers who are usually associated with these groups – such as Anatolii Afanas'ev, Vladimir Gusev, and Aleksandr Prokhanov – are not included in the present study. Another – Vladimir Krupin – has such a prominent association with the school of village prose that it seems most appropriate to discuss him under that rubric.

Vladimir Makanin (born 1937) is the same age as such long-established figures as Andrei Bitov and Valentin Rasputin. He has come to prominence much more recently than they, however, and he belongs to a later literary generation. A native of the Urals, he trained extensively at Moscow State University as a mathematician and then studied screen writing and directing. His first novel, *The Straight Line* (*Pryamaya Liniya*), came out in 1965, and he published numerous works of fiction in the succeeding decade. Only in the late 1970s, however, did he become known as an important writer.

Critics have identified Makanin, variously, as a member of the group of "forty-year-olds," such as Ruslan Kireev and Vladimir Krupin, who emerged in the late seventies and early eighties; as a representative of "city prose" and the "Moscow school"; as a legatee of the "confessional prose" of the 1960s; and even as a kinsman of "village prose." Despite some affinities with each of these loosely defined categories, Makanin's writing is too many-sided, complex, and dynamically developing to belong in any of them. Makanin is unique, and is clearly his own man.

The Urals provide a setting in many of Makanin's stories and novels (his favorite and most successful genre is the *povest'*, or short novel), but he is not a regional writer. Although a number of his works are located in cities, he is not notably a describer of urban life. Perhaps his favorite point of reference is the *poselok* – a small settlement or community where people usually live in barracks – but this is seldom depicted in detail, and serves, rather, as a large metaphor for the way of life, moral situation, and tensions of his countrymen. Although Makanin is an impressively observant, concrete, and tangible writer, the external world for him essentially provides a framework in which to brood about existence and to comment, implicitly, on the problems of the individual and his surrounding culture.

For instance: in "Man of the Suite" ("Chelovek svity," 1982), a middle-aged, middle-level bureaucrat suddenly, and for unknown reasons, ceases being invited to regular tea with the influential secretary of his superior – a loss of status that leads to profound anxiety over his career. In "Antileader" ("Antilider," 1980), a Moscow plumber becomes increasingly upset and enraged by men who "stand out" in his circle of acquaintances by being affluent, popular, or powerful. After a series of physical attacks on such persons he is sent to prison, where this behavior continues and is sure to bring about his death. "Safety Valve" ("Otdushina," 1977) features the married, colorless manager of a furniture factory who loses his mistress, wins her back, and then abandons her to settle down with his wife for good. In *A Man and a Woman* (*Odin i Odna*, 1987) we are given extended portraits of two Moscow loners, talented eccentrics who gradually, in different ways, repudiate society and in turn come to be scorned by it.

In each of these works, and numerous others, both the individual and society are portrayed dispassionately, sometimes in considerable ugliness, sometimes with humor, and often with irony. Makanin has been accused of being misanthropic, unfeeling, excessively cerebral, an "entomologist." He has also been defended as a writer who is loving in spite of his surface coolness, and who cares deeply about his aliens and outsiders. Surely his manner of writing – probing, analytical, and at the same time respectful of the mysteries and enigmas of the personality and the charm of spoken language – mark him as an artist with a strong attachment to the human race.

Until recently Makanin's characters, as a rule, have tended to be ordinary people, undistinguishable, at least on the surface, from the masses of their fellow-citizens. What makes them interesting, however, is conduct that shows them to be subject to inner impulses and torments that they cannot fully understand and which the reader himself often finds to be enigmatic and unexplained. Thus in "Citizen Runaway" ("Grazhdanin ubegayushchii," 1984) we see a highly qualified worker, attractive to other people but indifferent to them, who roams about Siberia seeking increasingly out-of-the-way job sites until he finds the most remote of all, far in the north, where he dies.

Clearly the hero of this story is running away from society, but what he is seeking is not specified and can only be conjectured. Makanin usually refrains from dwelling upon or analyzing the causes of his characters' alienation and yearning. The circumstances are usually such, however, as to make it evident that the characters are seeking some kind of freedom or repose that the man-made world does not provide. Ultimately it is in the peculiar and local nature of this man-made world – the Soviet Russian time and place – rather than in some cosmic discontent, that the motivation of this restlessness is to be sought.

The hero of *Where the Sky Met the Hills* (*Gde skhodilos' nebo s kholmami*, 1984), is a middle-aged, successful composer who is guilt-ridden because many of his serious compositions, and his popular songs as well, were adapted from folk themes that he learned in the *poselok* where he lived as a boy. In an effort to atone for his fancied transgression – the exploitation and betrayal of his cultural heritage – he returns to his boyhood settlement with the intention of teaching music and organizing choruses. The locals, who are now content with their transistor radios, are not interested. The composer discovers that the culture which nurtured him is irretrievably lost.

The slim story lines I have offered above, focusing as they do on central characters and ignoring others, do not give an indication of the social richness and psychological and moral complexity of his narratives. Most of his writing can confidently be called critical realism. His portrayal of everyday life is clear-eyed and unsparing. He looks at poverty, suffering, and social injustice, explores dark corners, discovers a host of characters that seem to be typical but heretofore unnoticed. Some critics have called him a sociologist, others an anthropologist. But he is much more than an analyst of the social fabric or a creator of types. Makanin digs deep for the historical, moral, cultural, and philosophical significance of the situations he features and the people he creates.

In nearly all of Makanin's works there is a prominent awareness of the transitional nature of recent Russian existence. His narratives switch freely back and forth in time to show contrast and development between past and present. The essence of this development is an increase in the individual's feeling of homelessness, of loneliness as he confronts the crowd and finds himself unable to identify with it. I have mentioned that the *poselok* as an institution plays an important part in his narratives. This kind of settlement, in which people tend not to live in individual houses as in the village or in apartments as in the cities, but in densely crowded barracks with a minimum of amenities and little or no privacy, is a product of the Soviet Five-Year Plans. The barracks were intended as temporary emerging housing for the masses of newly created industrial workers who were coming chiefly from the peasant villages. In the absence of new, more substantial dwellings they became, in the course of half a century, a shabby, cramped, and stifling kind of permanent housing. Over the decades the *poselok* became an established feature of the Soviet scene, with its own culture, mores, loyalties, frustrations, and special psychology. Makanin does not describe the *poselok* in detail, but he often refers to it, since it has been an essential part of the lives of many of his characters and the subject of many of their deepest emotions. As the image of a people ironically frozen in an ugly and painful transitional mode, perpetually on bivouac, it becomes in Makanin a metaphor for the Soviet historical situation.

Makanin is indeed a metaphorical writer. In his works of the 1980s, especially, his characters and situations are made subtly and unobtrusively, but nevertheless compellingly, to stand for something larger than themselves. Makanin provides no direct guidance; it is up to the reader to work out the metaphor for himself, and various interpretations are possible. But his images are so vivid and arresting that the attentive reader is forced to ponder their significance. For example, the self-destructive hero of "Antileader," with his compulsion to attack anyone who stands out in the crowd, may be a metaphor for a peculiar trait of Soviet society. Or the *poselok* in *Where the Sky Met the Hills*, which exists to fight sudden fires in an adjacent chemical factory, and many of whose inhabitants have died in fires over the years, seems to serve as the sign of a malevolent fate which can bring instant destruction at any moment, and particularly in the twentieth century.

Much of the tension and conflict in Makanin's stories comes from his characters' searches for various kinds of freedom and from the inharmonious relationship between the individual and the collective. The self-isolated male character in *A Man and a Woman*, for example, refers to society as a "swarm" in which the individual, if he is willing to subjugate himself, can be protected and happy. He himself, however, is unwilling to exist merely as a dependent bee. Others of Makanin's protagonists actively seek the warmth and comfort of the collective but find themselves rejected or incapable of blending into it.

In "The Blue and the Red" ("Goluboe i krasnoe," 1981), a story that may be at least partly autobiographical, Makanin emphasizes the feelings of tightness and confinement in a boy who lives cooped-up in a barracks and of his frequent loneliness in the midst of the dense barracks crowd. Paradoxically, this loneliness comes from the inability to assert one's self as an individual, to carve out a private life within the collective. Both the impulse toward liberation from the group and the striving toward an accommodation with that same group are prominent sources of conflict in Makanin. The implications of such conflict for Soviet society are obvious, but Makanin is probably not trying to teach lessons. Rather, he is making aesthetic use of material that is obtrusively at hand.

Constructed to serve the interests of a centrally administered planned economy, the *poselok* can be considered emblematic of much that has happened in the soul of the Soviet people. Many of Makanin's characters who have eagerly left such settlements still have psychological roots and allegiances there, and think of their former way of life with bitter-sweet nostalgia, a mixture of affection and revulsion. Although they may have hated the *poselok*, they are lonely without it. As Soviet critics have pointed out, the "collective unconscious" of the Soviet people is a major subject of Makanin's concern, and the "psycho-ideology" of the *poselok* is an important historic element in that unconscious.

In the last five years or so, Makanin has increased the historical dimension in his writing, which as a result has become even more interesting and complicated. Like Trifonov, he has always tried to provide an historical perspective to his situations and characters, to endow them with more than contemporary significance. Recently, however, he has taken to juxtaposing, within a single work, plots that are widely disparate in time and place and ostensibly unrelated. Under close scrutiny these plots can be found to reflect upon, penetrate, and reinforce one another, and ultimately to focus mutually on a single general theme. (Tatiana Tolstaya calls this his "holographic" method.) The aim of this method, it would seem, is to suggest the totality of the Russian experience.

Left Behind (*Otstavshii*, 1987) combines the retrospective, often ironic narrative of a middle-aged man about his days as a student, aspiring writer, and frustrated lover in the 1960s; the torments of his father, a veteran builder (from the period of "socialist construction") who suffers from a recurring nightmare in which he hopelessly tries to catch up with a truckload of his contemporaries; and several (often contradictory) versions of an ancient legend about a persecuted boy in the Urals who has an uncanny gift for divining the presence of gold ore. A common thread of being "left behind" runs through all three accounts. The novel embraces several generations, reflecting the total Soviet Russian experience, and the legendary passages go deep into the Russian past. The parts do not fit easily together, and there seem to be some loose fragments. Moreover, there is distracting, if fascinating, play with notions of illusion and reality. Nevertheless, the numerous and motley characters and subplots in their totality create a vigorous and arresting portrait of a people and its history.

Another short novel, *Loss* (*Utrata*), also published in 1987, is likewise preoccupied with history and its resonances in the present. The story, which is compounded of legend, dream, and stark reality, is often harsh and grim in showing age-old hardship, suffering, and cruelty. A central image is a tunnel dug for mysterious reasons centuries ago under the Ural river by a disorganized, drunken gang of drifters led by a mean-spirited but courageous bully whom posterity, through the distortions of legend, turns into a regional saint. Ruminative and loosely episodic, it contains much speculation on questions of memory and legend, social history and tradition, and the transitoriness of human life and of the things and institutions that men build. Images of ruin – graveyards and crumbled villages – are frequent. All in all, the novel shows a somber, brooding Makanin in what seem to be the depths of pessimism.

Although he is a versatile stylist, Makanin does not seem to aspire to elegance in language, preferring precision over beauty.

He has an acute ear for contemporary vernacular, and his dialogue is extensive and convincing. He is, however, a writer for whom finding the essence of matters is more important than describing them. This, I think, is why one usually feels in his works the presence of an ironic intelligence, and often a tragic one.

In Valerii Popov's (born 1939) story "Superfluous Virtuosity" ("Izlishnyaya virtuoznost'," 1988), the narrator's wife asks him: "What are your plans for tomorrow?"

He answers: "Get a shave and a haircut, get my picture taken, and hang myself."

He does not really mean this, of course, and she knows it. This is merely a typical wry quip from this poet of modest talent who is scraping by as a writer of lyrics for pop-songs. Although he is an unsuccessful poet, the narrator is a witty, engaging character, whose digs at his wife, comments on his likes, dislikes and frustrations, amorous adventures and accounts of episodes from the streets of Leningrad have a buoyantly humorous appeal. Popov's flavor is often best conveyed in dialogue. This same narrator takes a song to an editor:

> "You ought to get twenty rubles for this text."
> "And for the subtext?"
> "Do you have one?"
> "Of course."
> "Then twenty five."

Although Popov's narrator has various external guises, he is always essentially the same person – a city-fellow engaged in the rat-race, but not too absorbed in it to notice the ironies in the things that happen to himself and others, or to observe the sometimes painful but often funny incidents in the daily life around him. His appeal to a wide contemporary Russian audience, by all accounts, is precisely in this amalgam of closely watched urban cultural detail, leavened by a fine sense of the absurd. Many of his stories involve travel – within his native Leningrad and its environs, or sometimes to Moscow for a short visit – in the course of which there is an accumulation of small episodes and impressions – vexatious, dismaying, or simply amusing, with which Russian readers can readily identify.

At times the narrator's travels take him further afield, as in "The Thirds Shall Be Firsts" ("Tret'i budut pervymi," 1988), in which he goes to a resort hotel for a big business conference, only to find Homeric chaos: the rooms are being torn up for unnecessary "repairs" on which the swindling management are making enormous profits, and the bureaucrat-conventioneers are preoccupied with a drunken orgy. Their corruption is so frank and uninhibited that their behavior takes on an almost heroic, mythological dimension. Although Popov usually writes with a light touch, he sometimes resorts to the hyperbolic, and even the fantastic.

Popov's colorful accounts of the small details and trials of everyday life are conveyed in compact but relaxed, conversational language, with a usually ironic intonation. One of his most ingratiating traits is his narrator's ironical attitude towards himself: he realizes that he can seem just as absurd as the people around him. And although he does make fun of stuffed shirts, crooks, and nincompoops and can be wickedly caustic about them, his own self-critical awareness seems to prevent him from engaging extensively in satire. For example, in "Dreams from the Top Berth" ("Sny na verkhnei polke," 1987) he finds himself unable to protest about the abominable conditions on a freezing passenger train that is grotesquely mismanaged by its swindling crew, because he has obtained his own ticket through somewhat shady means.

Until recently, there has been a light-hearted quality about Popov's accounts of life's discomforts and misfortunes. He wrote with such gusto that the mere zest for living seemed to outweigh the torments he depicted. Beginning around 1987, however, his humor sometimes took on a sarcastic tinge, and his heretofore optimistic narrator began occasionally to brood and express self-doubt. In the *povest' A New Sheherezade* (*Novaya Shekherezade*, 1987), he even relegated his standard narrator to the role of listener to whom a woman in early middle-age tells the story of her life. Marina is a smart, spunky person who came as a country girl to Leningrad to seek her fortune. Her tale is not reliable: she is obviously a fantasist and sometimes a liar. But it is clear that she has had a variety of colorful and often painful experiences, that she has been both the exploited and the exploiter, that she has had several different occupations and been involved with a number of men, and that she has moved frequently up and down the social ladder. She has seen much of the dramatically seamy, Dostoevskian side of Leningrad life, and has herself been implicated in it: one of her men is a currency speculator, and she herself, as a hospital kitchen worker, had participated in routine wholesale thievery. In the end Marina, married and a mother, emerges as an only slightly soiled survivor. But she is quite a different person from the sunny narrator-hero whom readers had come to expect from Popov.

Svetopol' is an imaginary city in southern Russia, not far from the Black Sea. Its location, topography, and vegetation are similar to those of Simferopol', where the writer Ruslan Kireev (born 1941) lived as a youth. This fictive provincial metropolis, together with nearby resort towns, has become the locale of dozens of Kireev's stories and novels and the place of origin, home, or visiting place of hundreds of his major and minor characters. While Svetopol' has an identity and integrity of its own, it is not notable for ethnic or cultural peculiarities and uniqueness. Rather, its populace represents a motley collection of personal attributes as varied as humanity itself, with diverse quirks, talents, ambitions, and moral makeups.

Kireev's imagination is both expansive and democratic. It embraces driving, pushy local big-shots and lonely oddballs, the very old and the very young, the placid and the cranky, and all shades of morality and immorality, often in complex mixtures. His major characters tend to be persons of his own generation, educated urbanites who grew up after World War II and who remember its traumas dimly if at all. His manner of presenting characters – their problems, aspirations, conflicts and frustrations – has usually been dispassionate with frequent touches of irony, although from the beginning he has been capable of shocking the reader with stories of cruelty and suffering and, conversely, of amusing them with shrewd satire.

Cumulatively the large cycle of novels and stories centering on Svetopol' create a kind of saga. The main personage of a particular work appears as a secondary character in a number of others, so that, recurring in varying degrees of prominence, Kireev's *dramatis personae*, living and dead, represent a lasting and memorable community, which in turn represents both a localized population and Kireev's version of the human race at large.

Although Kireev began publishing in the 1960s, his reputation became established in the late 1970s. His best-known works of that period are the trilogy of novels *The Preparatory Notebook* (*Podgotovitel'naya tetrad'*, 1981), *Apologia* (*Apologiya*, 1980) and *The Victor* (*Pobeditel'*, 1972–79), each of which features major characters with prominent but complicated and not readily definable psychological and moral identities. The narrator of *The Preparatory Notebook*, for example, a journalist on the staff of the regional newspaper, is a perceptive, sensitive, alert observer of others who, however, is so incapable of perceiving his own shortcomings that he has become an ineffectual "loser." He cannot understand the poorly educated but highly successful, driving administrator of the city's clothing factories to whom Kireev contrasts him. Both these and other major characters in the trilogy are presented so objectively that critics searching for the author's own opinion have sometimes been baffled and irritated by Kireev's seeming lack of moral commitment. In this, as in purely stylistic respects, the influence of Chekhov on the writer is prominent.

In "The Staircase" ("Lestnitsa," 1968) a thirteen-year-old girl is seduced in an attic by a greasy-haired punk who has promised to teach her how to play the accordion; he then shows her off among his cronies. *Ulya Maksimovna, My Love and Hope* (*Ulya Maksimovna, lyubov' moya i nadezhda*, 1981) tells of an innocent triangle involving a busy factory manager, his charming and devoted wife, and the strange mechanical genius and loner who becomes his trouble-shooter but also becomes attached to the manger's wife. Essentially a psychological novel, its main concern is the threat to a marriage which has lost some of its bloom but is still firm. Much of the narrative interest comes from the belatedly alarmed husband's maneuvers to defend his marriage against an unprepossessing rival who seems improbable but is nevertheless genuine. The husband and wife, both interesting characters, are portrayed intimately and sympathetically. Although many external details are provided about the nemesis, he remains, and appropriately so, a largely enigmatic figure.

"The Furious Woman Tat'yana" ("Neistovaya zhenshchina Tat'yana," 1983) is the portrait of a one-armed war veteran – a single parent and grandmother – who has long planned and saved for a visit from a wartime friend and her husband. The visit is a disaster. Her lavish hospitality is smothering, and her behavior is so insufferably arrogant and domineering that the couple leave well ahead of schedule. Like many of Kireev's stories, this is essentially a character study. Another such study, but larger and more intricate, is the novella "There lived Poets..." ("Tam zhili poety...," 1983), featuring the irascible, eccentric painter Rybchuk who, after reviving from a heart attack during which he had been declared clinically dead, undergoes a personality change and becomes mild and tractable, although artistically inactive. The story includes contrasting and supplementary portraits: two diametrically opposite women who share Rybchuk's affections, and a rival, less talented painter with a totally different temperament and attitude toward art. The clash of these two painters, and the arguments they provoke, provide interesting commentary on the social role of the artist.

Kireev's stories have often included odd and unusual characters, but until relatively recently they have remained in the background, giving center stage to more conventional types. As we have seen, there are exceptions, and Rybchuk is one of them. Another is Yurii Ivanovich, the obscure and mousy but endearing librarian hero of *The Glow-worm* (*Svetlyachok*, 1985), who has compensated for an abused and miserable childhood by cultivating a vivid imagination and living vicariously through books. He identifies himself, in large measure, with

Adelbert von Chamisso, who created the legendary Peter Schlemihl and, like Schlemihl, Yurii Ivanovich has lost his shadow. This touch of the supernatural is most unusual for Kireev, who had heretofore been distinctly a realist.

A different kind of departure from Kireev's established mode is *The Sandy Acacia* (*Peschanaya akatsiya*, 1984), narrated as the rambling reminiscences of a stage and screen actor. The novel is both fantasy and parable: Svetopol' is physically threatened by creeping sands, which may eventually engulf the city. The hero is anxiously aware that previous civilizations have been obliterated and buried in desert, and he senses that with every indication of the city's cultural and moral lassitude the sands approach more closely. Although the novel contains much of Kireev's usual concrete, tangible, colorful life material, the predominant metaphorical element, which is new for Kireev, seems artificial and strained.

Kireev is clearly restless about his art, its sources, means, and directions, and seems eager to break out of the mold of his Svetopol' fiction. A most interesting indication of this mood is *A Feast Alone* (*Pir v odinochke*, 1989), which is a novel about the unsuccessful writing of a novel, and which undoubtedly has a prominent autobiographical ingredient. The narrator is trying to write about the youth and maturation of a schoolboy acquaintance, but he constantly finds himself exploring his own life, his writing problems, the nature of his art, and his psychology as a writer. Ultimately we learn much more about the narrator than we do about the person who is his subject. Although Kireev's tone is serious as he details the pain of growing up with only a grandmother (the father is dead and the mother is usually absent and irresponsible), and as he grapples with aesthetic issues and the agonizing subjective problems of creativity, there is also a relieving and engaging atmosphere of self-irony of the kind that has so often refreshed the Svetopol' saga. The very awkwardness and groping of the narrator in this novel are fascinating, for Kireev is indeed a fine literary craftsman.

Anatolii Kim (born 1939) is the most gifted of a number of

writers who, in the seventies and early eighties, began to employ the fantastic and supernatural as a means of commenting on the human situation. Of Korean ancestry and born in Kazakhstan, Kim attended an art institute and graduated from the Literary Institute in Moscow in 1971. He writes only in Russian and considers himself primarily a beneficiary of the Russian literary heritage of the nineteenth century. Many of his earliest and most charming stories, however, feature the lives, folk beliefs, social customs, and tribulations of Soviet Koreans in Kazakhstan and the Far East.

"The Eglantine of Myoko" ("Shipovnik Myoko," 1976) recounts the sacrifices of a girl on Sakhalin who is berated by her family and community for having become pregnant by a local boy, thus jeopardizing *his* future. They marry, he goes to Leningrad to study physics, and she remains to work long hours on a mink farm to support their son and send her husband money to maintain him in his studies. She dies of an infected animal bite and he single-mindedly completes his doctorate. After an eight-year absence, he makes a return visit to Sakhalin, and only then does a dramatic and bitter revelation make him realize what this simple, unloved, and devoted woman has done for him. "A Link of Tenderness" ("Zveno nezhnosti," 1976) uses deeply superstitious, supernatural family legend, the narrator's boyhood memories of his ancient great-grandmother, and ruminations on the beauties of nature to create a delicate amalgam of ethnological detail, folklore, and personal meditation. In another tale of Sakhalin, "The Smile of the Vixen" ("Ulybka lisitsy," 1976) a young man, returned on vacation from his studies in Leningrad, spends an evening drinking Scotch whisky with his village buddies and listens in lofty urban disdain to their ghost stories. On the way home he is confronted by a fox who weirdly grins at him, evoking the image of a local girl known as The Vixen.

The works that have attracted the greatest attention to Kim, although they may be artistically inferior to his stories, are such novels as *Lotus* (*Lotos*, 1980), *The Squirrel* (*Belka*, 1984), and *Father-Forest* (*Otets-les*, 1989). In these works and others, Kim attempts, through complicated means, to embrace large, eternal moral and metaphysical issues. He freely violates chronology, logical narrative sequence, the psychological integrity of characters, and the empirical laws of nature, in attempts to conjure up profound, generalized images of the human situation. Often these images are vivid and poignant, but they are also frequently blurred, confusingly and self-defeatingly intricate.

The central situation of the short novel *Lotus* is the visit of an artist from the metropolis to the deathbed of his mother on Sakhalin after an absence of sixteen years, his remorse over his neglect of the suffering old woman, and his gesture of expiation in cutting an orange into the shape of a lotus and presenting it to her, a gesture which he repeats as an old man, many years later, at her grave. The lotus itself becomes a many-layered symbol for the possibilities of spiritual regeneration through art and expanded human understanding. Supporting and supplementing this symbolism, Kim uses an array of devices to recount the tormented life of the mother, to detail the psychological conflicts of the artist, and to speculate on the mystical, panhuman significance of their story. His language is highly poetic and often rhetorical. Temporal planes (including the future) and settings are constantly shifted and mixed, and there is a multiplicity of narrative voices – including those of disembodied spirits (a chorus called "We," which represents the eternal essence of humanity into which the "I" of the hero is made to blend).

In *The Squirrel* (which Kim calls a "novel-fairy tale"), two main supernatural forces are at work: a "conspiracy" of part-animal, part-human creatures who seek to destroy all of mankind's loftier impulses – toward artistic creativity, morality, idealism, and the like; and the narrator himself (who does not disclose his real name but calls himself Squirrel), who shares these lofty impulses and who is capable of embodying himself in the souls of other persons at will, and who deplores this "conspiracy." The novel traces the careers of a group of four Moscow art students as their talents are developed but usually frustrated and spoiled through the workings of the conspiracy. We learn about these individuals and their fates through the presence of Squirrel in their psyches, although at times their voices cease to be independent as they blend together into one single, timeless, universal voice. The characters seem to be intended to represent, individually and collectively, the present moral state of humanity. The novel, which is a cautionary and to a great degree a pessimistic one, questions whether human evolution and the positive, creative abilities of man are capable of continuing or whether they may have stopped.

Father-Forest, perhaps Kim's most ambitious novel to date, is dominated by a forest spirit (representing the eternity of nature) who decides to inhabit periodically the souls of individual men, to study the difference between humans and trees. He visits chiefly the male representatives of three generations of the Turaev family from the turn of the century to the present. The Turaevs are all intelligent brooders who have seen much of the dark sides of existence but who lead lives of desperation largely because they think too much. All three, after bitter experiences, retreat from the "civilized" world to live in remote villages or the forest itself. The spirit's conclusion seems to be that humans (especially by making war and by irresponsibly threatening the environment) are stupidly and unnecessarily cruel and self-destructive, and that the main motive of the human race, both as individuals and as a collective, is suicide. Despite the novel's portrayal of pain and suffering – there are graphic accounts of the perverse cruelty of both German and Russian concentration camps in World War II and of the Gulag – and a prominent element of apocalyptic foreboding (the nuclear peril is frequently mentioned), it ends with a faint ray of Christian hope.

To support the novel's over-arching idea that all phenomena, human and natural, are interconnected and independent of the bounds of time and space, Kim shows various characters experiencing identical emotions under widely separated circumstances. He also joins third-person and first-person narration, sometimes confusingly, in the attempt to show how Father-Forest "becomes" one of the human characters. All of this is in an effort to show disparate but thematically related events as if they were occurring simultaneously, by a method which Kim calls "epic polyphony." Earnest and ingenious as the attempt may be, and despite the author's impressive powers of description – the majestic beauty of nature, the awesomeness of human cruelty and suffering – the novel often strains under the weight of its own devices and intellectual aspirations.

Any account of the literature of this period should mention a work which in 1980 streaked across the Moscow sky and then, like all meteors, soon disappeared. This was the novel *Danilov the Violist* (*Al'tist Danilov*) by Vladimir Orlov (born 1936), the account of a half-man, half-devil, who has been commissioned by the netherworld to make a kind of medium-level mischief in this world, e.g. helping prepare earthquakes and avalanches, causing divorces. Because of his human side, he has little taste for this work and much prefers his more respectable occupation as a first-class orchestra violist. His foot-dragging and unco-operative attitude so irritate his devil superiors that they undertake various disciplinary torments, such as stealing his precious Albani viola, and finally bring him to trial. There is a happy ending: he gets off with a light punishment and is allowed to live out his life on earth with his beloved (second) wife.

The novel abounds in phantasmagoric features; the hero can transport himself in an instant to any place in the world or universe, he has an array of supernatural tricks at his disposal, and at one point he engages in a magnificent, pyrotechnic inter-galactic duel. Such juvenile entertainment, however, is not the author's intention. The hero, when not engaged in skulduggery or avoiding it, lives in the real world of Moscow, whose manners and morals Orlov uses as the subject of humor, mild satire, and, possibly, political allegory, although the latter is too vague to identify with confidence. The novel is in fact too diffuse and whimsical to achieve great intellectual depth.

What is most significant about *Danilov the Violist* is its prominent element of grotesque, often surreal fantasy. Critics and readers immediately saw in it the influence of Mikhail Bulgakov's *The Master and Margarita*, and the resemblance, superficial as it turned out to be on closer examination, nevertheless explains in large measure the novel's great initial popularity among the public. The example of Bulgakov, and the natural need of Soviet literature for new modes and forms as a relief from the then prevailing psychological realism, undoubtedly inspired Orlov to embark on this work. As literature, *Danilov the Violist* is not distinguished, but it marks the beginning of a tendency that was to flavor significant amounts of literature in the 1980s.

A prominent writer of this generation is Sergei Esin (born 1935). His short novel *Memoirs of a Forty-Year-Old* (*Memuary Sorokaletnego*, 1984) is essentially a series of portraits of his contemporaries, beginning with World War II, concentrating on the immediate postwar years, touching upon the youth culture of the 1960s, and ending in the mid-1970s. It attempts to capture the spirit of his Muscovite generation through the details of its often impoverished existence, its changing moods, and its passage into full adulthood. There is no plot; the characters episodically interact with the narrator, but seldom with each other. Although there are fictional elements, the novel seems to be more a factual report than a work of imagination.

Esin's novels and stories give accounts of contemporary urban social and personality types and examine their moral flaws in detail. "The Present Day" ("Tekushchii den'," 1979) focuses on the ambitious, manipulatory wife of a forty-year-old executive who has pushed her husband into a job beyond his powers, that brings him a fatal heart attack. Her materialism and talent for intrigue seem well suited to the bureaucratic world of influence, pull, and preference in which her husband is both a participant and a victim. Obviously and heavily didactic, the story is an indictment of unscrupulous selfishness and a social milieu in which it flourishes. The heroine of "One's Work is Never Done" ("Nezavershenka," 1986) is an outright criminal – an arsonist and saboteur. Praskov'ya Kuz'minichna is a public baths attendant who makes a comfortable but illicit living peddling vodka and snacks to the customers. When a new young manager initiates changes that threaten her cushy regime, the crafty Praskov'ya secretly sets fire to the establishment and later floods it in hopes of forestalling reform. For all her corruptness, Praskov'ysa is rather engaging in her native cunning.

Among the literary critics, Esin's most widely discussed work was the novel *The Imitator* (*Imitator*, 1985), the frank and even boastful confession of a corrupt portrait painter and museum director whose cynical intrigues have made him famous and wealthy. A master of flattery, deception, maneuver, and betrayal, he has parlayed a mediocre talent, through brilliant self-publicity and power-plays, into a distinguished career of international proportions. What is striking, in fact appalling, about the individual is not so much his total lack of personal and artistic integrity, but the pride and candor with which he discloses the techniques of his ascent from rural obscurity to prominence and influence, and the depth of his misanthropy, which approaches that of Dostoevsky's Underground Man. One wonders, in fact, how a creature who understands himself so thoroughly can bear to live with himself. What has puzzled the critics about this arresting character is the motivation, or lack of it, for his confessional outpouring. Why should so totally and efficiently corrupt a person, a man without conscience, want to take the trouble to unmask himself and enumerate his sins? In answer, it is pointed out that the hero is actually a *grotesque* figure, not requiring psychological motivation. (At the novel's end, in fact, he fancies that he has become a raven – a sinister creature he has always admired.) One critic indeed argues that the story develops not as a drama but as a farce. However striking the image of Esin's hero, it has strong elements of caricature. It can be concluded that although the portrait has power, it is psychologically ill-conceived.

The writing of Anatolii Kurchatkin (born 1944) has characteristics in common with several of the individual authors discussed in this chapter. He writes, although not exclusively, about routine contemporary city life, often from a critical point of view, and is alert to the historical processes taking place within the Soviet period. At times, his interests take him to the smaller, drabber communities of the suburban *poselok*. Kurchatkin also has a gift for abstraction and metaphor, which sometimes lends his stories a mysterious, parabolic quality. In the story "The Maze," for example, an unnamed and unidentified narrator spends his life from young manhood to old age trying to work his way out of an impossibly flexible, semi-animated labyrinth of brick walls.

In "The Guillotine" a depressed man crushed by the crowding, jostling, and shortages of city life, with a miserable job, an oppressive wife, and a disappointing family, after several attempts at suicide stumbles upon an Institute of Quick and Easy Death, where they mercifully decapitate him. It is suggested that this is an hallucination and that he has actually died of a heart attack. Other ghostly aspects of the story, however, point to the workings of the supernatural. A harsher, crueler, completely earthly story is "Owner of a Cooperative Apartment" ("Khozyaika kooperativnoi kvartiry," 1978), which chronicles a day in the life of a thirty-year-old Moscow woman employed in a fur factory, who deals in winter hats she has acquired from her workplace through dubious means. After witnessing a suicide on her way to her job she calls in sick, returns home, and, in a series of nasty episodes with neighbors, a casual sex partner, her child's nanny, and her husband, shows herself to be a completely shallow, vulgar, dishonest individual, well equipped for material survival in a corrupt society.

"Gasification" ("Gazifikatskya," 1981) examines the relationship between a retired physician in her seventies, who lives frugally and uncomfortably in an old house in a *poselok*, and her grandson, who lives in Moscow with a wife, child, and unpleasant mother-in-law. The grandson is not a bad fellow, but he is rather selfish and irresponsible and so preoccupied with problems at work, and domestic complications, that he neglects the old woman. When she dies he finds in her attic trunks of papers that document her life from 1917 on, and this discovery kindles an interest not only in his grandmother's life-story but in his family's history in general. We are not told how deep or lasting this interest will be, but there is a strong suggestion that the awareness of roots and family tradition is an essential, and too-often overlooked, element of spiritual life.

In 1990 Kurchatkin combined his penchant for social

criticism with his taste for the bizarre to produce an anti-utopian novel *Notes of an Extremist: The Construction of a Subway in our City* (*Zapiski ekstremista: stroitel'stvo metro v nashem gorode*). In this tragicomic parable, a group of idealistic college students, after unsuccessfully petitioning the city authorities to build a long-promised and badly-needed subway system, undertake to do the job themselves. With enthusiastic support from the local populace, they make an impressive start, but wholesale persecution by the authorities so severely threatens the work that the young leaders decide to go, literally, underground.

To build their subway and donate it to the city, they create their own subterranean community, with factories, farms, schools, and hospitals – a whole self-sufficient, self-perpetuating civilization completely sealed off from the world above ground. The subway construction proceeds apace, but the project takes time – in fact, a whole generation. By the time it is completed, the founding fathers are elderly, and their children, who have never known the world above, are totally isolated from it. What is worse, their closed society has become totalitarian, complete with a system of coercion and thought control. The "extremists" who began the subway project had no ideology other than their desire to contribute to their city's welfare, and after a generation their society still has only one goal – to present the completed subway to the world above. Still, an insidious authoritarianism has poisoned their society, as if inevitably.

When the day comes for these hundreds of would-be altruists to emerge to the surface and donate their gift, it turns out that for years the city has been enjoying an efficient, lighter-than-air system of public transport, and that the gleaming subway is useless. Most of the "extremists" have grave nervous breakdowns; the others return to their subway to commit suicide. The narrator, after a period in a city hospital, ends his years as a humble night-watchman, avoiding those few fellow-extremists who still roam the city as broken casualties of a youthful dream.

It is tempting to read *Notes of an Extremist* as an allegory of the October revolution and its consequences, and also as a general parable about the dangers of a fanatical, exclusive pursuit of a single social goal. The work distinctly belongs to the category of

Russian dystopian novel, as exemplified by Evgenii Zamyatin's *We*, Andrei Platonov's *Kotlovan*, and works of recent Russian emigre literature such as Aleksandr Zinov'ev's *The Yawning Heights*, Vladimir Voinovich's *Moscow 2042*, and Abram Tertz/ Andrei Sinyavskii's *Lyubimov* (translated as *The Makepeace Experiment*). Although Kurchatkin's novel is neither as extensive and detailed nor as satirically pointed as these other anti-utopias, it is powerfully written and thought-provoking, and it undoubtedly belongs in their company.

Since the time, a decade and a half ago, when they were first identified as the "forty-year-olds," the writers with whom this chapter is concerned, who even then had only a limited number of characteristics in common, have diverged still more as their writing has continued to develop. In considering their careers to date, there is scarcely a generalization that could be made about them as a group to which there would not be at least one or two exceptions. Still, certain patterns seem fairly clear. These writers were originally nurtured on traditional Russian realism, and in their portrayal of life in the city and the *poselok* they pay close attention to the details of everyday existence and the psychology of ordinary persons. Although they are keenly aware of moral problems, their manner of depicting them tends to be dispassionate and objective. Satire among them is mild and not extensive. They avoid capacious or epic narration; the novels they write are fairly short. At the same time, there has recently been a movement among them toward increased narrative complexity – intricate mixtures of temporal planes, multiple voices, and points of view, a more active usage of metaphor and symbolism.

There is a prominent historical consciousness among these writers, an acute awareness of the entire Soviet period – not only of the changes over generations but also of the unique spirit of specific periods, such as the 1960s. Recently Makanin and Kim have attempted to capture the "collective unconscious" as it has developed over the years, and to introduce a dimension of folklore and legend into the structure of their narratives. Their efforts, it would seem, are part of a general tendency among this group to restore the richness of traditional Russian realism, on the one hand, and to move away from realism on the other.

The move has taken several directions. In recent works of Kim, Kireev, Orlov, and Kurchatkin, the real and the unreal are made to co-exist in a mixture of the ordinary, the fantastic, and the supernatural. Kim's mysticism and his increased interest in metaphysical matters, in fact, make him seem more a romantic than a realist; Orlov joins him in combining the romantic with the everyday. Orlov's use of phantasmagoria and Kurchatkin's depiction of dark powers at work in the otherwise ordinary world represent other kinds of departure from realism. Similarly, the use of parable by several of these authors seems at variance with realism. While Kurchatkin's anti-utopia is realistic in its narrative manner, the story manifestly exceeds the bounds of the possible.

Many of the works discussed in this chapter lend themselves readily to political interpretation. Nostalgic references to the *elan* of the early 1960s, and the sense of malaise and alienation so prominent in works set in the 1970s, can be seen to represent writers' impressions of the political climate of the times. When a writer features corrupt bureaucrats and opportunists, or a failure of sympathy and communication between members of different generations, he often appears to be making an implicit commentary on an oppressive, Party-dominated social and economic system. The anti-utopian novel of Kurchatkin is unmistakably a political parable. It would be a great over-simplification, however, to view the works of these writers primarily as political phenomena, for they are actually the products of a developing, multi-faceted, essentially *literary* process.

CHAPTER 6

Other voices

This chapter presents an assortment of writers who apparently have little in common. Some of them have partial affinities with other possible groupings – for example, the writers of fantastic or historical prose, "women's literature," the so-called "alternative literature," and the "tough" and "cruel" prose that is the topic of the following chapter. None of them, however, displays any of these tendencies with sufficient prominence to warrant an exclusive categorization. The range of their ages – they were born between 1934 and 1951 – is considerably wider than that of the "forty-year-olds," so that they cannot be considered as a generation.

These writers, in fact, give evidence of the increased *variety* in Russian literature as it developed during the latter years of the Soviet regime. In years to come, surely, a longer perspective will make possible a reasonably firm classification of each of these writers, and some may simply fade into the shadows of literary history. For the moment, however, each of them seems significant, in his or her unique literary contours.

In the late 1980s Mikhail Kuraev (born 1939), heretofore a film scenarist, made his debut as a prose writer by applying a fresh and original perspective to thematics that had already become well established in the immediately preceding years: Soviet history and the moral devastation caused by Stalinism. His novel *Captain Dikshtein* (*Kapitan Dikshtein*, 1987) tells of a sailor who, caught up in the Kronstadt uprising of 1921 against the Soviet government, protects himself from retribution by assuming the name and identity of another sailor who was

executed during the same events. Kuraev's depiction of the
uprising itself – factual, vivid, kaleidoscopic, and told from the
intimate perspective of participants – was innovative in its
delineation of the causes of the rebellion; his implicitly
sympathetic stance toward the mutineers challenged the time-
honored official interpretation.

Captain Dikshtein, however, was more than just another
glasnost'-inspired polemic against historical canon. The larger
part of the work tells of the mundane existence of the impostor
Dikshtein – supporting himself with a variety of petty jobs,
raising rabbits – until he dies of a heart attack in the mid-1960s.
He lives in a small, obscure city near Leningrad – Gatchina,
which itself has changed its name and visage more than once
over the years, and which therefore, like the hero, has a dubious
identity. In his attempt to transform his character and
personality, to adapt himself to his image of the man he has
"replaced" but whom he scarcely knew, this hero becomes
merely a phantom, a divided soul, an essentially faceless victim
of history. The influence of Gogol seems quite evident in this
part of Kuraev's work, not only in the image of a little man who
has lost his identity but also in the whimsical, ornamental style,
with intricate sentences and frequent asides to the reader.

The stylistic influence of Gogol, and also of two other
prominent St. Petersburg writers – Dostoevsky and Andrei Bely
– is even more pronounced in *Night Watch* (*Nochnoi dozor*, 1988),
which features the reminiscences, in monologue form, of an
NKVD–KGB operative and enforcer, Polubolotov, who has
retired after forty years of service. Proud of what he considers to
have been an honorable and constructive contribution to
society, absorbed in the details and procedures of his work,
Polubolotov enthusiastically shares his experiences – surveillance, interrogations, burials – like any other conscientious
technician. He speaks affectionately about the interesting
prisoners – especially the intellectuals – whom he has interro-
gated on their way to prison or execution, or their behavior
under arrest, their evasive maneuvers (such as feigning mad-
ness), and of the numerous enlightening things he has learned
from his educated and cultured subjects – for example, the

profession of gynecology. He is especially fond of birds and speaks lyrically of hearing nightingales singing in the woods while he is helping to bury executed prisoners and derelict secret policemen. Morally obtuse and limited in intelligence but not insane, he has simply been a dutiful, specialized workman in a system that, to the reader, is manifestly insane.

The voice of Polubolotov, grotesque in its unconscious irony, is only one of two in the story. Another voice, a kind of chorus evidently representing the views of the author, speaks of the historic Petersburg milieu in which Polubolotov's activities have taken place. It lovingly and at length describes the charm of Petersburg's white nights but at the same time dwells on the city's grim heritage, from the time when Peter the Great built his capital on the bones of thousands of slave laborers, through the creation of the city's architectural monuments, which are presented as tragic symbols of Russia's tradition of violent despotism. Thus the character of Polubolotov is shown in the wierd context of a city that is both fantastically beautiful and the embodiment of civic oppression and cruelty. At the beginning of *Night Watch*, Kuraev highlighted this anomaly by providing dual epigraphs – from Gogol and from Stalin.

The stories of Tatyana Tolstaya are crammed with images from the most diverse sources – the mundane and the supernatural, the kitchen and the classics, the exotic and the familiar. Her world is sharply, sensuously tangible, laden with sights, sounds, smells, colors, and objects in lively and dynamic association, so that the very interaction of these elements is of great intrinsic interest, regardless of logic or narrative significance. Tolstaya's intensely poetic prose is playfully inventive, often subtle in its shadings, often boldly arresting and sometimes grotesque. With a robust sense of humor and a grim sense of the tragic, keen moral awareness and a gift for sardonic satire, a searching compassion and a love of the absurd, she creates complex verbal artifacts that are frequently puzzling and just as frequently fascinating.

Born in 1951 to a distinguished literary and scholarly family (on both maternal and paternal sides), she made her debut in

1983 and has published some two dozen stories. As a rule these stories have been quite short, no more than twenty pages in length, although two recent works have run to forty and sixty pages. She presents practically no situations or events of public significance, but her topical range is extensive. Seemingly confined to the private lives of relatively obscure and unobtrusive individuals, the stories actually embrace a wide assortment of characters of various ages and makeups, most of them in poignant and some in bizarre circumstances. Although Tolstaya is sensitive to pain and suffering, she is not sentimental; she portrays both the cruelty of humans and the cruelty of fate with a clear eye and a firm voice. She is stern about human shortcomings, but she is more an observer than a moralist.

Many of Tolstaya's stories are essentially portraits of individual characters, usually involving an extended, but summarized and compressed, period of time. All of these characters are singular; many of them are distinctly odd. The hero of "Peters" ("Peters," 1986) is a librarian, a squat, pot-bellied loner who longs for love and friendship but who is doomed to live as an outsider because his emotional growth has been stunted by a domineering grandmother. In "Dear Shura" ("Milaya Shura," 1985) we see, sympathetically, an eccentric old woman, a vestige of pre-revolutionary Russia, who lives solely on the memory of past husbands and lovers. The heroine of "Sonya" ("Sonya," 1984) is an affectionate and generous, but gullible, ugly spinster, exploited by a callous circle of intellectuals who make cruel fun of her by secretly inventing for her a phantom lover. The central figure of "The Fakir" ("Fakir," 1986) is an imaginative fraud who poses as an affluent dilettante and art-collector and beguiles a scruffy and pathetic coterie with his phony culture and erudition. "Night" ("Noch'," 1987) is the portrait of a childlike, retarded middle-aged man who lives with his closely protective mother and exists largely, and happily, in a fairy-tale world of fantasy.

To summarize Tolstaya's stories solely in terms of their major characters, however, would be grossly inaccurate. Much is going on in the stories that is of a purely literary nature – the interplay of an abundance of tropes, whimsical digressions and flights of fancy, sly jokes and quizzical asides, a rich allusiveness. There is great formal virtuosity in Tolstaya – involved, elegantly shaped sentences, adroit combinations of lofty and earthy diction, precisely graphic detail in the midst of calculated ambiguity. Her narratives often involve multiple voices representing disparate points of view but without marks that clearly distinguish the speakers, so that the effect is one of generalized, although sometimes discordant, rumor.

The recurring concerns in Tolstaya's works are human behavior and personal relationships, life and death, time and memory. Although there are many admirable individuals in her cast of characters, she often displays a mordant view of the human race. One of the most frequently highlighted human shortcomings in her stories is the obtuse indifference of one person toward another, the lack of desire to understand the psychology or nurture the soul of another. A number of her most interesting characters are relative isolates at the very edges of society, misunderstood or neglected aberrants. Tolstaya's approach is not solemn; their strange behavior is often presented in a humorous, if sympathetic, light, and the fantasies with which these lonely individuals console themselves can be enchanting.

Tolstaya's writing is seldom far removed from irony, and this mood clearly dominates some of her stories. In "Hunting the Wooly Mammoth" ("Okhota na mamonta," 1985), the cold-blooded campaign of a pretty but vulgar young woman to induce a man to marry her is described through a governing metaphor in which her role is not that of the sentimental heroine she thinks herself to be, but rather that of a cave-man out for meat. Tolstaya often engages in outright satire. Here is an excerpt from her account, in "Limpopo" ("Limpopo," 1990) of a report which an orthodox Soviet communist, a "regional ideological dragon," is expected to make upon his return from a junket to Italy:

In the middle of Italy rises a black, gloomy fortress – the Vatican. A horrible, foul-smelling moat surrounds the fortress on all sides, and only once a year a squeaking drawbridge lowers its rusty chains to let in trucks full of gold. Crows circle the Vatican cawing ominously, and higher up helicopters zoom around, and even higher – Pershing missiles. Once in a while a wheezing laugh sounds from within the fortress walls – it's the pope of Rome, a dreary old man whom no one has ever seen. He's well-fed and rich, of course; he has his own fields and flocks, so he eats sausage, fats, and dumplings every day and pizza on holidays.

The world of Tolstaya is a highly animated, sometimes anthropomorphic one in which the distinction between reality and fantasy is often blurred, as is the distinction between past, present, and future. It can be the private world of an imagination, but we cannot always be sure just whose imagination it is. Not only is the narrator unidentified but she or he is often interrupted and intruded upon by the unidentified voice or voices of others. In one sense this is vexing to the reader, but in another sense it makes no difference, because what is actually at work is a flow of elaborate, variegated, witty, metaphorical language whose texture and density provide their own justification. While reading Tolstaya, one is in the presence of a stylist in the tradition of Gogol and Nabokov, a writer who is always in close touch with the roots of her national literature, both written and oral, who is erudite and joyously swept up in the power of words. She is a keen and detailed observer of her surroundings, and she is shrewd in her apprehension of human conduct. Her writing so often and so abruptly changes its tempo, focus, and direction within a given context that it can seem whimsical and capricious. But hers is a controlled capriciousness, with an eloquence and stylistic originality that make her absolutely unique among her Russian contemporaries.[1]

Like many works of fiction published after 1985, Nikolai Shmelyov's novel *Pashkov House* (*Pashkov Dom*, dated 1982, published 1987) evokes the atmosphere of the 1950s, 1960s, and 1970s and grapples with moral and ethical issues of the times. Its protagonist is Aleksandr Ivanovich Gort, a professor and scholar of Chinese history and literature, born and educated in Moscow, who fondly recalls such events as the prize-winning Moscow debut of Van Cliburn and the belated discovery of the paintings of Marc Chagall. He also recalls poignantly a session of an academic assembly in which, at the beginning of his career, he was the only person to speak and vote against the expulsion of a scoundrel who had been found guilty of secretly denouncing and informing on his faculty colleagues. Gort explains his quietly defiant stand:

> But is this louse really to blame for all this? It's not a question of him, but of the fact that this method, the method of enmity, has already exhausted itself. We don't need hostility – today against these, tomorrow against those, we need ordinary, hard, constructive work on the material we have, with all the good and bad that's in it.

Although Gort's refusal to go along with such scapegoating does not ruin his career, as it might have, it identifies him as an independent thinker of great moral stubbornness with a historian's proclivity for taking the long view. Later, the book manuscript representing the major intellectual effort of his lifetime and entitled "Mercy as a Political Instrument: An Attempt at a Comparative Analysis of Certain Medieval Doctrines" is rejected for publication on the ground that it does not represent "our" (i.e. official) kind of thinking.

Shmelyov himself (born 1936) is a leading liberal economist who has enjoyed great prominence both at home and abroad during and after the Gorbachev years. Although he has apparently dabbled in literature all his life, his public career as a writer began with *Pashkov House*. The novel's account of the philosophical and moral searchings of Gort, who rejects the notion that sudden political revolutions can solve mankind's problems and argues, instead, for a gradual intensification of a collective sense of humanity and social obligation, inspired considerable discussion among critics and readers. Also of interest to the contemporary reader was Shmelyov's portrayal of the Moscow intelligentsia of the sixties and seventies, especially its dissident element. At the end of the novel, Gort's stoical retirement to his library at the early age of fifty is partly a defeat, but also a positive, logical stage in his personal ideological development.

In *Pashkov House*, Shmelyov combined a concern for age-old

moral and ideological problems with an interest in contemporary Russian society and representative individuals. Since that novel those two topics have developed in his writing along separate and distinct lines: historical novels featuring the first set of concerns, and stories featuring portraits of contemporary Russians the second. It is almost as if Shmelyov were two different writers. *A Performance in Honor of Herr Prime Minister* (*Spektakl' v chest' gospodina pervogo ministra*, 1988) is a short novel portraying a day in the life of Johann Wolfgang von Goethe when, as Prime Minister of Weimar, the great man faced a complex political and moral decision and was forced by circumstances, and by his own personal ambition, to make an uncomfortable and humbling compromise. The novel *Sil'vestr* (*Sil'vestr*, 1991) tells of the moral and spiritual struggles of the sixteenth-century Archpriest Sil'vestr, the confessor and powerful adviser to Tsar Ivan the Terrible, and of his authoritarian ideology, a mixture of Christianity and cynicism. Both of these historical novels seem designed to bear contemporary relevance.

Shmelyov's stories of recent Russian life are unsparingly realistic and depressing. In "Presumption of Innocence" ("Prezumptsiya nevinnosti," dated 1977, published 1987) we are shown a selfish, opportunistic hedonist and his mistress, an unbearable shrew. "The Fur Coat Incident" ("Delo o shube," 1988) tells of a long, dismal marriage between a middle-level engineer, whose career is permanently stalled, and his profoundly dissatisfied and unfaithful wife; we last see them simply as resigned, aimless survivors. In "The Visit" ("Vizit," 1988) a theater manager and gambler, who is secretly wealthy and has extensive underworld connections, discovers that a call-girl whom a friend has procured for him is his own, adored daughter. "Night Voices" ("Nochnye golosa," 1988) is the transcript of three telephone calls, spaced several years apart, made by an alcoholic model to a former lover, which discloses the pathetic woman's decline into an existence of corpulent penury and loneliness.

There is nothing formally innovative about Shmelyov's writing. The stories of Moscow life are rich in contemporary detail and psychologically convincing, grim in their social implications but not startling. His novels are similarly conservative in style, but they are more interesting and profound than the stories because they feature complex characters who both think and feel deeply and responsibly.

Although she immerses her characters in the atmospheric detail of city life and is clearly an urban writer, Nina Katerli is primarily concerned with issues that transcend time and place – the relationships between men and women, women and women, parents and children, the fears and anxieties of middle-age, the onset of illness and approach of death, the cruelty or indifference of one person to another, the motives that bring people together and tear them apart, the sources of misunderstanding. Katerli is psychologically perceptive and constantly aware of human failings, but she also finds warmth and strength among her city-dwellers.

Born in Leningrad in 1934, Katerli was trained as an engineer and worked as such for a number of years before her literary debut in 1973. She has written children's fiction and also stories that mingle elements of the fantastic with elements of mundane reality. In "The Monster" ("Chudovishche," 1983), for instance, a one-eyed, scaly, dragon-like creature lives for years with a number of ordinary humans in a communal apartment. The association is not entirely pleasant, but it is peaceful and is enlivened by an occasional miracle, such as the monster's transformation of one apartment dweller into a saucepan for a month. As the monster ages, his magic powers wane, but two of the women begin to lend a hand, assisting him, for example, in turning one particularly obnoxious female dweller into a rat.

Katerli's strongest stories, however, are devoid of the supernatural. For example, *The Barsukov Triangle* (*Treugol'nik Barsukova*, 1977), whose English translation in 1984 first brought her to general attention in the West, is a harsh, episodic portrayal of a neighborhood of ordinary Leningraders as they live rather brutish, occasionally violent lives in close quarters, queue up at food stores, drink, and switch sexual partners. The story is heavily laden with coarse dialogue and the interior monologue that discloses the psychology of characters of various ages. The narration is intimate, as if emanating from one or more persons closely familiar, from long acquaintance, with all of the neighborhood characters. A feature of the story, unusual for its time, is the presence of a number of Jewish characters as they experience the climate of anti-Semitism and as they contemplate the pros and cons of emigration.

For all its virtues, *The Barsukov Triangle* seems kaleidescopic and overpopulated. As a rule, Katerli uses fewer characters in her stories and concentrates on one or two of them. "Polina" ("Polina," 1984) contrasts two women in early middle-age: Polina, an intellectually gifted, capable but slovenly and disorganized person who has loved many men and been badly used by most of them, and her friend Maiya, who in their student days carefully chose and cultivated a prospective husband and has prospered monogamously. The irony is that Polina's experiences have case-hardened her, so that although she remains prone to victimization by men she is buoyant, practical, and resilient, and loves life; the well-organized and prudent Maiya, for her part, discovers that her husband might be having an affair, goes to pieces and tries to kill herself. The ostensible realist turns out to have been a vulnerable romantic, and vice versa. If this were the sole burden of "Polina," the story would be rather an ordinary one. But Polina herself is such an open and engaging woman, with such an interesting combination of attributes and attitudes toward life, that she provides us with valuable general insights into the human condition.

On the whole, Katerli seems to like her teen-age characters and those in their early twenties better than she does their parents. In "The Farewell Light" ("Proshchal′nyi svet," 1981) we glimpse a selfless, idealistic girl whose parents criticize her for excessive devotion to a crippled friend. Only the girl's step-grandmother, a retired physician who is near the end of her life, has the sensitivity to understand her. "Between Spring and Summer" ("Mezhdu vesnoi i letom," 1983) shows us a spunky and independent young woman in love with a married man twenty years her senior. She is unwise, of course, but her disapproving parents seem incapable of lending her moral support. In "Colored Postcards" ("Tsvetnye otkrytki," 1987) a talented and totally honest young man on the verge of a promising scholarly career suddenly kicks over the traces and joins the army. The pressure of a well-meaning but prodding and overprotective mother and grandmother and neglect from his successful, divorced father have been too much for him to bear. In the story's most powerful scene, the young man's girl friend berates the amiable but remote father for his smugness and dishonesty as a big-shot administrator of science.

Katerli writes often about men, with impressive, although somewhat condescending, understanding. Her male characters, in the time-honored Russian tradition, tend to be weaker and morally less substantial than the women with whom they are associated. The middle-aged "scientific bureaucrat" in "The Farewell Light," a basically decent man, pales in comparison to his physician mother, whose diary, which he reads after her death, reveals her to have been a highly intelligent, accomplished, large-hearted woman. The husband in "Between Spring and Summer" is passive and subordinate, "under the thumb" of a wife who married him originally only because she was pregnant by another man. The central figure in "Colored Postcards," a driving scientific administrator with the rank of Academician, is weak in a different way: success has made him spiritually shallow and compromising, and neglectful of his obligations as a parent.

The world of Nina Katerli is authentically Soviet Russian in its social, psychological, and moral dimensions. Although many of her stories have an element of the fantastic, even these are fundamentally realistic in their characters and settings. Her writing is factual and critical, but it is also compassionate and leavened with humor. Her stories constitute a sensitive chronicle of life in post-World War II Leningrad and, in general, in the complicated late twentieth century.

Virtually every writer who is mentioned in this book has been concerned, directly or indirectly, with contemporary Soviet reality. Even those works that have focused on events and circumstances in previous Russian history, or on private lives, emotions, and relationships, have included some degree of awareness of the texture of Soviet life and of care for the problems and conflicts of the present. The novels of Leonid Latynin are an exception.

Although he had been active as a poet and translator for many years, Latynin (born 1938) did not publish fiction until the appearance in 1988 of his novel *The Face-Maker and the Muse* (*Grimer i muza*, written 1977–78). The setting – an unidentified city, with no particularly Russian characteristics, at an unspecified time – is deliberately vague, emphasizing the abstract and eternal quality of the novel's thematics. The hero is one of a large number of plastic surgeons employed by the all-powerful government to reshape the faces of the populace to conform to an ideal Image. Such surgery, which the hero proudly considers not a craft but an art, is a never-ending process, because the authorities keep changing the specifications of the Image to fit altered standards of perfection. (Many citizens have accumulated numerous layers of faces over the years.) Although the work is arduous and demanding, it gives the dutiful hero great aesthetic and moral satisfaction, as well as a privileged status and opportunities for social advancement. For one thing, members of the upper levels of society are given names, while the masses are only known by their numbers.

It is not clear what iron hand ultimately rules this robotic civilization – the aura of mystery is as dense as the constantly cloudy and rainy atmosphere. Discipline is severe; unruliness and nonconformity, as well as an unacceptable visage, are punished by death, which is quaintly called Departure (*Ukhod*). There is, however, intense political competition and intrigue within the higher echelons of authority, and the hero becomes entangled in, and ultimately the fatal victim of, this intrigue.

It is tempting to see this fantastic allegory as a kind of anti-utopian political parable, although as such it is not readily decipherable. The novel is also a study of the psychology and sufferings of the artist, who is increasingly disturbed about the morality of his ultimately absurd profession. A love story runs through the work, culminating in a tragic separation. In his Departure in the midst of a popular uprising, the hero leaves behind his beloved, who has just had another new face carved upon her.

Latynin's "novel" *Sleeper at Harvest Time* (*Spyashchii vo vremya zhatvy*, 1991) might better be called a compendium. Saturated with Russian history, it extends from the tenth century AD to a fantastic twenty-first century, but concentrates on those two extremes. (The twentieth century is mentioned in only a few passing references to "Joseph the Bloody" and one reference to the decayed and forgotten Lenin mausoleum.) Its hero, Emelya, who is capable of moving freely in time and was born in a small tribal settlement on the site of the future Moscow Kremlin, is the son of a pagan priestess and a bear. In the twenty-first century, this same Emelya is a citizen of a tightly regulated, xenophobic Moscow, one of the main features of which are flying squads of police known as "percentchiks," whose function it is to stop people on the streets, draw blood samples from them, and test the blood to determine the proportion of various racial and national strains in their makeups. Each area, block, and dwelling in the city is meticulously segregated according to these strains, and violators are executed.

When it is discovered that Emelya has "bear" in his blood, he is publicly stoned to death at a hallowed place of execution on Red Square. He dies happy in the knowledge that he is being sacrificed for the good of society, to protect its genetic purity. Emelya's mother, the priestess Leta, a thousand years earlier, had voluntarily sacrificed herself for the good of the tribe by being burned at the stake, after having ritually coupled the night before with each of the tribe's eleven heads of household.

These two episodes of sacrifice are designed as major thematic connections. Otherwise, there is very little plot in *Sleeper at Harvest Time*. The work depends for its cohesion not on story lines but upon a kind of historical pageantry, the juxtaposition of scenes and rituals, semi-Biblical, semi-pagan accounts of the Creation, and chronicle-like accounts of ancient Russian cities and rulers. Latynin lavishly recreates prayers, charms, and incantations, features magic, myth, and legend, and uses other folk themes and motifs in abundance. The total is a mosaic compounded of historical, religious, and anthropological materials.

Not only is Latynin's fiction thematically far removed from contemporary realism; it stands apart in its stylistic originality. In *The Face-Maker and the Muse* he had shown a fondness for figurative language, and notably the simile. The array of devices in *Sleeping at Harvest Time* is much broader. Many passages are written in an oral style that suggests the cadences and formulas of folk tales. Others have the stately tone of medieval chronicles and other religious and historical writings. There is much anaphora and repetition of phrases and clauses, and there are long catalogues of cities, rulers, nations, and regions. All of this produces arresting, often charmingly archaic rhetorical effects. Indeed, perhaps without intending to, Latynin has made the past, although surely tragic, seem more colorful and vibrant than the present.

The great virtue of Viktoriya Tokareva's stories is their style, which usually emanates from a colorful narrator with a vivid presence, a distinct point of view, and a gift for imagery and figurative expression. This is how the narrator tells about the attitude of a restless, discontented, and rapacious married woman toward the young man whom she has just seduced: "She had discovered Sasha, as though he were a new continent, and she intended to plant her flag and found her state on that continent." As a rule this narrator is detached and playful in manner, and she enjoys mocking her characters. Her sprightly, witty, epigrammatic observations can extend even to pathetic and tragic circumstances without seeming coarse or insensitive. Tokareva's subject matter – most often woman's unfulfilled need for love – is so painful that it could easily become lugubrious, but the author avoids this through her ability to sustain a lightly ironic tone and to apply wit and humor to the most serious situations.

Tokareva (born 1937) was trained as a scenarist and has many scripts, including several international prize-winners, to her credit. She has also written frequently for television. At the same time, she has been a steady and prolific writer of short fiction since the publication of her first story in 1964. Although sometimes slight and trivial, particularly in her earlier years, her stories are always bright and engaging, and she is never boring. She has mastered the craft of economy; her paragraphs, and often her sentences, are short and compact, her dialogue lean and swift. Unlike many writers of short fiction, however, Tokareva does not seem to prefer a small scale. Her stories often involve numerous episodes and developments and can cover long periods of time, even decades; she usually creates central characters through an accumulation of experiences rather than through the intensive treatment of merely one or two.

Monologue and first-person narration can be particularly effective with Tokareva. In "Center of Gravity" a woman makes such clever fun of herself in telling of the various ways in which she tried to commit suicide that the amused reader is in danger of missing the gravity of the situation. Tokareva's own favorite story is "The Happiest Day of My Life" ("Samyi schastlivyi den'," 1980), the charming monologue of a thirteen-year-old girl faced with a school assignment to write about her happiest day. Unwilling to write the obligatory civic-minded pap that will ensure a high grade, she speculates naively but shrewdly about her friends, her parents, herself, and life in general as she searches for a topic that will please *her*.

The problems and relationships of adults, however, are Tokareva's usual material. Although she writes well about both sexes, her most frequent and best-conceived subjects are women. Her heroines tend to be self-supporting urban professional women who have had more than one mate and who are either still seeking an ideal romance or are resigned to its impossibility. All of them are unhappy in love to one degree or another. Their children, if any, are usually confined to the background. The men in their lives are often alcoholic, or childishly dependent, or otherwise unworthy. Even those who seem to merit the heroines' love have other powerful obligations that prevent them from making a commitment. As a result, these women are compelled to be either fairly constantly on the alert for a man, or sadly, fatalistically, courageously alone.

Not all of Tokareva's heroines are so nobly pathetic. The

woman in the story "Between Heaven and Earth" ("Mezhdu nebom i zemlei," 1985), who on a flight from Moscow to Baku becomes powerfully attracted to a young basketball player (who in turn is infatuated with her) simply makes a practical, "mature" decision to avoid an affair with him. In "Five Figures on a Pedestal" (*Pyat' figur na postamente*, 1989), a journalist on a field trip to a provincial city has a brief affair with a local engineer but prudently terminates it because she realizes that, for her, life in Moscow, even with a drunken husband, unpleasant mother, and spoiled son, is preferable to life in Dnepropetrovsk. An extremely interesting, although perhaps overdrawn character is the heroine of "Dry Run" ("Pervaya popytka," 1989), a pushy, unscrupulous, fanatically ambitious sexual imperialist who lives at top speed and destroys everything in her path. Her story is narrated by a normal, decent, conservative, respectable acquaintance, who by contrast makes this garish manipulator seem even more outrageous, albeit exotically attractive.

As a rule, men appear in Tokareva's stories primarily as foils to the women who are the centre of attention, but some of these men have a genuine stature of their own. Such is Pasha, a teacher of mentally retarded children in the story "Pasha and Pavlusha" ("Pasha i Pavlusha," 1987) who, although easily victimized by the woman who betrays him with his best friend, stands out as a strong, staunch, morally and socially responsible individual. Interesting also is the crippled, seventy-year-old war veteran in the story "Hello!," whose aroused response to the heroine's casual greeting in a hallway makes her realize that Eros is ageless.

Although Tokareva's writing has usually been only minimally aware of social issues, this awareness has increased in recent years. Thus, "Dry Run" refers frequently to the political climate and developments during the Khrushchev and Brezhnev years, "Five Figures on a Pedestal" examines rural brutality and drunkenness, and "Pasha and Pavlusha" shows mental retardation in children as a social evil caused largely by dissolute and vagrant parents. The increased social ingredient, however, has not raised the aesthetic level of her stories. In the past, style for Tokareva has occasionally seemed so paramount that verbal felicity got in the way of her thematics, making her writing seem lightweight and superficial at times. It is ironic that for this deft and sparkling writer, a growing social concern has brought with it a degree of ponderousness.

Genadii Golovin (born 1941) was forty-five years old before his first stories were published. Until that time he had made his living as a journalist and had worked in television. With a relatively late start as a writer of fiction, he appears to have been exploring tentatively a variety of modes and themes in short novels. *The Sentence of the Executive Committee* (*Prigovor ispolnitel'nogo komiteta*, dated 1971, published 1988) is an historical novel about the People's Will movement; *Jack, Little Brother and Others* (*Dzhek, Bratishka i drugie*, 1988) is a story of the relationship between people and dogs; *Millions with Big Zeros* (*Milliony s bol'shimi nulyami*, dated 1980, published 1988) is a detective story set in the period of the Civil War; *The Birthday of the Deceased* (*Den' rozhdeniya pokoinika*, 1988) is a vicious satire of the Brezhnev period.

The work that brought Golovin to prominence is *Anna Petrovna* (*Anna Petrovna*, dated 1984–85, published 1987), an account of the last days and death of a very old woman who lives alone in a tiny Moscow apartment, neglected by her only relative – an exploitive granddaughter – and tended only by a young man who has chanced upon her situation. The novel combines details of her physical decline and emotional withdrawal as death approaches, with dream-like flashbacks to episodes from her earlier years. She has led a difficult life, with early illness, the violence and deprivation of the Civil War period, the hard years of socialist construction, the joys of love and sorrows of widowhood, and horror as her granddaughter, in a venomous rage, destroys the things in her apartment. Through it all, Anna Petrovna has remained unbroken in spirit and has retained her dignity.

Although the story is apolitical, there is social commentary in the description of the depressed and dingy atmosphere of Anna Petrovna's neighborhood and the repeated references to a pathetic line of people waiting at a glass-recycling station just outside her window. Golovin has said, in an interview, that in creating the flashbacks in which his heroine recalls her past, he tried to use a sentence construction that suggested the thought processes of an elderly person suffering from sclerosis. The story is indeed psychologically acute. Furthermore, although its portrait of the old woman is admiring and ingratiating, it avoids the temptation of sentimentality.

A Foreign Country (Chuzhaya storona, 1989) tells of the odyssey of Ivan Chashkin, a semi-skilled factory worker in his fifties who lives in a grimy, remote industrial *poselok*. Chashkin is a passive, timid, and depressed Soviet "everyman," who has long since fatalistically accepted his miserable, obscure existence. When he learns of the death of his mother in a Moscow suburb, 1,000 kilometers away, he decides, without enthusiasm but with a dull sense of duty, to attend her funeral. By coincidence, Leonid Brezhnev has also just died, a period of national mourning has been declared, and the Moscow area has been sealed off from all but influential travelers. Chashkin, with numerous ordinary citizens, is taken off his flight and must make his way to the Moscow area as best he can. Soon he is robbed of his suitcase, all his money, and, most important, his passport. Totally defenseless and without verifiable identity, he becomes the victim of a series of physical assaults and insults, cold and starvation, and of general abuse from sometimes taunting but usually merely indifferent countrymen. There are exceptions – truck drivers who give him lifts toward Moscow and occasional good souls who give him a bit of bread. Battered, infinitely lonely and dazed, but with a dawning understanding that all of Russia is just as forlorn and rotten as his native *poselok*, Chashkin dies just as he approaches the site of his mother's funeral.

Within this framework of a journey through purgatory, Golovin shows the tragic awakening of an individual soul that has lain dormant under a half-century of repression by a corrupt authoritarian regime. Toward the end of his tormenting trip, Chashkin begins, however clumsily, to think independently, to assert himself, and to lash out, though feebly, in indignation. In a kind of epiphany he comes to realize that the masses of compatriots he has met are "not guilty" and that they, like him, are the products of an entire system of oppression. But he also realizes that their passivity and indifference, like his own, have contributed to their wretched and morally diseased condition. As he nears the end of his journey he discerns, in the midst of a filthy and dreary settlement, the clean outlines of a church, and begins to think haltingly, but for the first time with some conviction, about God.

Golovin uses Chashkin's plight and wanderings not only to depict a symbolic journey but also as a device for excoriating the Soviet regime. His satire of Party fatcats and bureaucrats, the ruling class, "they," is both clever and virulent. The disruption of the transportation system in order to honor Brezhnev is shown as sadly farcical. The author often lets the Soviet populace, for whom their native land is a "foreign country," speak for themselves. In their outbursts and bitter anecdotes, the people whom Chashkin meets on his stumbling way show a contempt for their masters that is only equaled by their masters' contempt for them.

In several respects the writing of *A Foreign Country* resembles the "tough" and "cruel" prose that will be discussed in Chapter 7. But despite the fact that it presents a vivid, powerful, and disturbing image of an alienated population in a grim and ugly realm, it is not entirely successful as a work of art. For one thing, its sarcastic treatment of the parasitic Soviet regime is somewhat too insistent and heavy-handed. For another, its portrayal of Ivan Chashkin himself, of his mental processes and spiritual catharsis, is not entirely convincing. The narrow and supine Chashkin whom we see early in the story does not seem to be endowed by nature with sufficient acumen to come up with the kind of understanding he displays at the end. (The hint of a religious revelation remains merely a hint.) Nevertheless, this is an eloquent novel, and it gives evidence that finer things are yet to come.

Affinities with the writings of a number of contemporary authors can be found in the works of Leonid Borodin (born 1938). Like Solzhenitsyn and others, he is a veteran of the Gulag and writes authentically about it. A Siberian born in Irkutsk, he shares Rasputin's affection for Lake Baikal and the taiga, as well as that writer's anxiety over threats to the natural environment. Borodin shares the interest of many of his contemporaries in folk legend and the supernatural, and these features are prominent in much of his fiction.

As a dissident in the sixties, seventies, and early eighties, Borodin was denied publication in the Soviet Union and, like many others, was forced to print his works abroad. His writings have a pronounced anti-Soviet flavor and speak bitterly of the moral devastation of the Stalin era. He seems to be neither a liberal nor a Westerner, however, and in his manifest concern for human suffering and injustice he seems to aspire more to Christian understanding and behavior than to political solutions.

Themes of personal responsibility, guilt, and forgiveness run prominently through most of Borodin's fiction. The charming novel *The Year of Miracle and Grief* (*God chuda i pechali*, 1984) examines the psychology and moral fibre of a twelve-year-old boy as he confronts a situation in which an adult's blind passion for vengeance has brought cruel suffering to an innocent person.

Much of the story is a lively account of the everyday adventures of the schoolboy in a small community on the shore of Lake Baikal. Borodin also recreates, however, a Siberian legend about the creation of Baikal and plunges his young hero into a supernatural realm related to that legend, where the boy must confront overwhelming questions of good and evil. Because of his moral purity and instinctive compassion for the oppressed, the boy undergoes harrowing mental anguish, but the strength of his spirit prevails. The story thus combines a pagan legend, the supernatural, and Christian values.

A collection of stories first printed abroad in 1978 demonstrates the breadth of Borodin's literary concerns. In "The Meeting" ("Vstrecha"), the escape of two Russian soldiers from a German prison camp fails when one of them mistakenly identifies the other as a hated, sadistic officer who years before had persecuted him in the Gulag. "On Trial" ("Pered sudom") is an account of intrigue and betrayal among internal security officers who are hunting down postwar Ukrainian nationalist insurgents, with detailed and sometimes excessively lengthy authorial analysis of the situation's moral implications. The title story of the collection, "The Story of a Strange Time" ("Povest' strannogo vremeni"), the account of a family tragedy brought about by the Stalin purges, shows how decent, well-meaning individuals were trapped into collaboration with the insane injustices of a degenerate regime. In all three of these stories, problems of personal responsibility are dramatized with painful moral intensity.

In "The Option" ("Variant") Borodin chronicles the breakup of a cell of young Leningrad revolutionaries, disillusioned Young Communists who aspire somehow to destroy the Soviet system. Misguided idealism induces their quixotic leader to embrace terrorism and, having become isolated and a killer, he ends as a suicide. A story of quite a different nature is "The Visit" ("Poseshchenie"), in which a young atheist intellectual, who has suddenly discovered that he can levitate himself and fly at will, calls upon a village priest in an attempt to find an explanation for this miracle. Although stunned, the priest tries to persuade the young man that God exists. That night, still an atheist, the young man, disoriented, flies beyond earth's field of gravity. The next morning his broken body is found in the village street. Although this story is no more imbued with religious feeling than other works of Borodin, it comes the closest to being a parable.

In what is probably his gloomiest, most down-to-earth, and most profoundly religious novel, *The Third Truth* (*Tret'ya pravda*, 1981), Borodin traces the fates of two men – a Siberian game warden, swept up in the purges together with his wife (the daughter of a former White officer), and the warden's friend, a local eccentric who spends most of his time roaming the taiga but who also devotes himself to saving the imprisoned warden's daughter. In the person of the persecuted warden, who finds God in the Gulag, and of his loyal friend, who is a man of nature and a creature more of instinct than of intellect, Borodin embodies themes of religious belief and doubt, love for the environment and anxiety over its future, the waste and cruelty of Soviet power, and the search of simple people for peace and dignity. The "third truth" suggested by the novel's title is represented neither by the October revolution nor its opponents, but by the natural wisdom and aspirations of ordinary humans.

Borodin's world is one of violence, injustice, suffering, and difficult moral choices. As a rule his writing is tight and vigorous, and only occasionally does it become overburdened with moral speculation. He writes with a deep respect for mankind, compassion over the tragedies it experiences, and with a strong attraction for those who have found a religious faith, spoken or unspoken, in the course of a frequently discouraging existence.

It is hazardous to draw conclusions about a collection of writers as diverse as those who have been discussed in the present chapter. For instance, although three of them are women, often display a special feminine understanding of things, and do write, although by no means exclusively, about problems that are peculiar to women, it does not seem that any of them should be categorized as a "women's writer." Although Katerli, Latynin, Kuraev, and Golovin write, at times, about human coarseness, abuse and violence, there are many other features of their writing that would prevent their works from being identified merely as "tough" and "coarse" prose. Moreover, Tolstaya seems absolutely unique.

There are, nevertheless, certain characteristics which these eight writers have in common. In varying degrees they all preserve the traditional Russian interest in psychological analysis and moral exploration. Most of them are emphatically aware of the Russian historical context in which their narratives take place; the characters and situations in their fiction are, pointedly, historically conditioned. The peculiarities of Russian culture, and notably its ancient folk traditions, are prominent concerns of several of these writers, and in fact the Russian national culture, rather than its recent Soviet layer, seems to be at the center of their attention.

Several of these writers share the renewed interest in the

fantastic that has been a feature of recent Russian literature, and one of them, Latynin, is representative of its anti-utopian strain. Nearly all of them, finally, are self-consciously, openly, and unabashedly concerned with literary craftsmanship and experimentation as a self-justified activity. Gone are the days when "formalism" was a literary crime.

CHAPTER 7

"Tough" and "cruel" prose

Early in 1989, the critic Sergei Chuprinin introduced the term *drugaya proza* – "other prose" or, more precisely in the given context, "alternative prose."[1] Since then, Chuprinin's definition, augmented by the contributions of numerous other critics, has been applied to a growing body of writing that differs from the standard critical realism of the *glasnost'* period. The term came to signify a large and loose category of prose that was distinguished not by its political content (although it was generally liberal in tone) but by innovation in language, style, and narrative point of view. In the Soviet context much of this "alternative" literature was original, challenging, and even shocking, although by contemporary Western standards it did not seem notably daring or uninhibited.

The main characteristic of "alternative" prose is its emphatically *literary* orientation. Although it does not entirely repudiate the traditional sense of civic, social, or moral responsibility of a Tolstoy, Tendryakov, or Trifonov, it is much more concerned with unique angles of vision and with freshness and inventiveness of expression than it is with any educational mission. Its writers are interested, first of all, in exploring aesthetic possibilities, widening horizons, cultivating their creative idiosyncrasies, and developing away from the conventions of recent decades. Tatyana Tolstaya, for example, is frequently numbered among them, as is Mikhail Kuraev.

As a large aesthetic reaction against the restrains and taboos of the past, "alternative" prose has no particular ideological axe to grind. Its writers, in fact, seem singularly skeptical about systems of thought and belief and try to avoid extra-literary intellectual commitments. At the same time, they display great intellectual unrest, wide-ranging curiosity, and a powerful urge for self-expression. In their aggressively unconventional way, they have managed to explore dark corners and crannies of Russian life, to discover patterns of behavior and states of mind that had never before been shown to Soviet Russian readers. This has not been done in a spirit of muckraking or political engagement; there is no program of sensational exposure or social protest. Rather, the emphasis is on the artist's individual vision, his or her subjective and often complex reaction to puzzling, sometimes ugly reality.

The writer of "alternative" prose is likely to adopt an ironic mode, to dwell on the apparent absurdity of the life about him. Sometimes he or she appears as a frustrated romantic, brooding sarcastically on the discrepancy between ideal and actuality. Much of the humor in this Russian writing is at once hilarious and bitter, engaging and at the same time despairing. The lack of an ideological tendency in this writing, in fact, seems to come from a desperate consciousness of the absence of something to believe in.

"Alternative" prose has its immediate origins in two groupings of Russian writers, both of them illicit until the era of *glasnost'*. The first of these were the literary "underground" of the 1970s and early 1980s, who were unable to publish their work in the Soviet Union for both political and cultural reasons. Not only were their topics and viewpoints politically proscribed and "seditious" (although less decisively so than those of a Grossman or a Solzhenitsyn), their writing was also officially unacceptable because it was often ambiguous, its language too earthy, and its candid and explicit treatment of personal and social behavior too indelicate to pass censorship. Moreover, a number of writers adopted defiant attitudes that made them unacceptable to the authorities.

The other source of "alternative" prose was the Russian emigration, exemplified by such writers as Andrei Sinyavskii, Sasha Sokolov, Eduard Limonov, Yurii Mamleev, and Aksenov, who went abroad after the *Metropol'* affair and was stripped of his Soviet citizenship. As the works of these emigres became known in the USSR with the advent of *glasnost'*, they joined with the "underground" literature into a single broadening stream.

The writers with whom the present chapter is concerned are all prominent representatives of "alternative" prose, with a special distinction as creators of so-called *zhestkaya* (tough) and *zhestokaya* (cruel) prose. Their special distinction is in their assiduous investigation of the brutal, cruel, ugly, even depraved features of Russian life and their use of coarse, earthy language from the streets and from the very dregs of society in depicting that existence. Although they tend to concentrate on characters and situations on the bottom layers, their attention is distributed throughout various locations (both urban and rural), occupational groups, and stations in life. Many of their stories were written about, and during, the period of stagnation of the 1970s and early 1980s. They reflected the depressed psychology and mores of the time, and remained underground, unpublished, until the era of *glasnost'*.

These writers, however, are far from being mere chroniclers of the seamy side of existence. For one thing, although their frame of mind is generally pessimistic, none of them is unrelievedly gloomy or fixated on the cruel and the ugly. And although evil seems almost ordinary and routine in many of their stories, it is never posited as a norm. All of these writers are dramatic and vivid; they often resort to the grotesque and sometimes to the fantastic. Their art seems to be grounded on a painful and dreary reality, but it is a heightened reality, reshaped and distorted for emotional, moral, and, especially, aesthetic effect. The writer of this kind of prose often seems to want to astound the reader by showing him how iniquity and corruption lurk beneath placid surfaces. But among these writers evil is not usually subterranean; it is foregrounded, it proclaims its existence loudly and insistently.

Moscow-Petushki (translated as *Moscow to the End of the Line*) was first published in the Soviet Union in 1988 in the journal *Sobriety and Culture* (*Trezvost' i Kul'tura*), as a pamphlet in the government's fight against alcoholism. In 1989 it appeared in the almanac *News* (*Vest'*), in delayed recognition of its worth as a work of art. Its author, Venedikt Erofeev (1938–90), had been forced to wait twenty years for its Soviet publication, although the novel had long since appeared in the West in a number of languages and had circulated widely in Russia through *samizdat*.

The work is the fantastic account of an extravagantly inebriated journey on a suburban train from Moscow in the direction of a village a few dozen kilometers away. It features a thirty-year-old hero-narrator who is coarse and cultured, hilariously witty and abysmally despondent, romantically idealistic and hopelessly disillusioned. The people he meets on the train – nearly all of them, including the conductor, in various stages of drunkenness – talk of their sad, often brutal experiences. The only thing that makes life endurable for them, and the hero as well (his name is Venichka, the same as the author's), is vodka. It also makes life interesting and amusing – the alcoholic haze makes them see the funny side of things.

Erofeev called his novel a "poem" (*poema*) in the tradition of Gogol, who designated his novel *Dead Souls* similarly. The work is also in the tradition of Aleksandr Radishchev's eighteenth-century *A Journey from Petersburg to Moscow*, which uses the travelogue format as a device for meditating on the moral situation of Russia, its society, and its culture. One of Erofeev's favorite authors was Rabelais, and the Rabelaisian spirit of "carnival," of free, iconoclastic collective laughter is present throughout the novel. It is alcohol that provides the release that enables Erofeev's hero to present his tragic world as both absurd and comic. At the same time, his hero is so pathetically besotted that it is easy to see why his story could be misconstrued as a tract on the harmfulness of drink.

Moscow to the End of the Line is earthy, clever, sometimes obscene, touchingly wistful, and often wildly funny. The narrator is a "creative" drinker, who uses vodka as a means of escaping from his everyday gloom by building a bright artificial world filled with love, honesty, brotherhood, and happiness. He knows everything about alcohol – the rituals of drinking, the various stages of inebriation and kinds of hangovers, the exact price of every variety and brand of beverage. He offers a number of crazy, poisonous cocktail recipes, and he argues that all great writers, including Schiller, Gogol, and Pushkin, were epically heavy drinkers. It is alcohol that motivates the hero's extensive dialogues with angels and devils, as well as other hallucinatory visions and a series of nonsensical riddles presented to him by a sphinx.

Much of the novel's charm comes from the incongruity between its often elevated language, laden with literary and Biblical allusions, and its distinctly unrefined subject matter. Although it makes grotesque sport of Soviet society, it is not a satire but, rather, an anguished cry from the heart. Its creative irreverence and ultimately pessimistic view of life made it a model for writers of the 1980s who combine unsparing pictures of the seamy side of Russian existence with an entertaining sense of the ridiculous. Erofeev's work is now generally recognized as seminal in the development of "tough" and "cruel" prose.

Lyudmila Petrushevskaya (born 1938) has come to be known for her portrayal of crudity, malice, and brutality in the everyday lives of ordinary urban Russians. As both a playwright and a writer of short stories, she has shocked audiences and readers with her frank and seemingly merciless pictures of people tormenting, undercutting, betraying, exploiting, and even murdering one another, wasting away, behaving scandalously, indulging in sexual infidelities, and drinking themselves to death. The intensity and frequency of abuse and suffering in her works are so great that she is considered by some to be simply a repulsive distorter of the Russian scene. However, her knowledge of that scene is so intimate and detailed, and her ability to evoke the social and moral atmosphere so impressive, that she has commanded increasingly enthusiastic and respectful attention. She is now a leading contemporary literary figure, whose writing embraces much more than the gritty aspects of life, and whose interests are steadily developing.

Petrushevskaya's most frequent characters are downtrodden women. In "Nets and Traps" ("Seti i lovushki," 1974), a twenty-year-old girl, whose lover has cooled toward her, moves to the town where his mother lives (and also his legal wife and child), to have his baby. The mother receives her warily, then warmly, but then, suspecting that the expected child is not her son's, kicks her out. The girl has her baby, living in a bare rented room. Another woman, in "A Dark Fate" ("Temnaya sud'ba," 1987), tired of being loveless, invites a nonentity to her bed. Mechanical lovemaking takes place. This miserable initiation makes her joyous, but the cynical narrator opines that it will merely lead to a lifetime of agitation and suffering, the hell a woman goes through because of love. The central figure in "A Little Girl Like That" ("Takaya devochka," written 1968, published 1988) is a young Tatar woman, living in Moscow, who was sexually abused as a girl and now, married, passively accepts numerous extra-marital partners. When her neighbor's husband, an inveterate tomcat, prepares to leave his wife for another, the young Tatar woman brings him home by offering to sleep with him. The aggrieved wife, whom the young woman had earlier saved from suicide, does not appreciate this gesture. In "Vengeance" ("Mest'," 1990), a psychotic unwed mother, under the delusion that the woman with whom she lives is out to murder the baby, kills the roommate.

Several of Petrushevskaya's stories are set in hospital wards, where the misfortunes and maltreatment of women are displayed with a special poignancy. The stories are not exposés of poor medical treatment (the depiction of harsh hospital conditions seems matter-of-fact), but as the patients talk to and comfort one another, the cruel circumstances of their lives become painfully vivid. In "Panya's Poor Heart" ("Bednoe serdtse Pani") we see a hospital unit for women undergoing unusually difficult and dangerous pregnancies. The story focuses on an uneducated working mother of three with heart trouble and an invalid husband, who is aborted in her seventh month to save her life and leaves the hospital for the long journey home on foot. "Isolation Compartment" ("Izolirovannyi boks," 1988) is a "dialogue" between two cancer patients, a sixty-year-old who rambles on about her uncaring family, and a forty-three-year-old, who expects to live long enough to provide for the education of her adolescent son. The older woman knows what the younger one does not: they are in the room where terminal patients are sent to die.

Grim displays of pain and suffering such as these seem tainted with morbidity. On the whole, however, they are compassionate and deeply respectful of the strength of the human spirit. The narration is unsentimental, non-committal, and even hard-boiled at times, but it also shows great sensitivity to human feelings and a tragic understanding of the agonies which humans experience. The central figure in "Medea" ("Medeya," 1989), for example, is a taxi driver obsessed with guilt for not having foreseen that his wife, now in a ward for the criminally insane, would murder their fourteen-year-old daughter.

Not all of Petrushevskaya's characters are suffering souls, nor do all of them deserve a great deal of sympathy. Some are presented sarcastically, others with evident disgust, and still others with exasperated amusement. Most of them are normal, run-of-the-mill individuals. "Youth" ("Yunost'," 1987) is the account of a woman who parades her youthful charm and impetuousness, then becomes sour and querulous as she realizes her bloom is fading. Soon, however, she settles into a modest, graceful maturity. "Mania" ("Manya," 1973) is the portrait of a meek, timid girl who is unable to summon the artifice necessary to make herself attractive to men. On the darker and more unsavory side is the young woman in "Ali-Baba" ("Ali-Baba," 1988), an alcoholic and sometime thief, who tries to commit suicide when the beered-up man whom she has picked up in a bar turns out to be a bed-wetter.

Petrushevskaya has written several tightly and neatly organized stories, with straight and clear narrative lines and a steady focus. Often, however, her stories seem uncoordinated, with facts presented in illogical sequence, many repetitions and digressions, and numerous random fragments. The apparently chaotic structure is fully intentional, for Petrushevskaya invests heavily in the personality and attitudes of her narrator, who, despite the rambling and loose-jointed quality of her mono-logue, manages to maintain a consistent point of view.

The narrators vary in background, and degrees of intelligence and awareness. When she is writing in third-person, her narrator is usually a highly intelligent, skeptical eye-witness or reporter of community information, with an ironical outlook and free of illusions. This narrator is capable of producing self-consciously intricate prose, laden with literary allusions and parodic language taken from street jargon, officialese, and intentionally and amusingly clumsy and vulgar turns of phrase. Petrushevskaya's first-person narrators are comparatively un-lettered, and specialize in disorganized, gossipy monologues, full of free association, expressions of opinion, apologies, and slips of the tongue, in a coarse linguistic melange that reads like a literal transcript of everyday chatter. For all their undis-ciplined verbiage, these first-person narrators are often clever and psychologically acute. Just as often, however, we see narrators who do not seem to understand the full import of the experiences they relate. Such is the narrator of "A Little Girl Like That," a frequently betrayed wife who talks uninhibitedly about her abuse, seemingly without realizing the full horror of her situation. As with other of Petrushevskaya's narrators, however, it is possible that this woman simply lacks the means to express herself fully, and this adds to the impression of bleakness in her life.

Petrushevskaya has said that much of her material comes from "stories, gossip and anecdotes that circulate among her acquaintances and neighbors" in what amounts to a kind of "urban folklore."[2] She has also insisted that she does not write about ordinary life but rather about its exceptional events that mark turning points, "catastrophes." Her accounts have both psychological and moral depth. The story "Influenza" ("Gripp," dated 1969, published 1988) tells of a woman who walks out on her husband after a quarrel, returns five days later for her things, and finds him ill in bed. Too proud and angry to look at him, she turns away, and he jumps from their seventh-floor window. The story opens with his funeral and cremation, at which she is crushed with grief and guilt amidst silently accusing mourners. In "Our Crowd" ("Svoi krug," dated 1979, published 1988), a woman who thinks she has a fatal illness beats her little son in the face before a group of old

friends. Their indignation and sympathy for the lad, she has
calculated, will induce them to care for him after her death.

Although Petrushevskaya's stories are usually confined to
sober and recognizable reality, she has recently published
remarkable exercises in fantasy, using simple and straight-
forward narrators. These flights of imagination, sometimes
grotesque, take us outside Petrushevskaya's usually mundane if
tormented world. In "A Modern Family Robinson" ("Novye
Robinzony," 1989), subtitled "a chronicle from the end of the
twentieth century," we see a family retreating from the city to
live, they hope self-sufficiently, off the land. They discover that
they are merely the first wave and that ominously behind them
are rapidly increasing numbers of refugees who threaten to
engulf them and seize their remote lair. Another apocalyptic
story, "Hygiene" ("Gigiena") describes in grisly detail the
bestial behavior of a family in its efforts to save itself during a
mysterious plague. Even further removed from the ordinary
world is "The New Gulliver" ("Novyi Guliver," 1990), in
which a sick man fancies the presence of people the size of
cockroaches in his room and about his bed. He knows he is
hallucinating, but he watches with fascination as these tiny
humans busily proceed to build a civilization in his room,
regarding him, because of his size, as their God. Of still a
different nature is "Two Kingdoms" ("Dva tsarstva," 1990),
the story of a gravely ill woman who is being flown to a distant
city for surgery but winds up (it is not clear whether this is her
fantasy or the author's) in a kind of heaven in the form of a
beautiful, happy, tranquil foreign city. She has been transported
from one "kingdom" to another. It is tempting but, I think,
fruitless to look for heavy allegorical or prophetic significance in
Petrushevskaya's stories of the sort which these four represent.

Petrushevskaya first became well known as a playwright, and
she continues to write prominently for the stage. Many of her
stories, as we have seen, are essentially dialogues or dramatic
monologues, easily adaptable for the stage. The fact that her
reputation as a writer of prose developed later than her
reputation as a dramatist, however, may be attributable to censorship. There are large gaps between the dates of completion

and the dates of publication of several of her stories. It is quite possible that editors before 1985 simply found many of her stories too frank, gloomy, and disturbing. In this sense, Petrushevskaya's present prominence may be truly a product of *glasnost'*.

A landmark in the trend of "tough prose" was the publication in 1987 of the short novel *A Humble Cemetery* (*Smirennoe kladbishche*), with which Sergei Kaledin (born 1949) made his debut. Kaledin's subject matter alone – the lives of gravediggers at a Moscow cemetery – was unusual enough to create a stir, but his harsh and candid manner of displaying these lives in coarse and sometimes revolting detail augmented the novel's impact. Although the critics' reaction to the novel was generally positive, their praise was not unqualified. The general verdict was that Kaledin was a powerful but unpolished and sometimes clumsy writer who deserved credit for uncovering a new layer of Russian reality.

A major strength of the novel was its depiction of an extremely low level of Soviet society in the unique vernacular of its own members. The story, which was frequently identified with the nineteenth-century "physiological sketch" (*fiziologicheskii ocherk*), is told largely in rough and vulgar dialogue, and the narrative portions also make extensive use of the gravediggers' pungent idiom. The reader is intimately immersed in a cruel, depraved, even desperate milieu, but one in which a kind of forlorn humanity continues to sustain itself.

The gravediggers are mostly uneducated, alcoholic victims of social neglect and sometimes of child abuse. They have known violence, and they use and expect it. Many have criminal records, and most seem to be on the criminal fringe. Except for the nuns who help care for the church on whose grounds the cemetery is located, the women in the story are similarly pathetic – either beggars glimpsed at the church entrance or the battered and alcoholic mates of the gravediggers themselves. There is one baby – mentally defective because of its mother's prenatal drinking.

A Humble Cemetery, however, is not a work of unrelieved

gloom. The workers relish their gravedigging techniques and take pride in their deftness and efficiency. They are specialists in petty graft – the illegal re-use of old graves (with secret disposal of the bones therein), the harvesting of gold teeth from decayed skulls, the sale to mourners of a "special mix" of soil for growing flowers on graves – which consists of ordinary dirt. They engage in outlandish tricks such as garlanding the cemetery dogs with wreaths taken from graves and setting them loose in the streets. They have a code of ethics; for example, one must never refuse a drink from the bereaved at an interment. Violations, such as snitching on a fellow-grafter, are punishable by cruel, even fatal beatings. But the workers are also generous with each other, sharing bottles and holding impromptu feasts of food they have picked up here and there.

There are several sharply etched characters in the novel. Aleksei Sergevich Vorob'ev, known as Vorobei (Sparrow), the main character, lacks a portion of his skull, lost when his brother hit him three times with a rusty hatchet. Because of this hole, covered only by a thin skin, this former alcoholic knows that further drinking will bring certain death. Although an invalid subject to seizures, he continues digging graves and works well, until he sacrifices his job by taking responsibility for a comrade's transgression. As the novel closes, Vorobei takes a drink. Such is the suicidal fate of this representative of society's dregs. Kaledin provides a modicum of evidence to suggest that Vorobei, through innate inclination and his physical proximity to a church, may have found a rudimentary religious faith and consolation. This, however, is scarcely more than a hint, and it does little to dispel the novel's prevailing aura of hopelessness.

Equally depressing is Kaledin's story *Construction Battalion* (*Stroibat*, 1989), whose publication was long delayed by military censorship. It features a peacetime battalion of third-rate soldiers and officers, assembled from army misfits and augmented by criminals transferred from prison. Low in self-esteem and engaged in meaningless and unrewarding activity on the fringe of the national economy, the soldiers drink, fight among themselves, and trade in drugs under the loose supervision of officers even more corrupt than they. The story further enhanced Kaledin's reputation as a purveyor of the grim truth about dark pockets of society which literature had previously overlooked.

A native Siberian, Evgenii Popov (born 1946) lived in Krasnoyarsk until 1975, except for a three-year period as a student in a geological institute in Moscow. Most of his works are set in Siberia. He moved to Moscow for good in 1975, and by 1979 had published several stories. In that year, as one of the editors of *Metropol'*, he was expelled from the Writers' Union and blacklisted until the end of 1986. By 1988, by his own account, Popov had written over 200 stories but had published relatively few of them. In that year alone he published more stories than he had in his entire previous career. Since then, this backlog, together with numerous new works, has given him steadily increasing prominence and popularity.

Popov is capable of writing lean, compact prose – his stories are usually four to seven pages in length. On the other hand, he has also cultivated, particularly in his most recent works, a loose, easy, meandering, even whimsical manner that can involve non-stop sentences, repetition, sound play, *skaz*, startling combinations of elegant and vulgar language, and much parody. He obviously enjoys showing off, dazzling the reader with flights of complex, ornamental writing that is richly figurative and full of surprises and odd perspectives. His devices are indeed amusing and ingratiating, but their main purpose is to convey a complex, ironical, sometimes contradictory view of the world.

Popov employs a diversity of narrators, in which there are varying degrees of objectivity or involvement, moral concern or neutrality, earnestness or jocularity, toughness or sentimentality, indifference or sympathy. Often his narrator seems morally insensitive, as in "How They Ate the Rooster" ("Kak s'eli petukha," 1987), the portrait of a brutally quarrelsome old Siberian couple which depicts, as if in passing, the blinding of a woman by a street gang. Others of Popov's narrators seem utterly cynical, as in "Free Love" ("Svobodnaya lyubov'," 1984), in which two women, who discover that they are sharing the same man, make friends and join in teasing their mutual lover. The story is told in coarse good humor.

One of Popov's finest stories is "Pork-Kabobs" ("Svinye shashlyki," 1988), the account of a restaurant that enjoys enormous success until it is discovered that it has been serving dog meat instead of pork. Its manager is replaced by another, who does serve pork but embezzles by giving out short portions and goes to jail. The patrons engage in a pointless argument over who was the worse criminal, but the narrator interrupts this to end his story with an account of a man who fell into a vat of brewing beer and was not found for a month, causing some uneasiness among local beer fanciers. What makes the story a splendid one is not only its rollicking treatment of grisly themes but also its intimately confiding, sarcastic, opinionated, chatty, and seemingly undisciplined narrator, who interlards his story with charming irrelevancies and wild, tongue-in-cheek flights of imagination. In this study, as in many others of Popov, the rambling narrative manner suggests that of a folk tale.

Popov's world is sometimes weird – a mixture of earthy reality and the supernatural. In "An Old Idealist Fairytale" ("Staraya idealisticheskaya skazka," 1979), two men at a Ukrainian resort unblinkingly accept the fact that a companion can levitate himself in a beach chair; what angers them is that they cannot share his view of an adjacent walled-off beach for nude female bathers. In another spooky and somewhat weightier story, "The Reservoir" ("Vodoem," 1989), two attractive young men, probably a homosexual couple, come to an idyllic, park-like Siberian village, captivate its populace, and then quarrel in the village pond and drown. Their bodies are never found. Their ghosts haunt and poison the community and it decays. The story is told in first-person by a narrator, prone to digressions, who seems to represent the collective voice of the village. His pungent account is replete with irrelevant details and references that lead nowhere, but its intimacy and its very fallibility contribute to the richness of its local color. There is an aggressively zany quality about the narrator, who sometimes flagrantly defies logic and common sense. His manner is in keeping with the story itself, which suggests that the normal, everyday world is in fact a strange and fantastic place. This mixture of the ordinary and the unreal, and the discursive narrative manner, are reminiscent of the conventions of the traditional Russian *skazka*, and suggest that Popov, in parodic fashion, is writing contemporary Russian fairy tales.[3]

Although Popov often portrays moral obtuseness and cruelty, as in "Thick Hide" ("Tolstaya shkura," 1989), in which a reindeer is savagely clubbed in the face and the clubber argues that this is good for the herd, the narrators themselves can be tender and sensitive. "The Singing of the Brass" ("Penie mednykh," dated 1966, published 1988), for example, delicately presents the ruminations of a boy during the funeral of his father, and "The Circumstances of the Death of Andrei Stepanovich" ("Obstoyatel'stva smerti Andreya Stepanovicha," 1987) gives an account of the death and burial of a foreman in Yakutia and the inarticulate mourning of one of his roughneck workers. In "The Electronic Accordion" ("Elektronnyi bayan," 1987), a Siberian worker – a family man with a taste for material comforts – chances upon a demonstration of a new-fangled accordion. The sound so elevates him that for a moment he despises his mundane existence and flies into a rage, after which he calms down and resumes his way of life. The story, like many of Popov's, is somewhat enigmatic, but it is also compassionate and heartwarming.

A great many of Popov's characters are unhappy – unlucky (and, as a rule, inept) in love, work, and social relations, people who are poor and badly educated, who have had bad things done to them or are self-destructive. Many are derelicts unable to hold jobs or stay put, because of their drinking or irresponsible attitudes and behavior. Some of them have low horizons, others impractically high ones. Many are petty, selfish, or obtuse, and some are downright brutal. Several have criminal records. There is very little of the milk of human kindness in the world they inhabit. All are to some degree frustrated or dissatisfied, and few seem able to grasp the *reasons* for their discomfort or depression. Many are complainers – some wry and humorous, others bitter and despairing. Some blame themselves, but most blame others or general circumstances. A few simply suffer in obscurity, such as the main character in "It's Empty at Home" ("Doma pusto," 1987), a lonesome young laborer in a remote geological dig, who saves money to buy a house in which to live quietly with his widowed mother, only to discover by telegram that she is mortally ill.

Popov is a versatile, sophisticated writer with a wide topical and thematic range. Nevertheless, his attraction to the dismal world of these unfortunate characters, and his graphic portrayal of their lives, clearly identifies him with the trend of "tough" and "cruel" prose.

Although he continues to write short stories, Popov has recently undertaken longer works. The short novel *The Soul of a Patriot, or Various Epistles to Ferfichkin* (*Dusha patriota, ili razlichnye poslaniya k Ferfichkinu*, 1989) is cast in the form of a series of daily, meditative letters to a mysterious recipient who remains unknown to the reader. It begins with a lengthy, colorful, but often redundant chronicle of the narrator's Siberian family and ancestors, then switches to an account of his wandering about central Moscow, with a friend, on the day of Leonid Brezhnev's funeral. Within this simple framework there is great complexity, for the narration is loosely, almost randomly structured, with numerous digressions – many of them gossipy, verbose, querulous, and often silly.

The reason for this ostensible disorder and the justification for the narrator's irritating qualities is that, like Dostoevsky's underground man, he is striving for complete honesty and full self-disclosure. Despite the fact that he often plays the fool, he has important things to say. A professional writer who has yet to receive recognition, the narrator reveals in his musings not only the self-critical psychological agony that can accompany literary creation but also the profound frustration of the Soviet artistic community in the so-called period of stagnation.

The narrator's revelations and ruminations are not only an attempt to understand himself; they are an attempt to come to terms with history. As he details his ancestry he is trying to identify his historic roots, and as he strolls about Moscow regaling his friend with facts and figures about its streets, squares, and buildings (especially their *pre-revolutionary* names and circumstances), he is performing a kind of summing-up on the eve of a possible historical transformation as Brezhnev goes to his grave.

Like other writers of "alternative prose," Popov seems to have no ideological or political program; he is not an advocate. Nevertheless, he shows a profound sense of history and a keen sensitivity to the place of recent events in historical development. *The Splendor of Life* (*Prekrasnost' zhizni*, 1990), subtitled "chapters from a 'novel with newspaper' which will never be started and finished," is a 415-page volume with twenty-four chapters, titled by years from 1961 through 1985. Each chapter contains one story written during the given year, one story written in the early 1980s, and a large number of quotations, lists, and random data from a variety of sources in a manner somewhat reminiscent of John Dos Passos. Considered collectively, the stories constitute a kind of lyrical portrait of the developing artist. The quoted materials consist of newspaper headlines; selections from official speeches and proclamations (often pompous, bombastic, and mendacious); current Party slogans; news stories domestic and foreign; poems or excerpts from them; death announcements and obituaries; officially inspired public letters of indignation (for example, against Sakharov and Solzhenitsyn), with the names of signatories; and a variety of other contemporary information. Popov lets this mosaic of historic facts speak for itself, but it is so arranged that the ironies are inescapable: in a culture of mass deceit even good men become subtly corrupted, without realizing it. The ultimate irony of the work is the title itself.

Popov's most recent historically oriented work is "The Restaurant 'Beryozka'" ("Restoran 'Berezka'," 1991), with the subtitle "a poem and stories about Communists." It features mocking, although sometimes sympathetic, imaginary portraits of disillusioned Party functionaries and rank-and-file members and the shattering of their prescribed beliefs. Burlesquing official jargon, cliches, and mythology, including the reverential treatment of "great names," including Lenin, it pictures the dispossessed victims of historic upheaval as both comic and pathetic.

A complex and extravagant artist, Popov has often cultivated a joking manner that combines tragedy and comedy, lyricism and sarcasm, stark realism and the absurd. These combinations sometimes make it impossible to distinguish between levity and bitterness in Popov, and tempt one to conclude that he is a hopeless prisoner of irony. But in spite of his inclination to look at the dark and unfair side of life, he displays such good humor, alert intelligence, lively curiosity, and interest in human beings, and writes so abundantly and with such gusto, that his art goes far beyond the bounds of irony.

Like Popov, Vyacheslav P'etsukh was born in 1946. A native Muscovite, he graduated from a pedagogical institute in 1970 and taught history in the schools for a number of years. His first story was published in 1978, at about the time when Popov began his eight-year banishment from literature.

Also like Popov, P'etsukh is capable of writing tersely and economically (his stories are often very short), but he shares Popov's occasional fondness for non-stop Gogolian sentences and paragraphs. His narrator can be detached and neutral, as in "Three Under the Apple Tree" ("Troe pod yablonei," 1989), in which three ostracized Russians – a woman who had married a German occupying soldier, a man who had served the occupiers as a policeman, and a very old man who had served in Vrangel's army – discuss their fates (none feels guilty) as victims of history. The narrator simply "records" what they say. Often, however, P'etsukh's narrator is opinionated and enjoys interrupting his tale with side remarks and little essays on this and that – some of them obviously and intentionally nonsense. Thus, in "The Tsentral'no-Ermolaevskaya War" ("Tsentral'no-Ermolaevskaya Voina," 1988), the comic account of a violent feud between two villages, whose young men take turns trashing each other's public buildings, the narrator describes the "war" as would a military historian, and sometimes assumes the scientific posture of an anthropologist, engaging in spurious speculations on the influence of the natural environment, and even the grammar of the Russian language, on the people's behavior. In this, as in several other works of

P'etsukh, there are tongue-in-cheek digressions on the Russian soul.

When he is obviously in earnest, P'etsukh's narrator has important things to say about the Russian national character. The story "The Ticket" ("Bilet," 1989), which takes place in a remote mining settlement, features an itinerant worker – an ex-convict self-educated in the prison library – who is a natural leader, an independent thinker, and iconoclastic philosopher who identifies himself with a motley group from the past – Khlebnikov, Gorky, Aleksandr Grin, and Jesus Christ. He disdains material comforts, and prizes the freedom his poverty brings. Moreover, he argues, large numbers of Russians do not want the happiness associated with prosperity. Man, in fact, "is not obligated to be happy," and many intentionally and legitimately *seek* unhappiness.

P'etsukh has created a large gallery of colorful Russians – contradictory, inconsistent, given to extremes. His "Precious Traits" ("Dragotsennye cherty," 1989) is a collection of anecdotes and vignettes that illustrate various features of the Russian character – many of them perverse and absurd. He is fond of showing Russians in groups. In the story "Anamnesis and Epicrisis" ("Anamnez i Epikriz," 1990), the patients in a hospital ward – a varied collection of men broadly representative of the populace – discuss Russian history and society at length, until tempers flare and a bloody mass fight wrecks the ward. (Before the fight erupts, however, the patients generally agree that Russians do not *like* each other.) In "Novikov, the Feudal Lord" ("Novikov, feodal," 1992), the new director of a state farm, on overnight notice, restores serfdom, with all its oppressive and brutal trappings. Despite some grumbling and one weak attempt to assassinate the director, the peasants dutifully adapt to the new/old regime, and the farm prospers.

Submission to authoritarian rule is merely one of many seemingly incompatible features of the Russian character on display in P'etsukh's works. There is, for example, the opposite of this meekness – a rebellious streak that borders on the irrational and the self-destructive. Among his Russians one finds extreme pettiness and impractical, unworldly expansiveness, totally selfless generosity and utter miserliness, furious aggressiveness and passive timidity. P'etsukh's collective portrait of his countrymen is often so grotesque that the only characteristic they seem to have in common is their penchant for excess.

In almost every work of P'etsukh, however contemporary its setting, there is a prominent sense of history. He has also written a purely historical novel. *Rommat* (*Rommat*, 1989), whose title is an acronym for "romantic materialism" (*romanticheskii materializm*), is a study of attempts to overthrow Russian rulers in tsarist times, but it focuses mainly on the Decembrists. What makes it a novel and not simply a historical treatise is the prominent ingredient of inventiveness: there are numerous imaginary characters, and the historical personages themselves, such as Nicholas I and Ryleev, are given fictional treatment. There is even a lengthy fantasy in which the Decembrist uprising *succeeds*, with speculation on how Russian history and culture might have developed as a result.

The essence of *Rommat* is its irreverent attitude toward the Decembrist conspirators, whom it portrays as callow, impractical, undisciplined, capricious, romantic young dilettantes who were totally unqualified to lead an uprising. There is a fascinating "post-mortem" conversation among Petersburg intellectuals, including Somov, Khomyakov, and Pushkin, in which they express their scorn and disapproval of the Decembrists, both individually and as a group. P'etsukh's idea of "romantic materialism," developed laboriously at the end of the novel, seems to boil down to the rather obvious notion that history creates individuals, who in turn create history.

P'etsukh's narrator seems to hate and love his fellow-Russians in about equal proportions, but above all to view their extreme character traits, their uniqueness, with prideful astonishment. These traits, in great abundance, are demonstrated in the novel *The New Moscow Philosophy* (*Novaya moskovskaya filosofiya*, 1989). The novel, a modern-day travesty on Dostoevsky's *Crime and Punishment*, with numerous references to other nineteenth- and twentieth-century Russian writers and works, is set in a communal flat in contemporary Moscow. The plot is simple:

the flat's hereditary owner, an old woman who now occupies a tiny room in it since its post-revolutionary requisitioning, disappears. Foul play is suspected, and the occupants – a motley group of citizens of various ages – spend their time (1) speculating on the mysterious disappearance and (2) elbowing each other to get the old woman's room.

The detailed history of the flat represents a kind of microcosm of Soviet history itself, and the flat's inhabitants are an unflattering cross-section of the Soviet urban populace. There are many satirical references to the mores of the Gorbachev era. For example, the squabbling tenants decide to hold a "democratic" meeting to allocate the old woman's space in the spirit of "glasnost'," and then proceed to knife each other in the time-honored way. However, the novel is much more than a social satire. Widely discursive, it speculates at length, and usually with tongue in cheek, on the relation between literature and life, art and reality, good and evil, and philosophizes about human nature, criminal behavior, and the Russian national character. The persons who discuss these matters are a pair of not-too-bright amateur philosophers, but the narrator himself also makes his eccentric contributions.

This is a novel preoccupied with itself; it toys with its own aesthetic problems and freely, in a comic spirit, bares its own devices. It dilutes, cheapens, and trivializes the characters and themes of *Crime and Punishment*, but in doing so it makes fun of itself, not Dostoevsky. It is puzzling that P'etsukh, who is obviously seriously concerned about the fundamental moral and intellectual issues involved in this novel, should make them the object of so much ostensible foolishness. This ambiguous amalgam of earnestness and spoofery, however, constitutes a kind of narrative irony that, although sometimes exasperating, is arresting and attractive.

Viktor Erofeev (born 1947) is a literary critic and scholar with a wide knowledge of Western literature and considerable experience of living in the West, who emphatically disdains the heritage of Soviet literature and seems determined that it leave no traces in his own writing. His association with the avant-garde began early, when in 1979 his participation in the almanac *Metropol'* brought about his expulsion from the Writers' Union and several years of blacklisting. The *Metropol'* offense was probably not solely political: his novella and two stories in the almanac were scabrous far beyond the bounds of official tolerance at that time.

When the publication of his fiction resumed in the late 1980s, Erofeev continued to demonstrate his ability to shock. Not only were his works loaded with explicit physiological and sexual detail that made them seem nasty and cynical; their displays of sadistic cruelty, of extreme pain inflicted on innocent individuals – and often their destruction – were at times simply repulsive. At the same time, his stories did not seem to be simply mischievous challenges to public taste or mere self-indulgent exercises in indecency. For one thing, they were written with considerable literary sophistication and virtuosity; for another, their concern with the ugly and the pathological suggested the possibility of a deep moral dimension.

The most vivid and disturbing of Erofeev's stories is "The Parakeet" ("Popugaichik," 1988), the monologue of a professional interrogator-executioner directed at the father of a boy whom he and his cohorts had sodomized, tortured (using medieval methods, including the rack and sexual mutilation), and killed. Garrulous, self-satisfied, cold-blooded and weirdly objective about his activities, the killer details the ghastly tormenting and the death of the innocent boy with the relish of an expert. He speaks in a mixture of loftily formal and polite, and abysmally low and vulgar, language – a combination, as the author himself has testified, of four historic levels of Russian, from pre-Petrine speech to contemporary criminal jargon. This linguistic amalgam, and numerous other historically incompatible details, seem designed to lend a timeless quality to the story, to suggest the constancy of malevolence and inhumanity in an otherwise changing Russian scene.

Gruesome and grotesque, "The Parakeet" is bound to produce a visceral revulsion in nearly any reader. For all its sinister power, however, the story is too obviously an intellectual contrivance; the author's presence, his artifice, and manipulation in an effort to scare us are too evident. A somewhat similar criticism can be made of the story "Anna's Body, or the End of the Russian Avant Garde" ("Telo Anny, ili konets russkogo avangarda," 1989), in which the scene of a blowsy woman in bed with her recently returned, sleeping lover is made into an elaborate, disjointed allegory full of political, historical, and literary allusions, designed, presumably, to suggest something about the present state of Russian culture, and, possibly, the current condition of the author's own muse.

Erofeev is at his best when he is least evidently cerebral. The story "Galoshes" ("Galoshi," 1988), like "The Parakeet" a study in malice, is a self-conscious adaptation from the medieval genre of saints' lives. Despite its calculatedly derivative origin, it is the unassuming and unaffected story of a boy, persecuted and humiliated by his classmates and teachers. At the height of his suffering, he prays to God to forgive his tormentors, and miraculously acquires a nimbus. In this instance, Erofeev the intellectual, the writer-literary scholar, is a charming artist whose portrayal of good and evil and of the sufferings of the heart, is infectious and moving. When Erofeev does not seem to be trying to outdo Sologub and Dostoevsky, he is a very good writer indeed.

The six writers identified in this chapter as representatives of the trend of "tough" and "cruel" prose are obviously not a discrete group. Although their writing has important features in common, there are equally important differences among them. None of them, moreover, is self-consistent; within each individual writer, with the possible exception of Kaledin, there is a variety of intonation, themes, and modes. It is also evident that these six writers do not hold a Russian monopoly on the portrayal of harsh and bitter lives, mean and ugly people, eccentric and lonely sufferers. Other authors of "alternative prose", and more conventional writers as well, share their interest in the most unattractive and painful aspects of contemporary Russian existence and behavior.

What these six writers do display with a particular intensity, sufficient to warrant the claim that they represent a unique tendency, is an intimacy with contemporary Russian vulgarity of outlook, speech, and demeanor, a sense of the national roots of this vulgarity, and a fascination with the essential naked and rough humanity that underlies this vulgarity. A desire to observe ordinary Russians closely, to record their talk in all its coarseness, and to try to understand their folk peculiarities is what seems to motivate these writers. They do this with varying degrees of objectivity and involvement. Venedikt Erofeev writes as a passionate participant, Petrushevskaya for the most part as a cool listener, Kaledin as a dispassionate but somewhat sympathetic observer, Popov and P'etsukh as bemused ironists and Viktor Erofeev as a literary craftsman who sees Russian life primarily as building material for his fiction.

It has been indicated that "alternative" prose, within which these six writers loosely form a sub-group, represents a reaction against utilitarian art and therefore has no ideology or program. These six writers do, however, show a particular fascination with the peculiarities of "Russianness," a yearning to define and disclose its deep and mysterious essence. This aspiration accounts for their emphasis on the contemporary spoken language, on earthy, even obscene, wit and humor. Evgenii Popov, in fact, has argued that literature that deals in the comic, the illogical, and the absurd is much closer in spirit to the popular genius than that which is rationalistic and doggedly enlightening.[4] The prominent element of the fantastic in these writers (again, Kaledin excepted), and their use of folk legend and fairy-tale motifs, would seem to be aspects of their striving to conjure up an authentic image of the national character.

A striking feature of this writing is its combination of horror and humor. Fundamentally pessimistic, it dwells at length and in sometimes repulsive detail on violence, depravity, and hopelessness, but it is often exuberantly witty and wildly, buoyantly funny. It can be legitimately argued that the literary antecedents and spiritual inspiration of these writers are an inharmonious group consisting of Dostoevsky, Zoshchenko, Daniil Kharms, and Vasilii Shukshin. Such a listing of literary fathers, however, would neglect an important trait shared by much of the writing of Venedikt Erofeev, Popov, and P'etsukh.

These three writers often give the impression of being very close to their narrators. We are invited to believe that the narrators are thinly disguised, and sometimes completely undisguised, surrogates for the author. The narrators are all passionate, ironic, and idiosyncratic – characters in themselves. It would be dangerous to conclude, however, that these narrators do in fact represent the authors. But they do provide evidence that someone is deeply concerned about the contradictions within the contemporary Russian soul.

CHAPTER 8

New faces

It might have been expected that the obliteration of Communist Party control over the publication of literature in the late eighties and early nineties would result in a burgeoning of new talent, and that a multitude of young writers, freed of the restrictions that had frustrated and crippled their elders, would now rush into print. As of the end of 1991 this had not happened. Critics and editors complained, in fact, that the flowering which some had anticipated was not coming about for the reason that the talent was simply not there. There were also counter-complaints, however, by self-appointed spokesmen for the younger generation, who argued that the talent *was* there but that, with publication facilities in short supply, editors had elected to give priority to established authors.

Still other factors may account for the apparent relative dearth of fresh talents. If under the Soviet regime the experimentation and aesthetic daring which can be expected of young writers was discouraged for ideological reasons, a similarly powerful discouragement might now have been exerted by the market. Editors and publishers, pressed to keep their enterprises afloat in the presence of heavy competition, might well have shied away from printing inventively difficult or esoteric new writing because they feared it would not sell. It is also quite probable that, in this time of national crisis and turmoil, many talented young writers, like many of their seniors, were too preoccupied with multiple social and personal problems to devote much of their time to literary creativity.

The sampling of new authors in the present chapter will indicate that the situation was not as bleak as the above considerations might suggest. These seven writers, fortunate enough to be published during these trying times, display a genuine diversity of interests and modes. While they probably do not represent all the strains of contemporary prose fiction, they do suggest that both below and above the surface there is indeed life and variety. Since they are so new to the literary scene and have only begun publishing their fiction, it is impossible to foresee which ones of them will make enduring contributions and which will fade into obscurity. Likewise, it is entirely probable that other contemporary new writers, not mentioned here, will eventually surpass those who are about to be discussed. Nevertheless, it is hoped that these seven writers will serve as an accurate, if rough, indicator of current literary activity.

A new talent and fresh voice from the Afghanistan War appeared in 1989 in the stories of Oleg Ermakov, a writer from Smolensk who was twenty-eight years old when he made his debut. The intimacy and emotional authenticity of his stories are those not of a reporter but of a participant.

"Baptism" ("Kreshchenie") is told from the point of view of a soldier in his first military action. His patrol, out to occupy an Afghan village, meets with sniper fire, shoots up the houses, and captures the snipers. The soldier is ordered to execute one sniper on the spot and does so with a burst of automatic fire. Another rookie soldier finds himself unable to carry out a similar order and is killed by a member of the patrol. As the story ends, the young hero is brooding over what has happened: he hates his dead comrade for not having had the stomach to help kill the prisoners.

Thus, a boy has been transformed into a murderer of men defending their native village and, in his shock, misplaces his hostility. The author's sympathies seem divided equally between the newly brutalized boy and his Afghan victims: the village is described as a charming one, the Afghans as people trying to repel an invader. However, Ermakov does not strain to make his point. In fact, the entire narrative is spare and precise, with just enough physical and psychological detail (the enveloping dust and the constant fear of land mines) to give it authenticity. It is by following the thought of the hero and listening to the extensive dialogue of his fellow-soldiers that we learn enough to draw the conclusion that this is an ill-considered and unjust war.

In "The Yellow Mountain" ("Zheltaya gora") the central figure is a war veteran on the staff of a provincial youth newspaper. He refuses an order to make an inspirational speech in support of the war and, instead, writes an article ironically describing a bombastic, cliche-ridden pep-talk he had heard delivered by a major in Afghanistan in an effort to boost morale following the desertion of a soldier from his detachment. The article is clearly unacceptable to the Party watchdogs who control the newspaper. Early in the story the hero plays on his tape recorder a rock number whose dominant refrain is "don't believe anyone, any time, anything," and he repeatedly expresses profound disgust over dishonest jargon and formulas of journalism about the war. The hero is a young man morally scarred by the war and obsessed by images related to it – chiefly the slaughter of birds, which also suggest aircraft.

All of Ermakov's stories depict a Soviet military that seems to be at war with itself. "Safe Return" ("Blagopoluchnoe vozvrashchenie") begins with the extended account of a bloody and near-fatal fist-fight between two soldiers over who gets to occupy a particular bunk. One of the men is about to be discharged after his two-year term of duty, and as his troop transport proceeds through the wasteland to Kabul, under sporadic guerilla harassment, he encounters many new recruits and many full coffins. Neither in this nor any of Ermakov's other stories is there a depiction of heroism – even the modest, unglamorous, lonely heroism featured in works about World War II by such writers as Baklanov and Bykov. But there are frequent glimpses of the people of Afghanistan and their suffering under a Soviet army that has lost its morale.

In "Winter in Afghanistan" ("Zimoi v Afganistane") – a story of a relatively quiet time for Soviet troops while the enemy prefers to remain disengaged – Ermakov displays the social anatomy, the complicated pecking order, of a typical small detachment. He does this largely by means of the abundant, coarse, often abusive dialogue that frequently distinguishes his stories. In a strikingly contrasting style he shows, in "House Covered with Snow" ("Zanesennyi snegom dom"), the feelings of a young schoolteacher as she anxiously awaits the return of her husband from Afghanistan. The psychology in this story is impressive; Ermakov's portrait of this woman is delicate and sensitive, and at the same time respectful of her innate nobility and dignity. In this, as in his other stories, the young author makes deft, vivid, and richly evocative use of imagery taken from both nature and ordinary life.

"Zyoma, an Ironic Diary" ("Zyoma, Ironicheskii Dnevnik," 1989), by Aleksandr Terekhov, presents a different view of the military, but in its way it is no less harrowing than that of Ermakov. Now in his middle twenties, Terekhov served not in Afghanistan but, at least during part of his enlistment, in Moscow itself. His story recounts, in first person, the experiences of a nineteen-year-old recruit who, with a few comrades, is sent to the guard-house for a minor act of insubordination. Prior to his incarceration, he is shown briefly serving as a flunky to a childish and ridiculous, fat general. In this early part of the story, Terekhov displays both a gift for satirically humorous writing and a sensitivity to the sufferings of others.

In his account of life in the guard-house, however, Terekhov paints a shocking picture of routine, arbitrary cruelty. A guard nonchalantly, and for no reason, smashes the glasses of a young prisoner; a group of detainees is forced to stand at attention for hours in a stifling cell; the narrator's head is repeatedly immersed in a toilet. The officers in charge are capriciously, sadistically abusive, and systematic beatings and other forms of torture are common. In this regime, which seems little different from the Gulag, one of the narrator's friends tries to hang himself. Terekhov's accounts of army life aroused fierce protest from military authorities, who labeled them slanderous. The publication of "Zyoma" was delayed by the censors.

The outspoken, iconoclastic hero of *The Wintry Day of the Start of a New Life* (*Zimnii den' nachala novoi zhizni*, 1991), a student in geography at a Moscow institute, is burdened by a number of fairly normal frustrations and anxieties, but these are compounded by phobias and a weakness for alcohol. Some fellow-denizens of his cockroach-ridden, run-down coed dormitory consider him a natural leader, but his behavior seems so perverse and infantile that he has become a self-destructive object of pity and scorn. His psychological problems, however, are complicated by clear insights into a surrounding world that is manifestly unhealthy, corrupt, and out of kilter. The institute's teachers are inept, stupid, and pathetically paralyzed by the ideological poison they have been fed and in turn have prescribed for decades, and which, they now dazedly realize, must somehow be counteracted. The students have become cynical, their natural ambitions and idealism vitiated, at least temporarily, by a sense of purposelessness. Most of them are functioning minimally as students with one aim: to keep their government stipends coming.

A romantic individualist who appears a taunting misfit to the outside world, the hero plays little nasty tricks that exploit the all-too-evident personal shortcomings of his male classmates, clumsily and ineffectively pursues the girl of his dreams, and rejects the advances of others. Meanwhile, he obsessively tries to kill the rats, real and imagined, that he thinks infest his quarters. Finally, in a grand quixotic gesture he tries to free a prostitute whom a wealthy middle-eastern student has lured into the dormitory and who is being put to constant, punishing, universal use.

It is evident that, through the hero and his classmates, Terekhov is attempting to make a grim, although often humorous, statement about the crisis condition of a crucial element in contemporary Russian society. The prose that embodies this statement is rich in unpleasant detail, of which there is at times an overabundance. Although one wants to sympathize with his wryly intelligent but deeply confused hero and to see him as a plausible emblem of the times, his hysterical behavior and his troubled thoughts are portrayed so copiously that he is, more often than not, simply repelling.

A most startling and puzzling new talent in the late 1980s was Valeriya Narbikova, a writer in her early thirties. Narbikova combined in her stories a virtually total plotlessness, sexual fantasy, free association, and seemingly uninhibited word-play. The most interesting and surely the most dynamic feature of her writing is its language, which is loaded with puns, elaborate syntax, whimsical parallelisms and progressions, and illogical, often absurd, transitions, and which seems governed by a logic based on acoustic rather than semantic relationships.

Although Narbikova's prose affects a spontaneous randomness, and although the narrative voice seems undisciplined and capricious, there is also at work a calculating intelligence. The short novel that marked her debut, *The Equilibrium of the Light of Daytime and Nighttime Stars* (*Ravnovesie sveta dnevnykh i nochnykh zvedz*, 1988), displays (the word deserves emphasis) not only great linguistic virtuosity but also considerable erudition. There are allusions to numerous classical, Russian, and Western authors and schools of literary theory and practice, to historical and cultural figures and phenomena, to artists (Braque and Picasso), to the Holy Trinity, and to the Holy Family (she saucily refers to the Virgin Mary as "Masha"). In the absence of an evident unifying or justifying concept, however, this large collection of references seems merely contrived.

What we have in the stories of Narbikova is a strange, subjective amalgam of fragmentary erotic and linguistic musings, interlarded with sometimes girlishly naive, sometimes impressively perceptive speculations on the phenomena of time and space and on human nature. Occasionally her verbal texture and her small, idiosyncratic intellectual games are delightful. Her treatment of sexual themes, however, seems purely intellectual, designed to shock, perhaps to impress, but scarcely to seduce. One suspects that until she is able to fit the bits and pieces of her lively, imaginative world into a discernible system, Narbikova will remain a writer of unfulfilled potential.

The prose of Dmitrii Bakin (born 1964) strikes one immediately with its compression, grace, earthiness, and lively and tangible imagery. Whatever else he may be, Bakin is an impressively interesting and powerful stylist, a literary presence of great seriousness and promise. At the same time, Bakin is complex and enigmatic, and the frequently puzzled reader is swept along more by his compelling style and fascinating characters than by any confident comprehension of what is taking place.

Available biographical information about Bakin is scant. He is reported to be a Moscow truck driver whose real name is Dmitrii Bocharov. He has a secondary education, has done army service, and appears to have had no formal training as a writer – somewhat startling in view of the precision, maturity, and discipline of his style. It seems evident that he has absorbed a knowledge of common people, provincial life, and Russian folkways. Social settings and social issues, however, are not at the center of his attention. What interest him most, it would appear, are mysterious, and often supernatural, forces and impulses that motivate his characters, who themselves have symbolic significance.

In the story "Leaves" ("List'ya," 1988), we are shown the life of a young man from the time (immediately after World War II) when he returns to his native village as a twelve-year-old orphan, to the day when he immolates himself in a pile of burning leaves. A seeker who frequently detaches himself from other people and resists their advances, he has Christ-like characteristics of meekness and insight, but is also subject to dark, violent, self-destructive drives. The persons with whom he comes into closest contact are all bizarre – including the promiscuous village woman who forces herself upon him and becomes his wife, and an untalented painter who uses the hero's face as a model for icons which he peddles to the local church. The very strangeness of this story and its characters suggests that it may have been designed as a parable.

A simpler but equally haunting story is "Lagopthalmos" ("Lagoftal'm," 1989), the first-person account, by a young soldier, of being shadowed constantly by an awkward, disheveled, sickly comrade who tries to make friends with him. In a fury against this repulsive pest, whom he refers to as "my enemy," he even beats him up – to no avail. Finally, at a military exercise, he saves his maddening pursuer's life, and in doing so is crushed by a tank. The story has been told, it seems, in the narrator's dying words. Although this is not said, it appears clear that the pursuer has been the angel of death.

Bakin's most provocative story to date is "Land of Origin" ("Strana proiskhozhdeniya," 1991). It features another one of the author's possessed heroes, this time a man who carries about a cabalistic chart of his own genealogy and who carries within his heart a bullet inherited, through seven generations, from the Siberian hunter in whose heart it was originally lodged. He also carries about him a "cosmic coolness," which eerily chills his own house and coats his mother-in-law's crucifix with ice. Only his newly acquired, warm, and loving wife, who has selected him after fifteen years of seeking, fails to notice the chill. In a packet made for cigarette papers, he carries seven of his own baby teeth and a locket of hair from a seven-year-old girl whose name is, or was, Idea.

After excruciating, haunting torment, in the course of which he tries to rid himself of his obsession with his occult family tree by burying his genealogical papers under a heap of old revolutionary journals, the hero manages to achieve peace of mind, but we are not told how he has done this. Much mystery remains. The reader is tempted, however, perhaps even compelled, to see the entire story as a moral allegory of the relationship between the Russian nation and the idea of communism that dominated it for seven decades.

Aleksandr Kabakov has apparently been writing since the early 1980s, or possibly before, but his first notable publication was *No Return* (*Nevozvrashchenets*, 1989), which he labeled a "film-story" (*kinopovest'*). It is not likely that this story, despite its absorbing drama, will be made into a film in Russia in the near future. The thematics are politically so controversial and possibly inflammatory, the circumstances and action so lurid, that it could be foolhardy to present a cinematic version to a mass Russian audience in the early 1990s.

Clearly intended as a cautionary tale, *No Return* has as its main character a scientist with an uncanny ability to "ex-

trapolate" from present-day economic and political circumstances (the late 1980s) and thus to live, for short, intense
periods, in the Russia of the mid-1990s. This ability to foresee
the future makes him useful to a pair of secret agents, working
for an unspecified political organization, in their struggle
against other organizations, which also have their own "extra-
polators."

The hero's vision of Russia's immediate future is terrifying.
Perestroika has failed to bring about fundamental political and
economic reforms, and Russia is now in the hands of an
ineffective military dictatorship. Not only is there wild inflation
and, in places, famine; there is mass terror, caused by organized,
roving bands of assassins, representing various extreme political
groupings, which engage in mass roundups and executions.
Moscow is virtually a ruin, and the entire remaining population
of two other wrecked cities – Yaroslavl and Vladimir – is living
in the Moscow subway.

A Commission for National Security has confiscated all
clocks and watches, because these have been used as timers for
home-made bombs. In this nightmarish disorder, the presence
of a United Nations battalion and the trickle of material
assistance from abroad make little difference. Russia has sunk
into chaos, pogroms are widespread, and bloody battles are
going on between extremists of every stamp. Kabakov has
selected the most malign tendencies in the Russia of the 1980s
and shaped them into a worst-case scenario. One could only
hope that this dystopia would turn out to be a grotesque
exaggeration.

Kabakov's *A Cheap Novel* (*Bul'varnyi roman*, 1990) is totally
lacking in civic significance and displays a stylistic playfulness
and bizarre sense of humor that one would not expect from the
grimly concerned author of *No Return*. Its hero, Ignat'ev, a
gardener working for the city of Moscow, with a wife and teenaged daughter, hankers for the wife of Pirogov, a well-placed
bureaucrat who lives on the floor below in the same high-rise
apartment building. For his part, Pirogov hankers for Ignat'ev's
apartment, to add to his own, so that he can live in multi-level
splendor. Through his wife Pirogov tries to persuade Ignat'ev to

give up his flat, and fails. The unimaginative and rather dim Ignat′ev, on the other hand, winds up in bed not with Pirogov's wife, but with Pirogov's disaffected mistress. The story begins, in fact, with a steamy account of their lovemaking, an account which parodies banal, third-rate erotic fiction and includes a disconcerting detail – Ignat′ev does not know whether or not to leave his socks on.

There is possible symbolic significance in the fact that the easy-going Ignat′ev, on a tourist trip to Western Europe, is puzzled to discover that a German gardener whom he meets is so well disciplined that he cannot take time off from his work to enjoy a cigarette with him, and in the fact that Pirogov, who has also traveled abroad, lusts for Western material comforts. The real charm of *A Cheap Novel*, however, is in its narrative manner. The narrator, whom Kabakov insistently calls the "author," is constantly in the foreground, assiduously and with comic clumsiness manipulating his characters and situations, and nonchalantly introducing supernatural elements – Ignat′ev discovers his vocation of gardening only when flowers, shrubs, and even trees keep springing up through asphalt pavement which he, as a construction worker, has just poured. The narrator's language is abundantly interlarded with foreign words, which he often misuses. Frequently he addresses his characters and has little informal chats with the reader. A major source of interest is the "author's" humorous running commentary about his procedures and techniques in writing this story, and the problems involved. This narrator is self-confident, pompous, and inept, but at the same time he is wittily aware of his failings. His story is a farce with a creaky structure, and it is also an engrossing, sly joke.

Marina Palei, whose first publications were articles of literary criticism, has also been a physician, a cleaning woman, and an artist's model. A native of St. Petersburg, she first came to national attention as a prose writer with the publication of *Evgesha and Annushka* (*Evgesha i Annushka*, 1990), which offers portraits of two elderly women pensioners who share a three-room communal flat with the narrator, a considerably younger, professional woman. Both Evgesha, a retired nurse, and Annushka, a former factory worker, have had hard lives. Each of them has suffered from Stalinist persecution (although both are essentially apolitical), and each endured severe hardship during World War II. They are childless and poor, but both of them are exploited to the last kopek by scrounging nieces and nephews. Of peasant-origin, both are survivors, simple and unreflective. Neither has religious inclinations or convictions.

There the similarity ends. Annushka is slovenly, trusting, enormously forgetful, generous to a fault, and fearful of imposing on others. She spends much of her time in bed staring at the ceiling, and seldom leaves her room. Sickly and worn-out, she is "resting from life." Evgesha, on the other hand, is disciplined, cleanly, absorbed in her petty daily routine, gregarious, and a fount of up-to-date information on happenings in the neighborhood. She tends to be suspicious, prejudiced, and inflexible in her judgments. Although she seems narrow-minded and unimaginative, she is a reliable friend and a responsible citizen.

In creating these two characters, Palei seems to have had in mind not a contrast between two "types," but rather a composite showing two different reactions to the problems of existence. Although she shows the humorous, quirky sides of both women and sometimes seems a bit condescending toward each of them, her approach is essentially sympathetic and respectful. Her portraits are sprightly and psychologically acute, aimed at demonstrating how interesting ostensibly ordinary human beings can be.

What makes the characters especially fascinating, however, is the peculiar intensity and concern of the narrator, who becomes a prominent third character in her own right. This woman, who in contrast to her two apartment-mates has intellectual inclinations, suffers from periodic deep depression. Her interest in these two older women is closely related to an agonized search for meaning in her own life and life in general. As she observes these "simple" persons, she speculates on the light which their unlettered attitudes can shed on her own existential problems. The narrator is thus more involved in her characters than a purely objective observer would be. This involvement, perhaps, explains her sometimes nervously ironic and excessively witty portrayal of her two companions, and the sometimes arch quality of her comments on contemporary life.

In *A Cabiria from By-Pass Street* (*Kabiriya s Obvodnogo Kanala*, 1991),[1] Palei creates a heroine who does not even remotely resemble the characters in the previous story. Raimonda, known familiarly as Mon'ka, is a free spirit who, even as a grandmother, remains "eternally a fourteen-year-old." As an adolescent, she openly defies parental authority, leaves school early and for good, and begins a life of inveterate sexual promiscuity. She values her body only as a facility for attracting men and making love, and she otherwise totally neglects it. Persistent, heavy smoking hastens her death. She is undisguisedly unfaithful to her many husbands and lovers and sometimes carries bruises as a reward. Strangely, however, she seems both depraved and innocent.

Mon'ka is in fact quite an engaging person. She has many women friends and is never alone. As seen through the eyes of the narrator – a female cousin ten years younger than she, who is both disapproving and envious of her – she is a chatterer, both disorderly and lively, self-centered and sharing. As a result of two early suicide attempts, she comes to know and love hospitals, where she increasingly spends the last years of her life, painfully ill but also happily the center of attention. Frankly amoral, with little sense of responsibility, she lives her messy life with no apologies and no regrets.

Palei's supporting cast in this story is colorful and often grotesque. It includes Mon'ka's brutish father, an extravagantly lying mother who restlessly, constantly changes her apartments about Leningrad and meddles in her children's marriages, her brother, her straight-laced, practical and totally disapproving daughter, some of the numerous men in Mon'ka's life, and the narrator herself. Once again Palei creates a narrator with an extraordinarily complex attitude toward her subject. Like the narrator of *Evgesha and Annushka*, she is gifted with impressive verbal facility; her language is richly figurative (her sexual imagery is elaborate), wrily humorous, and often very amusing, although at times too clever and verging on verbosity. Most striking, however, is her concern for the ultimate significance of Mon'ka's life and character.

As a person who has followed a conservative, conventional, responsible pattern of life, the narrator finds herself awed by and perversely envious of her feckless older cousin. At one point she even experiences sympathetic symptoms of one of Mon'ka's illnesses. Toward the end, after Mon'ka's death, she seems to resurrect her heroine and to endow her with a continuing, happy life. She seems to want to celebrate, together with the author herself, a personality which, though deeply flawed, was honest, uninhibited, and free, and to raise that personality to the level of myth. Palei is an impressive stylist who, despite the minor excesses mentioned above, has created a most interesting narrator.

The first publication of Zufar Gareev (born 1955) was the story "When Other Birds Call" ("Kogda krichat chuzhie ptisty"), which appeared in 1989. It is an unrelievedly bleak tale of the twenty-four-hour visit of a young city women to the village where her parents live. Unruly and profligate as a girl, and now virtually estranged from the old couple, she arrives by train with no luggage. Instead of spending the night with her parents, she stays in a bathhouse with a pathetic local drunk, impotent and crippled from polio, whom she had known when they were children.

Gareev's account of these happenings is factual and dispassionate, but its apparent straightforwardness is deceptive. We are told so little about the young woman – she is poorly dressed, has a cold sore on her upper lip (which her father takes to be a chancre), is unmarried, and has "graduated in literature at Moscow University" – that she remains a mystery. She does not say why she has come, and even seems to be unaware of a reason. If she is essentially a malicious person, her malice is only exceeded by that of her father. When he is driving her from the train to the family cottage, they stop beside a river so that she can go for a swim; he tries to entice her to a deadly whirlpool.

By highlighting this attempted murder, and by omitting

essential details about the young woman's circumstances and motivation, Gareev creates an atmosphere of mystery and evil. He uses a prominent, and by now outworn, convention of "village prose" – the sad, nostalgic return of an urbanite to scenes of a rural childhood – to present an essentially desolate but arrestingly ambiguous and ominous vision of human relationships.

While it is possible that the heroine of this story is mentally unbalanced, the seventeen-year-old hero of Gareev's next published story, "On Holiday" ("Kanikuly," 1990), clearly is not. He is simply a confused adolescent, anxious for acceptance as a peer by a circle of more worldly classmates. To ingratiate himself, he spends an evening bumming around with them, drinking and smoking ineptly and with ill-concealed revulsion, until the police break up a dismal party they are having in a cellar. We see him the next day, lingering forlornly outside the dwelling of his favorite among the previous night's companions, engaging in wistful fantasies in which he is recognized as an equal.

"On Holiday" is not only a psychologically acute portrayal of youthful aspirations and emotions. It is also a story of initiation and corruption. Although it does not have as prominent an element of mystery as does "When Other Birds Call," with fewer essential facts "left out," this story, too, suggests a world that is basically ugly and evil. It opens with a depressing family dinner-table conversation in which the boy's cynical and vulgar uncle insists, between belches, that the boy's parents ship off his aged grandfather to an old folks' home and thus make more profitable use of his living space. The boy's initiating debauch that evening seems pathetically in keeping with the spirit of this conversation.

Gareev's most recently published work is fundamentally different from the two just cited. In "The Park" ("Park," 1991), which is basically phantasmagoric, a provincial "park of culture and rest" becomes the magic catalyst through which a number of typical, although caricatured Soviet citizens are released from their ordinary identities, freed of their earthly ties and inhibitions, and sent into fantastic, intoxicating realms of self-discovery and realization. Not only are they free to transcend the limitations of time and space; they find within themselves primordial spiritual drives and cultural depths of which they had been aware only subconsciously, if at all. "The Park" is also, and prominently, a melange of literary allusions, folklore, parody, grotesque transformations and happenings, and slapstick, with abundant cinematic effects. Gareev is clearly an experimenter with a taste for the fantastic, and with a robust sense of humor and the absurd. In view of his tastes and versatility, it is not surprising that his chief early literary sponsor is reported to have been Evgenii Popov.

By the time the writers discussed in this chapter began to appear in print – in the late 1980s – the flood of tendentious, topical fiction encouraged by *glasnost'*, most of it explicitly anti-Stalinist, had largely abated. Nevertheless, the traditional proclivity of Russian literature for social criticism remained prominent in several of these new authors. A case in point is Ermakov's strong expression of revulsion and protest against the war in Afghanistan; another is Terekhov's bitter and lurid portrayal of Soviet military life. Kabakov's *No Return* has a passionately civic message, and Terekhov's *A Wintry Day of the Start of a New Life* starkly describes malaise and alienation among Soviet youth.

The unsparing social candor of these new writers was reinforced by the now well-established practice of larding narratives with harsh, unpleasant, ugly, even shocking detail, in the manner of the writers of "tough" and "cruel" prose discussed in the preceding chapter. In this respect, Marina Palei, despite important individual differences, seems to have much in common with Lyudmila Petrushevskaya. The new candor is striking in respect to sexual matters; only a decade ago Russian writers seemed fastidious and reticent, but now they were explicit and detailed. There also seemed to be increased ingredients of social irreverence and satire, as evidence in the ironical narratives of Terekhov, Palei, Narbikova, and Kabakov.

A study, or perhaps multiple studies, should be made comparing the qualities of irony, and specifically of ironical narrators, in the Soviet Russian prose of the late 1950s and 1960s with that of the late 1980s and early 1990s, as exemplified by the young Vasilii Aksenov and Vladimir Voinovich, on the one hand, and such writers as Terekhov, Palei, and Kabakov on the other. There is evidence to suggest that such a study would conclude that the narrators of the sixties, for all their skepticism, would seem to be starry-eyed romantics in comparison to their present illusion-free successors.

There is great stylistic variety among these new writers. Ermakov, Terekhov, Kabakov, Palei, and Gareev seem to be fairly conservative and traditional in most respects, although each has elements of individuality and originality. The style of Bakin is extraordinarily powerful and arresting, that of Narbikova capricious and bewildering. Nearly all of these writers enjoy verbal play and ornamentation, confirming the fact that the bugbear of "formalism" has long been interred. Finally, the prominence of the fantastic and supernatural in the writing of Bakin, Kabakov, and Gareev indicates that these dimensions have now been fully restored to Russian literature.

CHAPTER 9

Conclusion

In the latter half of the sixteen-year period with which this book has been concerned, the Soviet Russian literary community made a giant, and largely successful, effort toward recovering those parts of the Russian literary heritage which the communist regime had denied it for many decades. Not only did it rediscover its own literature that had been lost or buried; it also resumed the full contact with twentieth-century world literature, especially that of the West, which Soviet rule had severely limited. And it made enormous progress toward joining forces with the community of Russian emigre literature after decades of compulsory separation.

A concomitant of these swift and dramatic developments was a marked growth of interest in the Russian national identity, the peculiarities of the Russian character, the essence of "Russianness." This interest, of course, had never died, and had increased in recent decades, notably through the efforts of the "village writers." The decay of Soviet rule, however, brought a marked decline in "Soviet" consciousness, as writers turned away from ideological categories and measurements and replaced them with cultural and ethnic concerns. Writers increasingly examined Russians not as political animals but as human beings with unique and ancient roots and patterns of behavior and belief, religion included.

A marked increase of writers' interest in the irrational and the supernatural is evident in this period. The exorcism of Stalinism, which occupied the literary community so intensely in the latter half of the 1980s, brought about, incidentally, the final interment of socialist realism. This, in turn, encouraged the development of a "fantasmagoric art," which Andrei Sinyav-skii, writing as Abram Tertz, had advocated three decades before in his famous underground article "On Socialist Realism." Although only a few writers now committed themselves to fantastic art in full, a great many increasingly freely included element of fantasy and the grotesque in contexts that were otherwise conservatively rational. This development is an illustration of the movement to recapture the Russian literary heritage and to rejoin a main stream of contemporary Western literature.

As of 1991, the Russian literary community was undergoing shock and confusion. The virtual abolition of censorship had given writers an unprecedented freedom of expression, and the demolition of Party controls and influence had given them new ideological and political latitude. Although writers, on the whole, welcomed their new liberty, their elation was not unqualified. During the last half-century of the Soviet period the literary community had been nurtured, protected, and financially sustained by the same official apparatus whose oppression had finally become intolerable. There was no question that Russian literature would endure and grow, but the new challenge of the marketplace was sure to influence this growth in strange and unpredictable ways.

Notes

1 THE LITERARY SITUATION

1 At least one contemporary critic, however, has argued that the *povest'* is an amorphous genre, a catch-all designation for prose works that do not fit other categories.

2 Igor' Dedkov, "'Kuplen' v 1956-m...,'" *Literaturnaya gazeta*, no. 23 (1990), p. 7.

3 Viktor Erofeev, "Pominki po sovetskoi literature," *Literaturnaya gazeta*, no. 27 (1990), p. 8.

2 FROM "STAGNATION" TO "OPENNESS"

1 For accounts of the earlier writing careers of Trifonov, Okudzhava, Zalygin, Tendryakov, Granin, Grekova, Bitov, Aitmatov, and Iskander, see Deming Brown, *Soviet Russian Literature Since Stalin*, Cambridge, Cambridge University Press, 1978.

2 For more thorough discussions of the stylistic and structural qualities of Trifonov's writing, see Josephine Woll, *Invented Truth: Soviet Reality and the Literary Imagination of Iurii Trifonov*, Durham, Duke University Press, 1991; Fiona Bjorling, "Yuri Trifonov's *The House on The Embankment*: Fiction or Autobiography?," in Jane Gary Harris (ed.), *Autobiographical Statements in Twentieth-Century Russian Literature*, Princeton, Princeton University Press, 1990, pp. 172–92; and Nina Kolsenikoff, *Yuri Trifonov: A Critical Study*, Ann Arbor, Ardis Publishers, 1991.

3 V. Maksimov, in "Beseda o sovremennykh russkikh pisatelyakh," *Strelets*, no. 8 (1987), p. 21.

4 For a fully study of Bitov, see Ellen Chances, *Andrei Bitov: Ecology of Inspiration*, Cambridge, Cambridge University Press, 1993.

5 Laura Beraha, "Compilation in the Art of Fazil' Iskander: A Chapter-Case Study from *Sandro iz Chegema*," paper delivered at IV Congress for Soviet and East European Studies, Harrogate, England, July 25, 1990.

3 RETROSPECTIVE WRITING ABOUT THE STALIN PERIOD

1 For an account of this novel, see Deming Brown, *Soviet Russian Literature since Stalin*, pp. 268–69.
2 For a thorough and sensitive treatment of this topic, see Margaret Ziolkowski, "A Modern Demonology: Some Literary Stalins," *Slavic Review*, vol. 50, no. 1, Spring 1991, pp. 59–69.

4 VILLAGE PROSE

1 The definitive study of village prose is Kathleen Parthé, *Russian Village Prose: The Radiant Past*, Princeton, Princeton University Press, 1992. I should like to acknowledge my indebtedness to this book for its analysis of the school and its history. For my own comments on village prose in the years of its greatest prominence, see *Soviet Russian Literature since Stalin*, Chapter 8, pp. 218–52.
2 E. Starikova, "Zhit' i pomnit'," *Novyi mir*, no. 11 (1977), p. 247.
3 For a thorough study of Mozhaev, see David C. Gillespie, "History, Politics, and the Russian Peasant: Boris Mozhaev and the Collectivization of Agriculture," *Slavonic and East European Review*, no. 2 (1989), pp. 183–210.

6 OTHER VOICES

1 For an excellent study of Tolstaya, the concepts and insights of which have influenced the present essay, see Helena Goscilo, "Tat'iana Tolstaia's 'Dome of Many-Coloured Glass': The World Refracted through Multiple Perspectives," *Slavic Review*, vol. 47, no. 2 (1988), pp. 280–90.

7 "TOUGH" AND "CRUEL" PROSE

1 Sergei Chuprinin, "Drugaya proza," *Literaturnaya gazeta*, no. 6 (1989), p. 4.
2 Nancy Condee, "Liudmila Petrushevskaia: How the 'Lost People' Live," *Institute of Current World Affairs Bulletin* NPC-14, p. 2.
3 I am grateful to Anatoly Vishevsky and Anthony Vanchu for drawing this feature of Popov's writing to my attention.
4 Evgenii Popov, "Prekrasnost' zhizni, ili poiski smysla prochnosti" (interview with S. Taroshchina), *Literaturnaya gazeta*, April 20, 1988, p. 6.

8 NEW FACES

1 In St. Petersburg, "Obvodnyi Kanal" is the name of a by-pass canal and of the street that runs along it.

Select bibliography

Hundreds of books, articles, and reviews – each devoted primarily to an individual author – have been consulted in the preparation of this study. These works are too numerous to list in the present context. The following bibliography consists of larger and more comprehensive studies, which I have found useful in designing the scheme of this book.

Ageev, Aleksandr, "Prevratnosti dialoga," *Znamya*, no. 4 (1990), pp. 213–22.
  "Konspekt o krizise," *Literaturnoe obozrenie*, no. 3 (1991), pp. 15–21.
  "Aktual'nye problemy izucheniya istorii russkoi sovetskoi literatury," *Voprosy literatury*, no. 9 (1987), pp. 3–78.
Anninskii, Lev, *Lokti i kryl'ya: Literatura 80-x: nadezhdy, real'nost', paradoksy*, Moscow, Sovetskii Pisatel', 1989.
Arkhangel'skii, Aleksandr, *U paradnogo pod'ezda: Literatura i kul'turnye situatsii perioda glasnosti (1987–1990)*, Moscow, Sovetskii Pisatel', 1991.
  "Toshchii sokhnet, tolstyi sdokhnet?," *Literaturnaya gazeta*, no. 25 (1991), p. 10.
Belaya, Galina, "O prirode eksperimenta: k sporam o khudozhestvennykh poiskakh v sovremennoi literature," *Literaturnoe obozrenie*, no. 7 (1985), pp. 21–26.
  "Pereput'e," *Voprosy literatury*, no. 12 (1987), pp. 75–103.
  "In the Name of Common Culture," *Soviet Literature*, no. 9 (1988), pp. 132–38.
  "Ugrozhayushchaya real'nost'," *Voprosy literatury*, no. 4 (1990), pp. 3–23.
Bocharov, Anatolii, *Literatura i vremya*, Moscow, Khudozhestvennaya Literatura, 1988.
  "Bol' i otvetstvennost'. O nravstvennykh aspektakh sovremennoi prozy," *Literaturnoe obozrenie*, no. 12 (1985), pp. 17–23.
  "Po strogomu schetu," *Novyi mir*, no. 7 (1985), pp. 215–34.
  "K yadru i po kasatel'noi," *Voprosy literatury*, no. 1 (1987), pp. 3–49.

"Sluzhit' pravdoi i veroi," *Znamya*, no. 11 (1987), pp. 205–13.

"Pokushenie na mirazhi," *Voprosy literatury*, no. 1 (1988), pp. 40–77.

"Mchatsay mify, b'yutsya mify," *Oktyabr'*, no. 1 (1990), pp. 181–91.

"Mify i prozreniya," *Oktyabr'*, no. 8 (1990), pp. 160–73.

"Dve ottepeli: vera i smyatenie," *Oktyabr'*, no. 6 (1991), pp. 186–93.

Bocharov, Anatolii, and Belaya, Galina, eds., *Sovremennaya russkaya sovetskaya literatura: v dvukh chastyakh*, Moscow, Prosveschenie, 1987.

Chalmaev, Viktor, "'Vozdushnaya vozdvigalas' arka…'," *Voprosy literatury*, no. 6 (1985), pp. 73–117.

Chuprinin, Sergei, *Kritika – eto kritiki*, Moscow, Sovetskii Pisatel', 1988.

"Come and Look," *Soviet Studies in Literature*, Winter (1988–89), pp. 83–90.

"Drugaya proza," *Literaturnaya gazeta*, no. 6 (1989), p. 4.

"Iz smuty: sub'ektivnye zametki o literaturnoi kritike 1988 goda," *Literaturnoe obozrenie*, no. 3 (1989), pp. 10–23.

"Situatsiya (bor'ba idei v sovremennoi literature)," *Znamya*, no. 1 (1990), pp. 201–19.

"Normal'nyi khod. Russkaya literatura posle perestroiki," *Znamya*, no. 10 (1991), pp. 220–34.

"Peremena uchasti. Russkaya literatura na poroge sed'mogo goda perestroiki," *Znamya*, no. 3 (1991) pp. 218–33.

Clark, Katerina, "Introduction," *Rethinking the Past and the Current Thaw, Studies in Comparative Communism*, no. 3/4 (1988), pp. 241–53.

Clowes, Edith W., "Ideology and Utopia in Recent Soviet Literature," *Russian Review*, July (1992), pp. 378–95.

Dark, Oleg, "Mir mozhet byt' lyuboi. Razmyshleniya o 'novoi' proze," *Druzhba narodov*, no. 6 (1990), pp. 223–35.

Dedkov, Igor', *Obnovlennoe zrenie*, Moscow, "Iskusstvo," 1988.

"Khozhdenie za provdoi, ili vzyskuyushchie novogo grada," *Znamya*, no. 2 (1988), pp. 199–214; Tr. as "The Road to Truth, or Those Who Seek a New Jerusalem," *Soviet Studies in Literature*, Winter (1988–89), pp. 5–41.

"Kogda rasseyalsya liricheskii tuman," *Literaturnoe obozrenie*, no. 8 (1981), pp. 21–32.

"Nashe zhivoe vremya," *Novyi mir*, no. 3 (1985), pp. 217–41.

"Mezhdu proshlym i budushchem," *Znamya*, no. 1 (1991), pp. 231–40.

Epshtein, Mikhail, "Posle budushchego. O novom soznanii v literature," *Znamya*, no. 1 (1991), pp. 217–30.

Erofeev, Viktor, "Pominki po sovetskoi literature," *Literaturnaya gazeta*, no. 27 (1990), p. 8.

Gillespie, David, *Valentin Rasputin and Soviet Russian Village Prose*, London, Modern Humanities Research Association, 1986.

Hosking, Geoffrey, *Beyond Socialist Realism: Soviet Fiction since Ivan Denisovich*, New York, Holmes & Meier, 1980.

"Istoriki i pisateli o literature," *Voprosy istorii*, no. 6 (1988), pp. 3–112.

Ivanova, Natal'ya, *Tochka zrenie: o prose poslednikh let*, Moscow, Sovetskii Pisatel', 1988.

"Vol'noe dykhanie," *Voprosy literatury*, no. 3 (1983), pp. 179–214.

"Ispytanie pravdoi," *Znamya*, no. 1 (1987), pp. 198–220; tr. as "Trial By Truth," *Soviet Studies in Literature*, Summer (1988), pp. 5–57.

"Otsy in deti epokhi," *Voprosy literatury*, no. 11 (1987), pp. 50–83.

"Namerennye neschastlivtsi? (o prose 'novoi volny')," *Druzhba narodov*, no. 7 (1989), pp. 239–53.

"Smena yazyka," *Znamya*, no. 11 (1989), pp. 221–31; tr. as "A Change of Language," *Soviet Studies in Literature*, Fall (1990), pp. 19–45.

"Zhizn prekrasna?," *Yunost*, no. 1 (1991), pp. 60–63.

Kamyakov, V., "Chto meshaet chuvstvom?," *Oktyabr'*, no. 2 (1988), pp. 184–93.

"Gde tonko – tam ne rvetsya," *Novyi mir*, no. 8 (1989), pp. 226–40.

Karyakin, Yurii, "Stoit li nastupat' na grabli?," *Znamya*, no. 9 (1987), pp. 200–24.

Kasack, Wolfgang, *Russian Literature, 1945–1988*, Munich, O. Sagner, 1989.

"Kopengagenskaya vstrecha deyatelei kul'tury," *Voprosy literatury*, no. 5 (1989), pp. 3–89.

Kustanovich, Konstantin, "Monologue of the Anti-Hero: Trifonov and the Prose of the Last Decade," *Slavic Review*, Winter (1991), pp. 978–88.

Latynina, Alla, *Znaki vremeni*, Moscow, Sovetskii Pisatel', 1987.
   Za otkrytym shlagbaumom: literatura situatsiya kontsa 80-kh, Moscow, Sovetskii Pisatel', 1991.

"Kogo uvenchivaet muza?," *Znamya*, no. 7 (1985), pp. 225–32.

"Dogovorit' do kontsa," *Znamya*, no. 12 (1987), pp. 211–20.

"Kolokol'nyi zvon – ne molitva," *Novyi mir*, no. 8 (1989), pp. 232–44.

"Ne meshaite konyu sbrosit' vsadnika," *Literaturnaya gazeta*, no. 16 (1990), p. 4.

Lavlinskii, L., "Nosha: o literaturnoi kritike nashikh dnei," *Literaturnoe obozrenie*, no. 2 (1989), pp. 3–19.

Lipovetskii, M., "Svobody chernaya rabota," *Voprosy literatury*, no. 9 (1989), pp. 3–45.

Marchenko, Alla, "Almanacs and Related Matters," *Soviet Studies in Literature*, Fall (1990), pp. 46–69.

Marsh, Rosalind, *Images of Dictatorship: Portraits of Stalin in Literature*, London, Routledge, 1990.

"Na perelome? kruglyi stol: proza – 89," *Literaturnoe obozrenie*, no. 1 (1990), pp. 9–21.

Nemzer, Andrei, "Net voprosov," *Literaturnaya gazeta*, no. 8 (1991), p. 10.

"Oblachno s proyasneniyami," *Literaturnoe obozrenie*, no. 2 (1991), pp. 26–36.

Novikov, Vladimir, "Novye dali romana," *Voprosy literatury*, no. 6 (1982), pp. 3–23.

"Dumaite postupkami. Rasskaz i sovremennost'," *Oktyabr'*, no. 6 (1987), pp. 192–99.

"Oshchushchenie zhanra (rol' rasskaza v rasvitii sovremennoi prozy)," *Novyi mir*, no. 3 (1987), pp. 239–54.

"Defitsit derzosti. Literaturnaya perestroika i esteticheskii zastoi," *Oktyabr'*, no. 3 (1988), pp. 186–95.

Nuikin, Andrei, "Novoe bogoiskatel'stvo i starye dogmy," *Novyi mir*, no. 4 (1987), pp. 244–59.

Olcott, Anthony, "Glasnost' and Soviet Culture," In Maurice Friedberg and Heyward Isham, eds., *Soviet Society under Gorbachev*, Armonk, N. Y., M. E. Sharpe, 1987, pp. 101–30.

Pankov, Aleksandr, "Zaboty zhizni i puti literatury," *Druzhba narodov*, no. 10 (1985), pp. 217–29.

Parthé, Kathleen, *The Radiant Past: Russian Village Prose from Ovechkin to Rasputin*, Princeton, Princeton University Press, 1992.

Peterson, Nadya, "Science Fiction and Fantasy: A Prelude to the Literature of Glasnost," *Slavic Review*, Summer (1989), pp. 254–68.

Piskunova, S., and Piskunov, V., "Uroki zazerkal'ya," *Oktyabr'*, no. 8 (1988), pp. 188–98.

Pittman, Riita, H., "Writers and Politics in the Gorbachev Era," *Soviet Studies*, no. 4 (1992), pp. 665–85.

Porter, Robert, *Four Contemporary Russian Writers*, New York, St. Martin's Press, 1989.

Potapov, Vladimir, "Na vykhode iz 'andergraunda'," *Novyi mir*, no. 10 (1989), pp. 251–7; tr. as "Coming out of the 'Underground'," *Soviet Literature*, no. 5 (1990), pp. 157–64.

Rassadin, Stanislav, and Urnov, Dmitrii, "Chto nas raz'edinilo?," *Literaturnaya gazeta*, no. 23 (1989), p. 10.

Rodnyanskaya, Irina, *Khudozhnik v poiskakh istiny*, Moscow, Sovremennik, 1989.

Rougle, Charles, "On the 'Fantastic Trend' in Recent Soviet Prose," *Slavic and East European Journal*, Fall (1990), pp. 308–21.

Shklovskii, Evgenii, *Proza molodykh: geroi, problemy, konflikty*, Moscow, Znanie, 1986.

Chelovek sredi lyudei, Moscow, Znanie, 1987.

Grani gumanizma: sotsial'no-nravstvennye problemy sovremennoi prozy, Moscow, Znanie, 1989.

Litsom k cheloveku, Moscow, Znanie, 1989.

"Po Verkhnemu sloyu...zametki o konflikte i geroe v zhurnal'noi proze," *Literaturnoe obozrenie*, no. 7 (1985), pp. 27–33.

"O sushchem i dolzhnom," *Voprosy literatury*, no. 10 (1986), pp. 3–40.

"Samoe glavnoe," *Literaturnoe obozrenie*, no. 11 (1987), pp. 25–34.

"Neugasayushchee plamya," *Literaturnoe obozrenie*, no. 2 (1989), pp. 20–38.

"Uskol'zayushchaya real'nost'," *Literaturnoe obozrenie*, no. 2 (1991), pp. 10–18.

Shneidman, N. N., *Soviet Literature in the 1970s: Artistic Diversity and Ideological Conformity*, Toronto, University of Toronto Press, 1979.

Soviet Literature in the 1980s: Decade of Transition, Toronto, University of Toronto Press, 1989.

"Should We Renounce Socialist Realism?," *Soviet Literature*, no. 4 (1989), pp. 127–37.

Vail', Petr, and Genis, Aleksandr, *Sovremennaya russkaya proza*, Ann Arbor, Hermitage, 1982.

"Novaya proza: ta zhe ili 'drugaya'?," *Novyi mir*, no. 10 (1989), pp. 247–50.

Vakhitova, T. M., "Perspektivy obshchestvennogo razvitiya i sovremennaya 'gorodskaya' proza," *Russkaya literatura*, no. 1 (1986), pp. 56–66.

Vil'chek, L., "Vniz po techeniyu derevenskoi prozy," *Voprosy literatury*, no. 6 (1985), pp. 34–72.

Ziolkowski, Margaret, "*Glasnost'* in Soviet Literature: An Introduction to Two Stories," *Michigan Quarterly Review*, Fall (1989), pp. 639–47.

"A Modern Demonology: Some Literary Stalins," *Slavic Review*, vol. 50, no. 1, Spring (1991), pp. 59–69.

Zolotusskii, Igor', *Ispoved' Zoila: stat'i, issledovaniya, pamflety*, Moscow, Sovetskaya Rossiya, 1989.

"Otchet o puti," *Znamya*, no. 1 (1986), pp. 221–40; tr. as "A Progress Report," *Soviet Studies in Literature*, Summer (1988), pp. 58–103.

"Vozvyshayushchee slove. Proza -87," *Literaturnoe obozrenie*, no. 6 (1988), pp. 23–32, and no. 7 (1988), pp. 7–18.

"Krushenie abstraktsii," *Novyi mir*, no. 1 (1989), pp. 235–46.

English translations of Soviet Russian prose

ANTHOLOGIES

Chukhontsev, Oleg, ed., *Leopard I: Dissonant Voices; The New Russian Fiction*, London, Harvill, 1991.

Decter, Jacqueline, ed., *The New Soviet Fiction: Sixteen Short Stories*. Compiled by Sergei Zalygin. New York, Abbeville Press, 1989.

Soviet Women Writing: Fifteen Short Stories, New York, Abbeville Press, 1990.

Goscilo, Helena, ed., *Balancing Acts: Contemporary Stories by Russian Women*, Bloomington, Indiana University Press, 1989.

Goscilo, Helena, and Lindsey, Byron, eds., *Glasnost: An Anthology of Literature Under Gorbachev*, Ann Arbor, Ardis Publishers, 1990.

The Wild Beach: An Anthology of Contemporary Russian Stories, Ann Arbor, Ardis Publishers, 1992.

The Human Experience: Contemporary American and Soviet Fiction and Poetry. Edited by the Soviet/American Joint Editorial Board of the Quaker US/USSR Committee. New York and Moscow, Knopf and Khudozhestvennaya Literatura, 1989.

McLaughlin, Sigrid, ed. and tr., *The Image of Women in Contemporary Soviet Fiction: Selected Stories from the USSR*, New York, St. Martin's Press, 1989.

Metropol. Literary Almanac, edited by Vasily Aksenov, Viktor Yerofeyev, Fazil Iskander, Andrei Bitov, Yevgeny Popov, New York, Norton, 1982.

Proffer, Carl and Ellendea, eds., *The Barsukov Triangle, The Two-Toned Blond and Other Stories*, Ann Arbor, Ardis, 1984.

INDIVIDUAL AUTHORS

Many works of the following authors appear in the anthologies listed above. They will be identified by abbreviated titles of these anthologies.

Abramov, Fyodor, *Two Winters and Three Summers*, tr. D. B. Powers and Doris C. Powers, Ann Arbor, Ardis Publishers, 1984. Also tr. Jacqueline Edwards and Mitchell Schneider, San Diego, Harcourt Brace Jovanovich, 1984.

"Olesha's Cabin," tr. Paul Gorgen, see *The Barsukov Triangle*, pp. 129–45.

Aitmatov, Chingiz, *The White Ship*, tr. Mirra Ginsburg, New York, Crown Publishers, 1972. Also *The White Steamship*, tr. Tatyana and George Feifer, London, Hodder and Stoughton, 1972.

The Ascent of Mount Fuji: A Play, tr. Nicholas Bethell, New York, Farrar, Straus and Giroux, 1975.

Tales of the Mountains and Steppes, Moscow, Progress, 1977.

A Day Lasts More Than a Hundred Years, tr. John French, Bloomington, Indiana University Press, 1983.

Mother Earth and Other Stories, tr. James Riordan, London, Faber, 1989.

The Piebald Dog Running Along the Shore and Other Stories, Moscow, Raduga, 1989.

The Place of the Skull, tr. Natasha Ward, London, Faber, 1989.

Time to Speak, New York, International Publishers, 1989.

"The Red Apple," tr. Raymond Stead, *Soviet Literature*, no. 12 (1982), pp. 8–22.

"White Rain," tr. Valentina Jacque, *Soviet Literature*, no. 6 (1986), pp. 5–13.

Aleksievich, Svetlana, "War's Unwomanly Face," tr. Richard Morton, *Soviet Literature*, no. 3 (1985), pp. 62–128.

"The Last Witness," tr. Allison John, *Soviet Literature*, no. 3 (1989), pp. 92–113.

"Boys in Zinc," tr. Arch Tait, *Granta*, Autumn (1990), pp. 146–61.

Astaf'ev, Viktor, *The Horse With the Pink Mane*, tr. Robert Daglish, Moscow, Progress Publishers, 1978.

To Live Your Life and Other Stories, Moscow, Raduga, 1989.

"Six Short Stories," tr. Alice Ingman, *Soviet Literature*, no. 5 (1984), pp. 96–114.

"The Hands of a Wife," tr. Robert Daglish, *Soviet Literature*, no. 3 (1985), pp. 12–25.

"Vimba," tr. Peter Greenwood, *Soviet Literature*, no. 6 (1986), pp. 14–29.

"To Live your Life," tr. Alex Miller, *Soviet Literature*, no. 1 (1988), pp. 3–44.

"Happiness," tr. Sergei Sossinsky, *Soviet Literature*, no. 8 (1988), pp. 3–9.

"Lyudochka," tr. David Gillespie, *Soviet Literature*, no. 8 (1990), pp. 3–39.

"The Blind Fisherman," tr. Robert Porter, see *Leopard I*, pp. 351–70.

Bakin, Dmitrii, "Lagopthalmos," tr. Sylva Rubashova and Milena Michalski, see *Leopard I*, pp. 235–44.

Belov, Vasilii, "Parting Hill," tr. S. Roy, *Soviet Literature*, no. 12 (1982), pp. 26–34.

"Hills," tr. Eve Manning, see *The Human Experience*, pp. 341–43.

"Morning Meetings," see *The Image of Women*, pp. 135–47.

"A War Like That," tr. George Bird, see *Leopard I*, pp. 131–43.

Bitov, Andrei, *Life in Windy Weather: Short Stories*, ed. Priscilla Meyer, Ann Arbor, Ardis Publishers, 1986.

Pushkin House, tr. Susan Brownsberger, New York, Farrar, Straus and Giroux, 1987.

A Captive of the Caucasus, tr. Susan Brownsberger, New York, Farrar, Straus and Giroux, 1992.

"The Doctor," tr. John Crowfoot, *Soviet Literature*, no. 5 (1989), pp. 15–29.

"The Doctor," tr. Susan Brownsberger, see *Leopard I*, pp. 103–18.

"The Door," tr. T. A. Monks, *Soviet Literature*, no. 4 (1990), pp. 80–88.

"The Little Devil," tr. Alexandra Nadezhdina, *Soviet Literature*, no. 4 (1990), pp. 88–92.

"Days of Leavetaking," tr. George Saunders, see *Metropol*, pp. 273–315.

"Pushkin's Photograph," tr. Priscilla Meyer, see *The New Soviet Fiction*, pp. 15–60.

Borodin, Leonid, *The Year of Miracle and Grief*, tr. Jennifer Bradshaw, London, Quartet Books, 1984.

Partings, tr. David Floyd, San Diego, Harcourt Brace Jovanovich, 1987.

The Third Truth, tr. Catriona Kelly, London, Collins Harvill, 1989.

The Story of a Strange Time, tr. Frank Williams, London, Collins Harvill, 1990.

Bykov, Vasil' (also listed by his Byelorussian surname, Bykau), *Pack of Wolves*, tr. Lynn Solotaroff, New York, Crowell, 1981.

L. Lazarev, *Vasil Bykov*; Vasil Bykov, *On Craftsmanship*, tr. Amanda Calvert, Moscow, Raduga, 1987.

Sign of Misfortune, tr. Alan Myers, New York, Allerton Press, 1990.

"The Wolf Pack," tr. Robert Daglish, *Soviet Literature*, no. 5 (1975), pp. 15–115.

"To Go Never to Return," tr. Hilda and Janet Perham, *Soviet Literature*, no. 12 (1979), pp. 3–143.

"The Quarry," tr. Tamara Zalite, *Soviet Literature*, no. 5 (1987), pp. 3–78.

Chukovskaya, Lidiya, *To the Memory of Childhood*, tr. Eliza Kellogg Klose, Evanston, Northwestern University Press, 1988.

Davydov, Yurii, "Evenings at Kolmovo," tr. Mark Buser, *Soviet Literature*, no. 6 (1990), pp. 62–71.

Dombrovskii, Yurii, "An Arm, a Leg, a Gherkin too...," tr. Alan Meyers, see *Leopard I*, pp. 199–214.

Ekimov, Boris, "House for Sale," tr. Diana Turner, *Soviet Literature*, no. 3 (1988), pp. 48–56.

"What's All the Crying About?," tr. Mary Plume, *Soviet Literature*, no. 4 (1989), pp. 3–13.

"The Boy on the Bicycle," tr. David Gillespie, *Soviet Literature*, no. 2 (1990), pp. 71–98.

"A Greeting from Afar," tr. Shirley Benson, see *The Human Experience*, pp. 174–96.

"Safe Return," tr. Howard Swarts, see *Leopard I*, pp. 245–59.

"The Chelyadins' Son-in-Law," tr. Jan Butler, see *The Wild Beach*, pp. 117–45.

Ermakov, Oleg, "Springtime Outing," tr. Thomas Dumstorf, *Soviet Literature*, no. 8 (1990), pp. 133–44.

Erofeev, Venedikt, *Moscow Circles*, tr. J. R. Dorrell, New York, Writers and Readers Publishing Cooperative, 1981. Also *Moscow to the End of the Line*, tr. H. W. Tgalsma, New York, Taplinger, 1980.

Erofeev, Viktor, "Two Stories and a Novella," tr. Martin Horwitz, see *Metropol*, pp. 457–526.

"The Parakeet," tr. Leonard J. Stanton, see *Glasnost*, pp. 367–82.

"Sludge-gulper," tr. Catherine Porter, see *Leopard I*, pp. 268–74.

Esin, Sergei, "The Present Day," tr. Andrew Bromfield, *Soviet Literature*, no. 10 (1989), pp. 58–79.

Genatulin, Anatolii, "Rough Weather," tr. Mary Fleming Zirin, see *Glasnost*, pp. 303–65.

Ginzburg, Lidiya, *The Semiotics of Russian Cultural History*, ed. Alice Stone Nakhimovsky, Ithaca, Cornell University Press, 1985.

On Psychological Prose, tr. and ed. Judson Rosengrant, Princeton, Princeton University Press, 1991.

"Conscience Deluded," tr. Ludmilla Groves and Mary Plume, *Soviet Literature*, no. 9 (1990), pp. 3–29.

"The Siege of Leningrad: Notes of a Survivor," tr. Gerald Mikkelson and Margaret Winchell, see *Soviet Women Writing*, pp. 23–50.

Golovin, Genadii, "Anna Petrovna," tr. John Beebe, see *Glasnost*, pp. 383–453.

Granin, Daniil, *The Bison: A Novel About the Scientist Who Defied Stalin*, tr. Antonina W. Bouis, New York, Doubleday, 1990.

"Thou Art Weighed in the Balance...," tr. Alex Miller, *Soviet Literature*, no. 7 (1984), pp. 3–24.

"The Forbidden Chapter," tr. Charles Rougle, see *The White Beach*, pp. 243–64.

Granin, Daniil, and Adamovich, Ales', *A Book of the Blockade*, tr. Hilda Perham, Moscow, Raduga, 1983.

Grekova, I., *Russian Women: Two Stories*, tr. Michel Petrov, San Diego, Harcourt Brace Jovanovich, 1983.

A Ship of Widows, tr. Catherine Porter, London, Virago, 1985.

"The Faculty," tr. Melinda Maclean Jr., *Soviet Literature*, no. 9 (1979), pp. 3–107, and 10 (1979), pp. 16–128.

"World Without Smiles," tr. Alex Miller, *Soviet Literature*, no. 3 (1988), pp. 19–48.

"No Smiles," tr. Dobrochna Dyrcz-Freeman, see *The New Soviet Fiction*, pp. 79–110.

"One Summer in the City," tr. Lauren Leighton, see *The Barsukov Triangle*, pp. 245–72.

"A Summer in the City," see *The Image of Women*, pp. 20–48.

"Introduction," see *Soviet Women Writing*, pp. 9–14.

"Masters of Their Own Lives," tr. Dobrochna Dyrcz-Freeman, see *Soviet Women Writing*, pp. 85–106.

Grossman, Vasilii, *Forever Flowing*, tr. Thomas P. Whitney, New York, Harper and Row, 1972.

Life and Fate, tr. Robert Chandler, London, Collins Harvill, 1985.

Iskander, Fazil, *The Thirteenth Labor of Hercules*, tr. Robert Daglish, Moscow, Progress, 1978.

The Goatibex Constellation, tr. Helen Burlingame, Ann Arbor, Ardis Publishers, 1982.

Sandro of Chegem, tr. Susan Brownsberger, New York, Vintage Books, 1983.

The Gospel According to Chegem, tr. Susan Brownsberger, New York, Vintage Books, 1984.

Chik and His Friends, tr. J. C. Butler, Moscow, Raduga, 1984.

Rabbits and Boa Constrictors, tr. Ronald E. Peterson, Ann Arbor, Ardis Publishers, 1989.

"Broadbow," tr. Valentina Jacque, *Soviet Literature*, no. 3 (1988), pp. 57–85. Also see *Leopard I*, pp. 288–322.

"Two Stories," tr. Carl R. Proffer, see *Metropol*, pp. 322–73.

"Grandfather," tr. Kristine Erickson, see *The Barsukov Triangle*, pp. 275–302.

"Old Hasan's Pipe," tr. Joseph Kiegel, see *Glasnost*, pp. 25–58.

Kabakov, Aleksandr, *No Return*, tr. Thomas Whitney, New York, William Morrow and Company, 1990.

Kaledin, Sergei, *The Humble Cemetery*, tr. Catriona Kelly, London, Collins Harvill, 1990.

Katerli, Nina, "The Barsukov Triangle," tr. David Lapeza, see *The Barsukov Triangle*, pp. 3–71.

"Between Spring and Summer," tr. John Fred Beebe and Regina Snyder, see *Balancing Acts*, pp. 229–55.

"The Farewell Light," tr. Valeria Sajez, see *Balancing Acts*, pp. 143–63.

"The Monster," tr. Bernard Mears, see *Soviet Women Writing*, pp. 107–16.

Kim, Anatolii, "Father Frost" (excerpts from the novel), tr. Alexander Postnikov and Charlotte Foster, *Soviet Literature*, no. 7 (1989), pp. 6–111.

"Road stop in August," tr. Leo Gruliow, see *The Human Experience*, pp. 235–70. See also "A Stop in August," tr. S. Roy, *Soviet Literature*, pp. 65–96.

"Cage with Color TV," see *The Image of Women*, pp. 149–58.

Kireev, Ruslan, "From the 'Svetopol Chronicle'," tr. Andrew Bromfield, *Soviet Literature*, no. 10 (1989), pp. 95–110.

"Aphrodite the Firewoman," tr. Gordon Livermore, see *The Human Experience*, pp. 70–85.

Kondrat'ev, Vyacheslav, "At Freedom Station," tr. Louis Wagner, see *The Wild Beach*, pp. 225–42.

Krupin, Vladimir, "While the Tall Candles Still Burn," tr. Andrew Bromfield, *Soviet Literature*, no. 10 (1989), pp. 111–15.

Kuraev, Mikhail, "Captain Dikshtein," tr. Margareta Thompson, see *Glasnost*, pp. 59–185.

Kurchatkin, Anatolii, "The Guillotine; The Maze; A Midsummer Night's Dream," tr. Rachel Polonsky, Rosamund Shreeves, Graham Povev, *Soviet Literature*, no. 12 (1990), pp. 3–40.

Latynin, Leonid, "The Face-Maker and the Muse" (excerpts), tr. Andrew Bromfield, *Soviet Literature*, no. 8 (1989), pp. 3–81.

"Sleeper at Harvest Time" (excerpts), tr. Andrew Bromfield, *Glas: New Russian Writing*, no. 1 (1991), pp. 118–37.

Lichutin, Vladimir, "Lyubostai or the Devil of Passion" (excerpts), tr. Andrew Bromfield, *Soviet Literature*, no. 10 (1989), pp. 122–44.

"The Itinerants," tr. Arch Tait, *Soviet Literature*, no. 6 (1990), pp. 90–124.

Makanin, Vladimir, "Antileader," tr. Jamey Gambrell, see *The New Soviet Fiction*, pp. 163–204.

"Left Behind," tr. Nadezhda Peterson, see *Glasnost*, pp. 195–270.

"Those Who Did Not Get Into the Choir," tr. Michael Duncan, see *Leopard I*, pp. 119–30.

Nagibin, Yurii, *Island of Love*, tr. Olga Shartse, Moscow, Progress, 1982.
  The Peak of Success and Other Stories, ed. Helena Goscilo, Ann Arbor, Ardis Publishers, 1986.
  Arise and Walk, tr. Catherine Porter, London, Faber, 1990.
  "Envoy from a Mysterious Land," tr. Valentina Jacque, *Soviet Literature*, no. 12 (1982), pp. 84–94.
  "Chocolate Drops," tr. Valentina Jacque, *Soviet Literature*, no. 6 (1986), pp. 128–33.
Okudzhava, Bulat, *The Extraordinary Adventures of Secret Agent Shipov in Pursuit of Count Leo Tolstoy, in the Year 1862*, tr. Heather Maisner, London, Abelard-Schuman, 1973.
  A Taste of Liberty (Poor Avrosimov), tr. Leo Gruliow, Ann Arbor, Ardis Publishers, 1986.
  "Lots of Luck, Kid!," tr. Robert Szulkin, see *The Barsukov Triangle*, pp. 305–70.
  "Girl of My Dreams," tr. Leo Gruliow, see *The Human Experience*, pp. 91–101. Also tr. Alex Miller, *Soviet Literature*, no. 3 (1988), pp. 88–97.
  "The Art of Needles and Sins," tr. Michele A. Berdy, see *The New Soviet Fiction*, pp. 213–34.
Orlov, Vladimir, *Danilov the Violist*, tr. Antonina W. Bouis, New York, W. Morrow, 1987.
  "A Ringing Sound," tr. Andrew Bromfield, *Soviet Literature*, no. 10 (1989), pp. 145–63.
Petrushevskaya, Lyudmila, "I'm for Swedes," tr. June Goss and Elena Goreva, *Soviet Literature*, no. 3 (1989), pp. 79–91.
  "The Violin," tr. Marina Astman, see *Balancing Acts*, pp. 122–25.
  "Mania," tr. Helena Goscilo, see *Balancing Acts*, pp. 256–60.
  "Nets and Traps," tr. Alma H. Law, see *The Image of Women*, pp. 100–110.
  "Through the Fields," tr. Stefani Hoffman, see *The New Soviet Fiction*, pp. 235–8.
  "Our Crowd," tr. Helena Goscilo, see *Glasnost*, pp. 3–24. Also in *Michigan Quarterly Review*, Fall (1989), pp. 676–98.
  "The Overlook," tr. Stefani Hoffman, see *The New Soviet Fiction*, pp. 235–8.
  "A Modern Family Robinson," tr. George Bird, see *Leopard I*, pp. 414–24.
P'etsukh, Vyacheslav, "Saturday" (from *The New Moscow Philosophy*), *Soviet Literature*, no. 1 (1990), pp. 86–107.
  "Anamnesis and Epicrisis," tr. Andrew Reynolds, see *Leopard I*, pp. 389–413.
  "The Ticket," tr. Byron Lindsey, see *The Wild Beach*, pp. 264–75.

"Novy Zavod," tr. Jan Butler, see *The Wild Beach*, pp. 277–82.

Popov, Evgenii, "A Baker's Dozen of Stories," tr. George Saunders, see *Metropol*, pp. 85–153.

"Three Tales," tr. Joel and Monica Wilkinson, see *The Barsukov Triangle*, pp. 217–27.

"The Situation," tr. Robert Porter, see *Leopard I*, pp. 275–87.

Popov, Valerii, "Dreams from the Top Berth," tr. Valentina Baslyk, see *Glasnost*, pp. 293–301. Also tr. George Bird, see *Leopard I*, pp. 342–50.

Rasputin, Valentin, *Live and Remember*, tr. Antonina W. Bouis, New York, Macmillan, 1978. Also, with a foreword by Kathleen Parthé, Evanston, Northwestern University Press, 1992.

Money for Maria and Borrowed Time, tr. Kevin Windle and Margaret Wettlin, London, Quartet Books, 1981.

Money for Maria: Stories, Moscow, Raduga, 1989.

You Live and Love and Other Stories, tr. Alan Myers, New York, Vanguard, 1986.

Siberia on Fire, tr. Gerald Mikkelson and Margaret Winchell, De Kalb, Northern Illinois University Press, 1989.

Farewell to Matyora, tr. Antonina W. Bouis, New York, Macmillan, 1978. Also, with a foreword by Kathleen Parthé, Evanston, Northwestern University Press, 1991.

"Downstream," tr. Valentina Brougher and Helen Poot, in Carl and Ellendea Proffer, eds., *Contemporary Russian Prose*, Ann Arbor, Ardis Publishers, 1982, pp. 379–430.

"The Fire," tr. Alex Miller, *Soviet Literature*, no. 7 (1986), pp. 3–55.

"Rudolphio," tr. Meredith M. Heinemeier and Liza Valova, see *The Barsukov Triangle*, pp. 113–26.

"French Lessons," tr. Eve Manning, see *The Human Experience*, pp. 9–33.

"Vasily and Vasilissa," see *The Image of Women*, pp. 74–97.

"What Should I Tell the Crow?," tr. Gerald Mikkelson and Margaret Winchell, *The New Soviet Fiction*, pp. 239–60.

Rybakov, Anatolii, *Heavy Sand*, tr. Harold Shukman, New York, Viking Press, 1981.

Children of the Arbat, tr. Harold Shukman, Boston, Little, Brown, 1988.

Rzhevskaya, Elena, "On the Tarmac," tr. Catriona Kelly, see *Leopard I*, pp. 386–8.

Semyonov, Georgii, "A Play of Fancy," tr. Faina Solasko, see *The Human Experience*, pp. 305–23.

Shalamov, Varlam, *Kolyma Tales*, tr. John Glad, New York, W. W. Norton, 1980.

Graphite, tr. John Glad, New York, W. W. Norton, 1981.

Shmelyov, Nikolai, "Night Voices," tr. Henri-Paul Pezet, *Soviet Literature*, no. 8 (1990), pp. 50–61.

"The Visit," tr. Michele A. Berdy, see *Glasnost*, pp. 271–92.

"The Fur Coat Incident," tr. Michele A. Berdy, see *The Wild Beach*, pp. 173–90.

Shukshin, Vasilii, *I Want to Live: Short Stories*, tr. Robert Daglish, Moscow, 1973.

Snowball Berry Red and Other Stories, Ann Arbor, Ardis Publishers, 1979.

Roubles in Words, Kopeks in Figures, and Other Stories, tr. Natasha Ward and David Iliffe, London, Marion Boyers, 1985.

"Stories," *Soviet Literature*, no. 3 (1990), pp. 3–111.

Soloukhin, Vladimir, *Laughter Over the Left Shoulder*, tr. David Martin, London, Peter Owen, 1991.

Tendryakov, Vladimir, "A Day That Ousted a Life," tr. Robert Daglish, *Soviet Literature*, no. 9 (1985), pp. 3–54.

"Donna Anna," tr. Lila H. Wangler and Helena Goscilo, see *The Wild Beach*, pp. 191–217. Also in *Michigan Quarterly Review*, Fall (1989), pp. 648–75.

"On the Blessed Island of Communism," tr. Michael Duncan, see *Leopard I*, pp. 76–102.

Tokareva, Viktoriya, "On the Set," tr. Clare Brailsford, *Soviet Literature*, no. 3 (1975), pp. 66–73.

"Sidesteps," tr. Valentina Jacque, *Soviet Literature*, no. 6 (1986), pp. 184–88.

"Thou Shalt Not Make...," tr. Vladimir Korotky, *Soviet Literature*, no. 3 (1989), pp. 48–68.

"Dry Run," tr. Michael Glenny, *Granta*, Summer (1990), pp. 77–112.

"Centre of Gravity," tr. Michael Glenny, *Granta*, Winter (1990), pp. 92–105.

"Hello!," tr. Paul David Gould, *Soviet Literature*, no. 8 (1990), pp. 40–49.

"Nothing Special," tr. Helena Goscilo, see *Balancing Acts*, pp. 49–78.

"Between Heaven and Earth, tr. Helena Goscilo, see *Balancing Acts*, pp. 273–84.

"Five Figures on a Pedestal," tr. Debra Irving, see *Soviet Women Writing*, pp. 153–202.

"The Happiest Day of My Life," see *The Image of Women*, pp. 161–83.

Tolstaya, Tatyana, *On The Golden Porch*, tr. Antonina W. Bouis, New York, Alfred A. Knopf, 1989.

Sleepwalker in a Fog, tr. Jamey Gambrell, New York, Alfred A. Knopf, 1992.

"Peters," tr. Mary Fleming Zirin, see *Balancing Acts*, pp. 6–18.

"Loves Me, Loves Me Not,"·tr. Antonina W. Bouis, see *The Human Experience*, pp. 43–53.

"Dear Shura," see *The Image of Women*, pp. 204–12.

"Fire and Dust," tr. Jamey Gambrell, see *The New Soviet Fiction*, pp. 297–310.

"Night," tr. Mary Fleming Zirin, see *Glasnost*, pp. 187–94.

"Sleepwalker in a Fog," tr. Jamey Gambrell, see *Soviet Women Writing*, pp. 51–84.

Trifonov, Yurii, *The Impatient Ones*, tr. Robert Daglish, Moscow, Progress Publishers, 1978.

The Long Goodbye: Three Novellas, tr. Helen P. Burlingame and Ellendea Proffer, New York, Harper and Row, 1978.

Another Life and The House on the Embankment, tr. Michael Glenny, New York, Simon and Schuster, 1983.

The Old Man, tr. Jacqueline Edwards and Mitchell Schneider, New York, Simon and Schuster, 1984.

The Exchange, tr. Michael Frayn, London, Methuen, 1990.

The Disappearance, tr. David Lowe, Ann Arbor, Ardis Publishers, 1991.

The Exchange and Other Stories, ed. Ellendea Proffer and Ronald Meyer, Ann Arbor, Ardis Publishers, 1991.

"A Short Spell in the Torture Chamber," tr. Alex Miller, *Soviet Literature*, no. 3 (1988), pp. 179–88. Also tr. Byron Lindsey, see *The Wild Beach*, pp. 3–12.

"Games at Dusk," tr. Jim Somers, see *The Barsukov Triangle*, pp. 59–66.

"Vera and Zoyka," see *The Image of Women*, pp. 53–74.

"Archetypal Themes," tr. Michael Duncan, see *Leopard I*, pp. 380–85.

Zalygin, Sergei, *The South American Variant*, tr. Kevin Windle, St. Lucia, University of Queensland Press, 1979.

"Pilot First-Class Kulikov," tr. Monica Whyte, *Soviet Literature*, no. 12 (1983), pp. 165–79.

"The Night of the Angels," tr. Valentina G. Brougher and Helen C. Poot, see *The Barsukov Triangle*, pp. 193–213.

"Women and the NTR," see *The Image of Women*, pp. 215–38.

"Prose," tr. Catharine Theimer Nepomnyashchy, see *The New Soviet Fiction*, pp. 363–85.

Index

The main discussions of individual authors and topics are indicated by page numbers in italics.

DATE DUE

GAYLORD			PRINTED IN U.S.A.